Child Care and Protection

Law and Practice

7th Edition

Child Care and Protection
Law and Practice

7th Edition

Safda Mahmood
Julie Doughty

WS
&H

Wildy, Simmonds & Hill Publishing

© Safda Mahmood and Julie Doughty, 2024

ISBN: 9780854903061

British Library Cataloguing in Publication Data

A catalogue record for this book is available from the British Library

First edition 1989
Second edition 1996
Third edition 2001
Fourth edition 2009
Fifth edition 2013
Sixth edition 2019

This edition published in 2024 by

Wildy, Simmonds & Hill Publishing
Wildy & Sons Ltd
Lincoln's Inn Archway
Carey Street
London WC2A 2JD
www.wildy.com

Printed in Great Britain by Ashford, Unit 600, Fareham Reach, Fareham Road, Gosport, Hampshire PO13 0FW.

Preface

I am delighted to have updated this essential publication with Dr Julie Doughty from Cardiff University, now in its seventh edition.

Our thanks go to both Barbara Mitchels and Helen James, for having been our co-authors on some of the previous editions and providing an excellent account of their experiences.

Since the previous edition in 2019, Julie and I have extensively updated the book with practicality, accessibility and strong roots in practice.

By way of background, I have practised as a solicitor in private practice and more latterly, in the local authority sector, now approaching 30 years. Currently, I continue to practise as a solicitor, manager and team leader in advocacy with Coventry City Council, Legal Services Department. I also continue to run training courses, predominantly in family and children law, across both England and Wales to various members of the legal profession and other professionals. This often involves Professional Development training for, amongst others, members of the Law Society Children Law Accreditation Scheme. My practice involves running children law cases in all areas, and aspects of adult services, including advising on the interrelationship between children proceedings and the Court of Protection, particularly with the continued developments in the law relating to deprivation of liberty (DoL), for both children and adults. I have written extensively in various legal journals on family and children law related matters for almost 30 years, including for the Law Society.

Julie Doughty has practice experience as a former solicitor and guardian ad litem panel manager, and as a senior lecturer and researcher for 20 years at Cardiff University School of Law and Politics. Julie writes widely in journals on child law topics and is a trustee of The Transparency Project and of Family Mediation Cymru.

Both Julie and I have been long-standing members of the CoramBAAF Legal Advisory Group. In this edition, we have updated the text with academic and research information in child law and protection.

Child care and protection in England and Wales is a vast and dynamic area of law and practice. In compiling this revised book, it has become clear how much has changed in child protection law and practice since the previous edition in 2019. We cannot cover everything here, but this book provides an overview and practical guide through the complexities of the Children Act 1989 (CA 1989) and subsequent child protection legislation, guidance and case law.

Since the previous edition, there have been significant developments, and the law in this book is up to date as at 10 July 2024. This new edition covers material, including developments, in terms of case law, statute, regulations and practice guidance, on a wide range of matters surrounding both private children law areas and public child care.

Inter-agency co-operation in child protection practice in England is currently based upon the revised edition of *Working Together to Safeguard Children 2023: A guide to multi-agency working to help, protect and promote the welfare of children* (DfE, December 2023) (*Working Together*), which has updated, particularly, the position with safeguarding and child death reviews. The guidance in 2018 referred to the Safeguarding and Child Death Review Partners, and the Child Safeguarding Practice Review Panel following the transition from Local Safeguarding Children Boards (LSCBs) and Serious Case Reviews (SCRs) to the reformed system of multi-agency arrangements and local and national child safeguarding practice reviews. The Children Act 2004 had been amended by the Children and Social Work Act 2017 so that LSCBs, set up by local authorities, were to be replaced. In Wales, the substantial changes to the law on children and families through the Social Services and Well-being (Wales) Act 2014 (SSW(W)A 2014), which was designed for improving the well-being of people who need care and support, and carers who need support, have been bedded in. The SSW(W)A 2014 brought about key changes to the position with voluntary accommodation, duties towards children in need and safeguarding, and was accompanied by varied secondary legislation.

With regard to safeguarding, in Wales, the LSCBs, which were responsible for carrying out safeguarding functions, have been replaced with the Safeguarding Children Boards, and their functions are set out in the Safeguarding Boards (Functions and Procedures) (Wales) Regulations 2015 (SI 2015/1466). They were established under section 134 of the SSW(W)A 2014.

In both England and Wales, there has been significant secondary legislation and case law surrounding special guardianship orders, particularly with the implementation of the Special Guardianship (Wales) (Amendment) Regulations 2018 (SI 2018/573) (W 102).

In this edition, we provide the developments in the law surrounding public child care proceedings, particularly in relation to care and supervision order applications. Since the previous edition, there have been various recommendations put forward by the Public Law Working Groups set up by the President of the Family Division. These recommendations, together with the re-launch of the *Public Law Outline* (PLO) in January 2023 are considered.

Since the introduction of the Legal Aid, Sentencing and Punishment of Offenders Act 2012, from April 2013, there has continued to be an impact on the availability of public funding in family law matters. The Act removed from the scope of public funding most private law family cases (with exceptions for those involving child abuse or domestic abuse), along with cases in other areas of law that impact on the lives of children and families. The Legal Aid Agency also brought in the *Guidance on the Remuneration of Expert Witnesses in Family Cases* (September 2022, Version 7). This relates specifically to experts on foreign law, communicating with clients at court, transcripts, translation, intermediaries, lay advocates and fees payable to experts. There have been recent developments surrounding public funding as a result of changes that were brought into effect in May 2023, which, although very welcome, some would argue have fallen short of what is required to ensure that children and families have adequate access to legal representation. Funding for various types of applications is considered in this updated edition, as well as the impact of the changes of May 2023.

There has been much-needed guidance to assist in relation to matters on capacity and disability, including *Capacity to Litigate: Guidance on the Capacity to Litigate in Proceedings Involving Children* (April 2018) and *President's Guidance: Family Proceedings: Parents with a Learning Disability* (10 April 2018), both issued by the then President of the Family Division, Sir James Munby. These publications have been assisted by practice directions on addressing 'vulnerability' in particular, and essential guidance on the court's approach to the use of 'intermediaries' and 'lay advocates'. Furthermore, the *Practice Guidance: Standard Children and other Orders* (June 2018) is also available, which is regularly updated and sets out detailed precedents in both private and public children law, and personal protection cases. This guidance is an invaluable aid for family law practitioners.

There has also been an abundance of case law over the last few years relating to DOL applications as they relate to children, with particular regard to the interface between care proceedings and Article 5 of the European Convention for the Protection of Human Rights and Fundamental Freedoms 1950 (ECHR). These applications have been considered at length by the Supreme Court in *Re T (A Child)* [2021] UKSC 35. We have ensured that this updated edition encapsulates a lot of the current thinking surrounding DoL applications, including the more recent regulations, such as the Care Planning, Placement and Case Review (England) (Amendment) Regulations 2021 (SI 2021/161), the Supported Accommodation (England) Regulations 2023 (SI 2023/416), and the most recent Practice Guidance by the President of the Family Division on DoL applications and the 'National DoL List'. In this context, given ongoing resource difficulties for local authorities across England and Wales, as well as the need to tackle more complex and varied circumstances surrounding the safety of children, such as those involving county lines, online child abuse and child sexual exploitation, public authorities have continued to struggle to keep up with the volume of cases and to put in place adequate measures to tackle them. This is clearly an area which many professionals working with children and families, as well as the judiciary, agree requires greater political intervention, financial investment and redirection.

We have also encapsulated the current developments surrounding the Family Court Reporting Pilot, the private children law Pathfinder Pilot, and the recent changes to police disclosure, as set out in the *Disclosure of Information Between Family and Criminal Agencies and Jurisdictions: 2024 Protocol*.

Both Julie and I were very pleased that the earlier editions of this book have continued to prove popular amongst practitioners, and we have maintained our aim to make this edition practical, easy to use and, above all, readable. 'He' and 'she' are used interchangeably in the text, for variety, and include either gender, where appropriate. This book sets out the salient points in child care and protection law and practice mainly as it operates in England. We highlight where the most significant differences between England and Wales occur but cannot make this comprehensive because of space constraints. Scotland and Northern Ireland are covered where specifically mentioned. In a book intended to be concise and portable, it is always difficult to decide how much to include or omit, and we provide as many pointers as we can to additional cases and useful reference points.

We feel that practice is enhanced by inter-disciplinary liaison and discussion between lawyers and practitioners from other disciplines working with children, sharing ideas and experience, debating challenging issues and tackling challenges. There have been many challenges facing practitioners over the last 5 years since the previous edition, and challenges will continue in the future, but we must not forget that we all get an immense sense of satisfaction from working in this field. We are all passionate about working in this area, and through 'joined up thinking' and 'working together' we have all played our part in effecting change, and no doubt we will all continue to do so.

Safda Mahmood (Editor)

Acknowledgements

Many thanks to all those who have given their permission to include quotations, references and materials.

We have both really appreciated the experience and help of Andrew Riddoch from Wildy's for his time and patience in working with us to substantially update this edition of the book to incorporate the significant developments in law, practice and procedure since the previous edition.

Thank you, too, for the advice and help of the many professionals, volunteers, children and families over the years with whom we have worked.

Our special thanks to our own families, work colleagues and friends for their tolerance, encouragement and patience while this book was being written. This has gone a long way in ensuring that we have completed the book at a timely stage, so as to pull together as many updates as possible, given the current and continuing challenges facing all those involved in child protection.

Safda and Julie

Contents

List of Abbreviations

1980 Hague Convention	Hague Convention on the Civil Aspects of International Child Abduction 1980
1996 Hague Convention	Hague Convention on Jurisdiction, Applicable Law, Recognition, Enforcement and Co-operation in Respect of Parental Responsibility and Measures for the Protection of Children 1996
2010 Regulations	Care Planning, Placement and Case Review (England) Regulations 2010 (SI 2010/959)
2015 Regulations	Care Planning, Placement and Case Review (Wales) Regulations 2015 (SI 2015/1818) (W 261)
BIIR	Brussels II Regulation: Council Regulation (EC) 2201/2003 of 27 November 2003 concerning jurisdiction and the recognition and enforcement of judgments in matrimonial matters and the matters of parental responsibility
CA 1989	Children Act 1989
Cafcass	Children and Family Court Advisory and Support Service
Cafcass Cymru	Children and Family Court Advisory and Support Service Wales
CASP	care and support plan
CFA 2014	Children and Families Act 2014
CMH	case management hearing
CYPA 2008	Children and Young Persons Act 2008
DfE	Department for Education
DfES	Department for Education and Skills
DoH	Department of Health

DoL	deprivation of liberty
ECHR	European Convention for the Protection of Human Rights and Fundamental Freedoms 1950
FCMH	further case management hearing
FPC	family proceedings court
FPR 2010	Family Procedure Rules 2010 (SI 2010/2955)
HFEA 2008	Human Fertilisation and Embryology Act 2008
HMCTS	His Majesty's Courts and Tribunals Service
IRH	issues resolution hearing
IRO	independent reviewing officer
LAA	Legal Aid Agency
LASPO	Legal Aid, Sentencing and Punishment of Offenders Act 2012
LSCBs	Local Safeguarding Children Boards
MIAM	mediation information and assessment meeting
Part 3 Code of Practice	*Social Services and Well-being (Wales) Act 2014 – Part 3 Code of Practice (assessing the needs of individuals)* (Welsh Government, 2015)
Part 6 Code of Practice	*Social Services and Well-being (Wales) Act 2014 – Part 6 Code of Practice (Looked After and Accommodated Children)* (Welsh Government, Version 2, April 2018)
PACE	Police and Criminal Evidence Act 1984
PD	Practice Direction
PLO	*Public Law Outline*
SCRs	Serious Case Reviews
Secure Accommodation Regulations 1991	Children (Secure Accommodation) Regulations 1991 (SI 1991/1505)

SSW(W)A 2014	Social Services and Well-being (Wales) Act 2014
SWET	Social Worker Evidence Template
UK GDPR	UK General Data Protection Regulation: Regulation (EU) 2016/679 of the European Parliament and of the Council of 27 April 2016 as retained by the UK Government
UNCRC	UN Convention on the Rights of the Child
Working Together	*Working Together to Safeguard Children 2023: A guide to multi-agency working to help, protect and promote the welfare of children* (DfE, December 2023)

List of Figures and Tables

1 Glossary and Legislative Framework

1.1 Glossary of basic definitions

Interpretations of many terms used within the Children Act 1989 (CA 1989) are given in section 105. The source of definitions created by other sections, other Acts or by case law and other sources are cited. Unless otherwise stated, sections cited are from the CA 1989.

Adoption agency

> Defined in section 2(1) of the Adoption and Children Act 2002 and includes local authorities and approved adoption organisations. Their work is regulated by the Adoption Agencies Regulations 2005 (SI 2005/389) (as amended), and in Wales by the Adoption Agencies (Wales) Regulations 2005 (SI 2005/1313) (as amended).

Authorised person

> (a) In care and supervision proceedings, and in child assessment orders, this means the NSPCC or its officers, under sections 31(9) and 43(13) of the CA 1989. A person (other than a local authority) may be authorised by order of the Secretary of State to bring proceedings under section 31 for a care or supervision order, but no other person has been so authorised.
>
> (b) In emergency protection orders, proceedings may be brought by an 'authorised officer' of the local authority, an 'authorised person' (as defined in (a) above), a 'designated' police officer or 'any other person'; see sections 31(9) and 44 of the CA 1989.

Authority

> The local authority of a geographical area, including county councils, district councils, unitary authorities in England and Wales, Welsh county councils and Welsh county borough councils.

Care and support plan (CASP)

> A plan agreed for services to be provided by a local authority for a child in need of care and support in Wales, under Parts 3 and 4 of the Social Services and Well-being (Wales) Act 2014 (SSW(W)A 2014).

Care order

An order made under section 31(1)(a) of the CA 1989, placing a child in the care of a local authority. By section 31(11), this includes an interim care order made under section 38. By section 105, any reference to a child who is in the care of an authority is a reference to a child who is in the authority's care by virtue of a care order.

Child

A person under the age of 18.

Child arrangements order

An order made under section 8 of the CA 1989 regulating arrangements about with whom, and when, a child is to live, spend time or otherwise have contact. These orders replaced former residence and contact orders under section 8 from April 2014.

Child assessment order

An order under section 43 of the CA 1989 to produce the child and to comply with the court's directions relating to the assessment of the child. There are restrictions on keeping the child away from home under this section.

Child in need

Under section 17 of the CA 1989:

a child is taken to be in need if:

(a) he is unlikely to achieve or maintain, or to have the opportunity of achieving or maintaining, a reasonable standard of health or development without the provision for him of services by a local authority;

(b) his health or development is likely to be significantly impaired, or further impaired, without the provision for him of such services; or he is disabled.

Section 17 was repealed in Wales by the SSW(W)A 2014 with effect from April 2016.

Child looked after

Defined in section 22(1) of the CA 1989 and refers to a child who is subject to an interim care order made under section 38 or a full care order made under section 31(1)(a). It also includes a child who is accommodated by the local authority under section 20.

The relevant legislation about children looked after in Wales is contained in Part 6 of the SSW(W)A 2014.

Child minder

Defined in section 71 of the Care Standards Act 2000 as a person who looks after one or more children under the age of 8, for reward; for total period(s) exceeding 2 hours in any one day.

Child of the family

In relation to the parties to a marriage, under section 52 of the Matrimonial Causes Act 1973, this means: (a) a child of both of those parties; and (b) any other child, not being a child who is placed with those parties by a local authority or voluntary organisation, who has been treated by both of those parties as a child of their family.

Children and Family Court Advisory and Support Service

The Children and Family Court Advisory and Support Service (Cafcass) is responsible for Family Court social work services in England. In Wales, this service is provided by Cafcass Cymru.

Children's guardian

A social work practitioner appointed by the court to represent the child's interests in court proceedings. Children's guardians are provided by Cafcass.

Children's home

Defined in section 1 of the Care Standards Act 2000 as a home which usually provides or is intended to provide care and accommodation wholly or mainly for children. Obviously, the section lists several exceptions, including the homes of parents, relatives or those with parental responsibility for the children in question.

Community home

Defined in section 53 of the CA 1989 and may be: (a) a home provided, equipped and maintained by a local authority; or (b) provided by a voluntary organisation but in respect of which the management, equipment and maintenance of the home shall be the responsibility of the local authority or the responsibility of the voluntary organisation.

Contact order

This was defined in section 8(1) of the CA 1989 as 'an order requiring the person with whom a child lives, or is to live, to allow the child to visit or stay with the person named in the order, or for that person and the child otherwise to have contact with each other'. Orders about contact made since April 2014 are child arrangements orders.

Contact with a child in care

Section 34 of the CA 1989 creates a presumption that a child subject to a care order will have contact with his or her parents, and contains provisions for determination of contact issues by the court.

Development

Defined in section 31(9) of the CA 1989 as physical, intellectual, emotional, social or behavioural development.

Disabled

Defined in section 17(11) of the CA 1989 and in relation to a child, means a child who is blind, deaf or dumb, or who suffers from mental disorder of any kind or who is substantially and permanently handicapped by illness, injury or congenital deformity, or such other disability as may be prescribed.

Education supervision order

An order under section 36(1) of the CA 1989, putting the child with respect to whom the order is made under the supervision of a designated local education authority.

Emergency protection order

Under section 44 of the CA 1989, this order is a direction for a child to be produced and authorises the local authority either to remove the child to a safe place or to stop the child from being removed by others from a hospital or other safe place.

Family assistance order

An order made under section 16 of the CA 1989 appointing a probation officer or an officer of the local authority to advise, assist and (where appropriate) befriend any person named in the order for a period of 12 months or less. Named persons may include parents, guardians, those with whom the child lives or the child himself.

Family Court adviser

A social work practitioner directed by the court to assist it by providing dispute resolution services in section 8 applications and/or reports under section 7 of the CA 1989.

Family proceedings

Defined in section 8(3) and (4) of the CA 1989 as including any proceedings:

(a)   under the inherent jurisdiction of the High Court in relation to children, including wardship but not applications for leave under section 100(3) of the CA 1989;

(b)   under Parts I, II and IV of the CA 1989; the Matrimonial Causes Act 1973; Schedules 5 and 6 to the Civil Partnership Act 2004; the Adoption and Children Act 2002; the Domestic Proceedings and Magistrates' Courts Act 1978; Part III of the Matrimonial and Family Proceedings Act 1984; the Family Law Act 1996; and sections 11 and 12 of the Crime and Disorder Act 1998.

(Note that the definitions in section 8(3) and (4) do not include applications for emergency protection orders, child assessment orders or recovery orders.)

Guardian

A guardian, appointed under section 5 of the CA 1989, for the child, but not for the child's estate. A guardian appointed under section 5 has parental responsibility for the child, following the death of one or both parents, depending upon whether the situation comes within section 5(7) and (8).

Harm

Defined in section 31(9) of the CA 1989, meaning the ill treatment or the impairment of health or development. Where the question of whether or not the harm is significant turns on the child's health and development, his health or development shall be compared with that which could be reasonably expected of a similar child (section 31(10)).

Health

Under section 31 of the CA 1989, includes physical and mental health.

Hospital

Under section 105 of the CA 1989, any health service hospital and accommodation provided by the local authority and used as a hospital. It does not include special hospitals, which are those for people detained under the Mental Health Act 1983, providing secure hospital accommodation.

Ill treatment

Defined in section 31(9) of the CA 1989 and includes sexual abuse and forms of ill treatment which are not physical.

Independent reviewing officer

An independent reviewing officer (IRO) is appointed by the local authority to monitor the care planning process for looked after children. The IRO's functions are set out in *IRO Handbook: Statutory guidance for independent reviewing officers and local authorities on their functions in relation to case management and review for looked after children* (DfE, 2010). There is separate guidance under the SSW(W)A 2014.

Kinship care

Care for a child by family members or friends of the family. Kinship care may be arranged privately, on a voluntary basis, or as part of a care plan in the context of a care order.

Local authority

Under section 52 of the CA 1989, a council of a county, a metropolitan district or a London borough, or the Common Council of the City of London; in Scotland, it means a local authority under section 12 of the Social Work (Scotland) Act 1968.

Local authority foster carer

Defined in section 22C(12) of the CA 1989 as a person with whom a child has been placed by a local authority under section 22. Local authority foster carers may include a family member, a relative of the child or any other suitable person.

Local housing authority

Defined in the Housing Act 1944, meaning the district council, a London borough council, the Common Council of the City of London or Council of the Isles of Scilly.

Parent

The natural (birth) mother or father of a child, whether or not they are married to each other at the time of the birth or conception. In the CA 1989, when it states 'parent', it means the birth parents of a child, including, therefore, natural fathers without parental responsibility. Where it intends to mean 'a parent with parental responsibility', it states so specifically.

Parent (in relation to adoption)

Under the Adoption and Children Act 2002, the consent of each 'parent or guardian of the child' must be obtained for adoption or dispensed with by the court. Section 52(6) defines 'parent' as 'a parent having parental responsibility for the child …'.

Once a child has been adopted, his or her birth parents are no longer legally 'parents' of the child. Former parents would therefore need leave to apply for orders under section 51A of the Adoption and Children Act 2002 after adoption, if they wish to apply for contact after adoption.

Parent with parental responsibility

All mothers have parental responsibility for children born to them.

Fathers also have parental responsibility for their child if they married (or entered into a civil partnership with) the child's mother before or after the child's birth. The father of a child who is not married to the mother (nor in a civil partnership with the mother) is able to acquire parental responsibility in various ways under the CA 1989. This term therefore excludes the natural birth father of a child who has not acquired parental responsibility under the Act. See Chapter 3.

Parental responsibility

Defined in section 3 of the CA 1989 and includes all the rights, duties, powers, responsibilities and authority which by law a parent of a child has in relation to the child and his property. It can be acquired by an unmarried father in respect of his child by registration of the birth with the mother after 1 December 2003, by court order or by a parental responsibility agreement under the CA 1989; by others through child arrangements orders, specifying living with or special guardianship orders; or by a local authority under a care order and an emergency protection order. Parental responsibility can be shared with others. It ceases when the child reaches 18, on adoption, death or cessation of the care order. See the discussion in Chapter 3.

Parental responsibility agreement

Defined in section 4(1) of the CA 1989 as an agreement between the father and the mother of a child providing for the father to have parental responsibility for the child (a father married to the mother or in a civil partnership with the mother of their child at the time of the birth will automatically have parental responsibility for that child, but a father not so married will not). The format for the agreement is set out in the Parental Responsibility Agreement Regulations 1991 (SI 1991/1478) (as amended). See Chapter 3. Other persons can also acquire parental responsibility through a parental responsibility agreement, including step-parents and a second female parent (as defined in the Human Fertilisation and Embryology Act 2008).

Private fostering

Defined in section 66 of the CA 1989. To 'foster a child privately' means looking after a child under the age of 16 (or, if disabled, 18), caring and providing accommodation for him or her, by someone who is not the child's parent or relative, or who has parental responsibility for the child.

Prohibited steps order

Defined in section 8(1) of the CA 1989. An order that no step which could be taken by a parent in meeting his or her parental responsibility for a child, and which is of a kind specified in the order, shall be taken by any person without the consent of the court.

Public Law Outline

Referred to colloquially in court as 'the PLO', the *Public Law Outline* was originally issued as a Practice Direction in 2008. It is now set out in FPR 2010 PD 12A and provides guidance on how public law proceedings should be prepared, timetabled and presented in court. The term PLO is often used to describe the pre-proceedings stage.

Relative

In relation to a child, this means a grandparent, brother, sister, uncle or aunt (whether of the full blood or of the half blood or by affinity) or step-parent, see section 105 of the CA 1989.

Residence order

This was an order under section 8(1) of the CA 1989 settling the arrangements to be made as to the person with whom a child is to live that confers parental responsibility on the person who holds the order. Residence orders were replaced by child arrangements orders from April 2014.

Responsible person

Defined in Schedule 3, paragraph 1 to the CA 1989. In relation to a supervised child, it means:

(a)   any person who has parental responsibility for the child; and

(b)   any other person with whom the child is living.

Service

In relation to any provision made under Part III of the CA 1989 (local authority support for children and families), this means any facility.

Special educational needs

These arise when a child has a learning difficulty or disability which calls for special educational provision to be made. These terms are defined in section 20 of the Children and Families Act 2014 (CFA 2014) in England. In Wales, provision is made under the Additional Learning Needs Education and Tribunal (Wales) Act 2018.

Special guardian

A special guardianship order confers parental responsibility on the holder of the order, which she or he may exercise alone, excluding the parent. The provisions are found in sections 14A–F of the CA 1989.

Specific issue order

An order under section 8(1) of the CA 1989 giving directions for the purpose of determining a specific issue which has arisen, or which may arise, in connection with any aspect of parental responsibility for a child.

Supervision order

An order under section 31(1)(b) of the CA 1989 and (except where express provision to the contrary is made) includes an interim supervision order made under section 38.

Supervised child/supervisor

In relation to a supervision order or an education supervision order, these terms mean, respectively, the child who is (or is to be) under supervision and the person under whose supervision he is (or is to be) by virtue of the order.

Transparency order

An order made by a Family Court specifying the reporting restrictions imposed on journalists or legal bloggers who attend court hearings with a view to reporting on them. A template order is attached to *The Transparency Reporting Pilot, Guidance from the President of the Family Division*.

Upbringing

In relation to any child, this includes the care of the child but not his maintenance.

Voluntary organisation

A body (other than a public or local authority) whose activities are not carried on for profit.

1.2   Orders available under the Children Act 1989

Order	Section	Maximum duration*
Parental responsibility	4	Age 18
Guardianship	5	Age 18
Child arrangements orders, specifying living with	8	Age 18
Child arrangements orders, specifying spending time with, or otherwise having contact with	8	Age 16 (18 in exceptional circumstances)
Prohibited steps	8	Age 16 (18 in exceptional circumstances)
Specific issue	8	Age 16 (18 in exceptional circumstances)
Special guardianship order	14A	Age 18 (or earlier revocation)
Family assistance order	16	12 months
Care order	31	Age 18
Interim care and supervision order	38	Cannot extend beyond the duration of the proceedings
Supervision order	31	Age 18; one year, may be extended to max total 3 years
Contact with a child in care	34	Duration of care order
Education supervision order	36	One year; repeatedly extensible for 3 years; ceases at age 16
Child assessment	43	Seven days
Emergency protection	44	Eight days; extensible for further 7 days

Note

*   These orders may be brought to an end by court order, variation or discharge and subject to additional provisions. For details, please refer to the relevant chapter.

1.3   Introduction to the Children Act 1989

The CA 1989 came into force on 19 October 1991, containing 108 sections and 15 Schedules, and was accompanied by the Family Proceedings Courts (Children Act 1989) Rules 1991 (SI 1991/1395), the Family Proceedings (Children) Rules 1991 (SI 1991/910) and several volumes of *The Children Act 1989 Guidance and Regulations* (DCSF, 2008) (*Guidance and Regulations*). The rules were replaced by the Family Procedure Rules 2010 (SI 2010/2955) (FPR 2010), and most of the *Guidance and Regulations* have been gradually updated.

The CA 1989 created a new unified court system consisting of three tiers: the High Court, the county court and the family proceedings court (FPC), each of which had concurrent jurisdiction and powers. From April 2014, the FPC and county court jurisdiction was merged into the Family Court. The avoidance of delay is one of the underlying principles of the CA 1989. This Act, along with its subsidiary rules, created a new system of directions hearings to enable the courts to take firmer control of the timing of cases, admission of evidence and administrative matters, which has been strengthened by amendments made by the CFA 2014.

The CA 1989 encourages families to stay together, imposing a duty on local authorities to provide services for children in need and their families, to reduce the necessity for children to be looked after away from home and for child protection proceedings. Unless the criteria for the making of care or supervision orders are met, an order cannot be made. The courts, if concerned about the welfare of a child, may order a local authority to investigate the child's circumstances, but the courts have no power of their own volition to order a child into the care of a local authority.

The CA 1989 introduced a new concept of parental responsibility, which unmarried fathers may gain in relation to their children, and which was accessible to other adults, such as grandparents or step-parents, who could apply for residence orders or special guardianship. It also created orders governing aspects of a child's life, i.e. contact with others, residence and resolution of disputed aspects of child care – prohibited steps (forbidding actions) and specific issues (permitting actions to take place).

The principles behind the CA 1989 and its guidance are that children are people whose rights are to be respected, not just 'objects of concern', and that children should, wherever possible, remain with their families, helped if necessary by provision of services, provided that their welfare is safeguarded. An atmosphere of negotiation and co-operation between professionals is encouraged. The welfare of the child is paramount in court proceedings, and, in the field of child care and protection, professionals are expected to work together in a non-adversarial way for the benefit of the child.

Part III of the CA 1989 (sections 17–30) was repealed in Wales by the SSW(W)A 2014 with effect from April 2016. The sections relating to children in need have been replaced by Parts 3 and 4 of that Act; sections relating to looked-after children have been replicated in Part 6.

Statutory guidance on child protection, known as *Working Together*, was issued under the CA 1989 and has been regularly updated and replaced by government. The current guidance in England was issued by the Department for Education in December 2023 as *Working Together to Safeguard Children 2023: A guide to multi-agency working to help, protect and promote the welfare of children* (*Working Together*). Safeguarding guidance in Wales is issued as Codes under the SSW(W)A 2014 and in the *Wales Safeguarding Procedures: Children and young people at risk of harm*.

Section 6 of the Human Rights Act 1998 makes it unlawful for public authorities to act in ways incompatible with the rights set out in the European Convention for the Protection of Human Rights and Fundamental Freedoms 1950 (ECHR). This includes courts, tribunals and local authorities, including both acts and omissions (section 6). Those affected may bring proceedings or rely on the ECHR (section 7) by way of an appeal, complaint or judicial review.

1.4   Changes to the Children Act 1989 introduced with the Family Court in 2014

In April 2014, a number of amendments to the CA 1989, made by the CFA 2014, took effect. These were:

(a)   Attendance at a mediation information and assessment meeting (a MIAM) as a requirement before issuing an application for a child arrangements order.

(b)   Introduction of a presumption in a section 8 application that it is in a child's welfare to have continued parental involvement by both parents, where this is safe.

(c)   Introduction of child arrangements orders.

(d)   Control and limitation of the use of independent expert evidence in children proceedings.

(e)   Introduction of an expectation of a 26-week limit on duration of care proceedings.

2 Principles Underlying the Children Act 1989

2.1 Paramountcy of the welfare of the child

The CA 1989 commences with a clear direction in section 1(1) that:

> When a court determines any question with respect to—
>
> (a) the upbringing of a child; or
>
> (b) the administration of a child's property or the application of any income arising from it,
>
> the child's welfare shall be the paramount consideration.

This means that after weighing all the factors, the court's decision will be made in accordance with the child's welfare. The child's welfare is not paramount if the decision is not about his or her upbringing or is not one being made within court proceedings.

The child's welfare is not always easy to determine, and so the CA 1989 sets out a list of criteria in section 1(3), known as the 'welfare checklist'. It is primarily intended as an *aide-mémoire*, particularly useful for judges, children's guardians, professionals and expert witnesses, but the court must have regard to it when considering an application to vary or discharge an order under Part IV (a child protection order), a special guardianship order, a section 8 order for child arrangements or specific issue or prohibited steps, and magistrates should always refer to the checklist when considering their findings of fact and reasons for their decisions.

The welfare checklist is not compulsory in other circumstances, but it is always useful for practitioners to consider it. If experts refer to these criteria whilst writing their reports, they will ensure that they are complying with the principles of the CA 1989.

2.1.1 Welfare checklist

The welfare checklist is set out in section 1(3) of the CA 1989:

> (a) the ascertainable wishes and feelings of the child concerned (considered in the light of his age and understanding);
>
> (b) his physical, emotional and educational needs;

(c)   the likely effect on him of any change in his circumstances;

(d)   his age, sex, background and any characteristics of his which the court considers relevant;

(e)   any harm which he is suffering or which he is at risk of suffering;

(f)   how capable each of his parents, and any other person in relation to whom the court considers the question to be relevant, is of meeting his needs;

(g)   the range of powers available to the court under this Act in the proceedings in question.

In private law cases (those between individuals as opposed to those involving state intervention in a family's life), in proceedings that are not 'specified proceedings' listed in section 41 of the CA 1989, the court may ask the Family Court adviser to investigate the child's circumstances and to report back to the court the child's wishes and feelings, also advising the court on the best way to safeguard the child's welfare.

The court should be alert to any unusual circumstances or factors of concern in private law cases, even if the parties themselves are in agreement. The court may, where there is a concern, make a direction to the local authority to investigate the child's circumstances under section 37 of the CA 1989 and appoint a children's guardian to safeguard the welfare of the child at the same time.

The court may also make orders under section 8 or section 16 of the CA 1989 (family assistance orders) of its own volition, if necessary.

Where there is more than one child subject to an application, the court must consider the welfare of each child and try to achieve the right balance. However, in *Birmingham County Council v H* [1994] 1 FLR 224, the court held that in a Part IV application concerning a child whose parent was herself still a minor, the welfare of only the child subject to the application was paramount.

2.2   Delay is deemed prejudicial to child's interests (the impact of the *Public Law Outline*)

In proceedings in which any question with respect to the upbringing of a child arises, the court shall have regard to the general principle that any delay in determining the question is likely to prejudice the welfare of the child (section 1(2) of the CA 1989).

The courts have been greatly concerned about delays in the Family Court system. One attempt at grasping the nettle was an interim *Protocol for*

Judicial Case Management issued in 2003. This was replaced by the PLO, issued as *Practice Direction: Guide to Case Management in Public Law Proceedings* by the President of the Family Division, and operative from 1 April 2008. The Direction has been revised as FPR 2010 PD 12A and is available on the Ministry of Justice website, www.justice.gov.uk. The President of the Family Division re-launched the PLO on 16 January 2023.

Under the PLO, the cases progress through four stages:

(1)   pre-proceedings up until the end of the first appointment in court;

(2)   the advocates meeting and the case management stage;

(3)   issues resolution hearing (**IRH**) and the preceding advocates meeting;

(4)   final hearing and directions for disclosure at the conclusion of the case.

The court regulates the conduct of cases by use of questionnaires, pro formas, meetings, hearings and directions. In these, the court establishes who are parties to, or who should have notice of, the proceedings. The court ensures that the evidence is in order and service is carried out. A timetable is set for preparation of the case and disclosure of evidence to other parties and the children's guardian, and a hearing date is fixed. Directions given carry the force of court orders, failure to comply with them will be viewed by the court seriously and a full explanation for non-compliance will be required. Sanctions include wasted costs orders against those parties to a case who cause (or negligently allow) unnecessary delay. For the Court of Appeal's guidance on wasted costs, see *Ridelhalgh v Horsfield and Watson v Watson* [1994] 2 FLR 194.

A recommendation from the *Family Justice Review Final Report* (Ministry of Justice, 2011) was that care proceedings under section 31 of the CA 1989 should have a time limit imposed of 6 months. This recommendation was tested and subsequently enshrined in legislation under section 32 of the CA 1989 (as amended). Possible justifications for an extension to the 26-week period are contained in the case management order template.

2.3   No order unless necessary in the interests of the child

The CA 1989 assumes that the parties will do their best to resolve differences by negotiation and co-operation. Section 1(5) provides that the court has a positive duty not to make an order unless it is in the interests of the child to do so. This is referred to as the 'non-intervention' principle and applies primarily to applications in private law disputes where agreement may have been reached.

However, the Court of Appeal held in *Re G (Children) (Residence: Making of Order)* [2005] EWCA Civ 1283 that section 1(5) of the CA 1989 does not create any presumption against making an order, just that, before making an order, the court will ask whether it will be better for the child to make an order than not to make one.

3 Parental Responsibility

On 19 October 1991, sections 2 and 3 of the CA 1989 changed the status of parents in relation to their children, by creating the concept of 'parental responsibility'.

Amazingly, many parents are still unaware of these changes, and they are also unaware that not all parents will have parental responsibility for their children. Parental responsibility may be shared with others, and it may be delegated in part, but it may not be surrendered or transferred entirely, save by adoption or a parental order. Each person who has parental responsibility may exercise it without a duty to consult others who also have it, with certain exceptions, but in the event of disagreement or a need for child protection, its exercise is also subject to orders of the court. Subject to limited exceptions, people who have a special guardianship order in their favour may exercise their parental responsibility to the exclusion of all others with parental responsibility other than another special guardian for the child.

3.1 Definition, powers and duties of parental responsibility

Section 3(1) of the CA 1989 defines parental responsibility as, 'All the rights, duties, powers, responsibilities and authority which by law a parent of a child has in relation to the child and his property'.

This wonderfully vague definition is not clarified anywhere in the CA 1989 except in section 3(2), which states that parental responsibility includes the powers of a guardian in looking after a child's property, for example, to give a valid receipt for a legacy.

Some statutory powers are reliant upon parental responsibility:

(a) appointment of guardian for a child in the event of death (section 5(3) of the CA 1989);

(b) consent to the adoption of the child (section 19(1) and (2) of the Adoption and Children Act 2002); parent in this context is defined as a 'parent' with parental responsibility under section 52(5);

(c) access to the child's medical records (sections 4, 5 and 12 of the Access to Health Records Act 1990 (as amended));

(d)   consent to a child's marriage (as previously set out in section 3 of the Marriage Act 1949 (as amended by Schedule 12, paragraph 5 to the CA 1989, but since repealed by virtue of the Marriage and Civil Partnership (Minimum Age) Act 2022)). Note that the 2022 Act has increased the minimum age for marriage and civil partnership to 18 as from 27 February 2023;

(e)   subject to limited exceptions, consent of all those with parental responsibility or leave of the court is required for removal of a child from the United Kingdom, failing which a criminal offence is committed (section 1 of the Child Abduction Act 1984). This provision applies even if there is in place a child arrangements order, specifying living with; but under s 13(2) of the CA 1989, the person holding the child arrangements order, specifying living with, in his or her favour, may take the child abroad for up to one month. The court may, of course, grant additional or general leave to take the child abroad for longer periods or permanently.

Other decisions and powers of those with parental responsibility include:

(a)   *Consent to medical assessment, examination or treatment.* See para 3.1.2 and Chapter 12. 'Nearest relative' in the Mental Health Act 1983 is defined under section 26(1). Also, section 27 of the Act provides that where: '(a) a patient who is a child or young person in the care of a local authority by virtue of a care order within the meaning of the Children Act 1989; or (b) the rights and powers of a parent of a patient who is a child or young person are vested in a local authority by virtue of section 16 of the Social Work (Scotland) Act 1968, the authority shall be deemed to be the nearest relative of the patient in preference to any person except the patient's husband or wife, or civil partner (if any)'.

(b)   *Ill treatment, neglect and other forms of harm.* See section 1 of the Children and Young Persons Act 1933, which provides that if any person who has attained the age of 16 years and has responsibility for any child or young person under that age, wilfully assaults, ill-treats, neglects, abandons or exposes him, or causes or procures him to be assaulted, ill-treated, neglected, abandoned or exposed, in a manner likely to cause him unnecessary suffering or injury to health (including injury to or loss of sight, hearing, limb or organ of the body, and any mental derangement), that person shall be guilty of a misdemeanour and is criminally liable.

(c)   *Application for or veto of child's passport.* In particular, note FPR 2010 PD 12P, which sets out the situations surrounding the removal from the jurisdiction, and the issue of a passport for a child who is a ward of court. PD 12P, paragraph 2.1 provides that it is the practice of the

Passport Department of the Home Office to issue passports for wards in accordance with the court's direction. This frequently results in passports being restricted to the holiday period specified in the order giving leave.

(d) *Right to represent child as 'litigation friend' in all court proceedings where the child is a party, except cases involving child protection or the upbringing of the child.* Note that for those cases where the child is a party in children cases, that child is classed as a 'protected party' under Part 15 of the FPR 2010. Part 15 provides for the appointment of a litigation friend to conduct proceedings on behalf of the protected party. The terms 'next friend' and 'guardian ad litem' have been removed. Part 16 of the FPR 2010 contains provisions for the representation of children in 'specified proceedings', as well as other proceedings. In this context, note the *Practice Note: The Official Solicitor to the Senior Courts: Appointment in Family Proceedings and Proceedings under the Inherent Jurisdiction in Relation to Adults* (17 May 2023). This replaced the Practice Note dated March 2013, and relates principally to the appointment of the Official Solicitor as 'litigation friend' of a 'protected party' or child in family proceedings, where the Family Division of the High Court is being invited to exercise its inherent jurisdiction in relation to a vulnerable adult, or where proceedings in relation to a child aged 16 or 17 are transferred into the Court of Protection.

(e) *Right to name or re-name child.* If both parents have parental responsibility and they agree, there is no problem. Please note Practice Direction [1995] 1 FLR 458 and *Re PC (Change of Surname)* [1997] 2 FLR 730 for guidance. In cases where one parent wishes to change a child's name, the consent of all others with parental responsibility is required, or in the absence of consent, the leave of the court is required. See, also the Enrolment of Deeds (Change of Name) (Amendment) Regulations 2005 (SI 2005/2056) and the Enrolment of Deeds (Change of Name) Regulations 1994 (SI 1994/604) (reproduced in the Appendix to FPR 2010 PD 5A). Also, as to the position with parental responsibility and change of surname, see the comments of Ryder LJ in *Re W (Children)* [2013] EWCA Civ 1488 at [12].

(f) *Registration of child's name.* Under section 2 of the Births and Deaths Registration Act 1953, a baby's name must be registered within 42 days of birth. Parents with parental responsibility may register the name. Fathers without parental responsibility, therefore, in most cases will have no power to register the baby's name without an order of the court. See *Re PK, Re A, and Re B (Change of Name)* [1999] 2 FLR 930 and the House of Lords in *Dawson v Wearmouth* [1999] 1 FLR 1167, but note joint registration of birth at para 3.4.3. See, also, the case of *F v F* [2007] EWHC 2543 (Fam), [2008] 1 FLR 1163, which considers the situations where a change of surname may be warranted, in order to generate an improvement in the child's welfare.

(g) *Deciding child's education and sending child to school.* The right to decide a child's education and the duty to send a child to school or to provide suitable alternative schooling are set out in the Education Act 1966. Section 7 of the Act requires the parent of a child of compulsory schooling age to ensure that the child receives full-time education, suitable to the child's age, ability and aptitude, and to any special education needs that child may have. It may be appropriate to withhold information to a parent relating to the child's education in appropriate cases. In particular, consider *H v A (No 1)* [2015] EWFC 58 about withholding information as to the children's schooling from the father. At [57]–[63], MacDonald J decided that, given the exceptional circumstances of the case, it was proportionate that the father was prohibited from receiving, in the exercise of his parental responsibility, any information from the children's schools. The children had a continuing physical and emotional need for a family and home life that was stable, secure and safe from further trauma instigated by the father.

(h) *Decisions about child's religion.* The courts will not interfere unless the welfare of the child is threatened. Consider the sensitive cases involving circumcision, such as *Re S (Specific Issue Order: Religion: Circumcision)* [2005] 1 FLR 236. In this case, the court decided that children of dual religious heritage should be entitled to practise both faiths in appropriate cases, and that they should be allowed to decide for themselves which, if any, religion they sought to follow. Also, see the case of *Re N (A Child: Religion – Jehovah's Witness)* [2011] EWHC B26 (Fam), where the court stressed that parental responsibility is joint and equal, and that one parent does not have a right to unilaterally determine the child's religion. The issue of religion, culture and contact was addressed by the Court of Appeal in the case of *Re M (Children)* [2017] EWCA Civ 2164, in which the then President of the Family Division, Sir James Munby, handed down the leading judgment. His Lordship provided that this case raised the question of how, in evaluating a child's welfare, the court is to respond to the impact on the child of behaviour, or the fear of behaviour, which is or may be unlawfully discriminatory as involving breaches of Article 14 of the ECHR. Also, at [86], His Lordship provided that the trial judge appeared to have had in mind that there may be breaches of the Equality Act 2010. It would seem that if a school were to ostracise a pupil, because of his or her father's transgender status, that would amount at the very least to 'any other detriment' within the meaning of section 85(2)(f) of the Equality Act 2010. That would constitute direct discrimination, within the meaning of section 13(1), and would be unlawful. More recently, in *A Local Authority v WSP & Others (A Child) (Vaccination: Religious Objection)* [2023] EWHC 2622 (Fam), there was an application brought by the mother, seeking for the court to exercise its inherent jurisdiction to injunct the local authority from exercising its parental responsibility under section 33(3) of the CA 1989, to arrange for the child to receive routine childhood vaccinations. She objected to the vaccinations on the grounds of her religious beliefs. In deciding against the mother, the judge took the view that given the lack of any cogent and credible evidence of contraindication on health or welfare grounds in the child's case, it was necessary to direct the vaccinations and that these were a necessary and proportionate interference with the mother's right to manifest her religion. Furthermore, more recently, in *BC v A Local Authority* [2024] EWHC 1639 (Fam), it was reinforced that the paramount consideration is the child's best interests.

3.1.1 Duration

Parental responsibility lasts until a child is 18 years old if it belongs to the mother, the child's married father, the father with a parental responsibility agreement, legitimation or joint registration, or other person with a court order. Parental responsibility can be ordered with child arrangements orders, specifying living with, and through guardianship. See paras 3.4.4 and 3.5.4.

3.1.2 Parental responsibility and medical consent

Save in emergencies, no person may be given medical treatment without consent. Whatever the motivation, this may constitute an assault for which practitioners may incur liability in tort or criminal law. Detention in hospital or any other place without consent could constitute false imprisonment. Those with parental responsibility, or a court, may give consent for medical assessment or treatment of a child. In emergencies, where there is no person capable or available to give or withhold consent, the doctor may lawfully treat the patient.

Medical records should note who has parental responsibility for a child. With unmarried parents, in the absence of a parental responsibility agreement, joint registration or court order, only the mother will have parental responsibility for the child. Should she (or any lone person with parental responsibility) die, there will be no one with parental responsibility for the child. Single parents should therefore appoint a guardian for their child; see para 3.5.4.

Young people aged 16 and over

Section 8 of the Family Law Reform Act 1969 confers on a person aged 16 and over the right to give informed consent to surgical, medical or dental treatment. Examinations or assessments could also impliedly be included. Those who suffer mental illness, disability or psychiatric disturbance will be subject to the same mental health provisions and safeguards as adults.

Children aged under 16

See Chapter 12, paras 12.1 and 12.2.

In *Gillick v West Norfolk and Wisbech Area Health Authority* [1986] AC 112, Mrs Gillick challenged her local health authority's provision of contraceptive advice to her daughters, aged under 16, without her consent. The House of Lords supported the health authority's actions. In giving judgment, it formulated the concept known colloquially as '*Gillick* competence'. A child under 16 may make medical decisions according to her chronological age, in conjunction with mental and emotional maturity, intelligence, her comprehension of the nature and consequences of the decision to be made and the quality of the information provided.

The rationale of the *Gillick* case has been considered and approved in *R (Axon) v Secretary of State for Health* [2006] EWHC 37 (Admin), in which abortion for a child under 16 was the subject of the court's consideration. Although distinctions could be made between the issues in *Gillick*, i.e. advice and treatment for contraception and sexually transmitted illnesses, on the one hand, and abortion in the *Axon* case, on the other hand, which gave rise to more serious and complex issues, the guidelines set out in *Gillick*, properly adapted, were considered appropriate as guidance in respect of all sexual matters. That was because the majority in *Gillick* did not indicate that their conclusions were dependent on the nature of the treatment proposed. The *Gillick* guidelines are of general application to all forms of medical advice and treatment.

In the case of *Re R (A Minor: Consent to Medical Treatment)* [1992] 1 FLR 190, the Court of Appeal held that a '*Gillick*-competent' child acquires a right to make decisions equal to that of each of his parents and only the absence of consent by all having that power would create a veto. However, the *Reference Guide to Consent for Examination or Treatment* (DoH, 2nd edn, July 2009), Chapter 3, paragraph 13 advises that where a young person of 16 or 17 who could consent to treatment in accordance with section 8 of the Family Law Reform Act 1969, or a child under 16, but *Gillick* competent, refuses treatment, it is possible that such a refusal could be overruled if it would in all probability lead to the death of the child/young person or to severe permanent injury. In this context, *Consent: Patients and doctors making decisions together* (General Medical Council, 2008), paragraph 79 provides that when an emergency arises in a clinical setting, and it is not possible to find out a patient's wishes, a doctor can treat the patient without his consent, provided the treatment is immediately necessary to save the patient's life or to prevent a serious deterioration of his condition. The treatment must be the least restrictive of the patient's future choices.

In relation to medical examination of children, there is the *Physical Signs of Child Sexual Abuse* publication of 2015, which relates to the physical signs of child sexual abuse. This guidance has been produced in collaboration with the American Academy of Pediatrics, the Royal College of Physicians of London and the Faculty of Forensic and Legal Medicine. The 2015 book updates the evidence of the physical signs of child sexual abuse from the 2008 publication and includes reviews on anogenital signs of accidental injuries in girls and boys, genital bleeding in prepubertal girls and healing in anogenital injuries.

If there is disagreement or refusal concerning medical treatment for a child when a doctor considers it medically necessary, and negotiation fails, then the matter can be resolved under section 8 of the CA 1989 by a specific issue order. The High Court in its inherent jurisdiction or under the CA 1989 can override the wishes of anyone in relation to the medical treatment of a child if this is adjudged to be in the child's best interests. The case of *Re SL (Permission to Vaccinate)* [2017] EWHC 125 (Fam) is a helpful illustration of the use of the inherent jurisdiction. Here, the local authority had applied under the inherent jurisdiction for a declaration that it was in the child's best interests for the authority to arrange for the child to receive the Haemophilus Influenza Type b (Hib) vaccine, and the pneumococcal conjugate (PCV) vaccine, in circumstances where the mother objected to these. This case showed that if the child is in the care of the local authority, as a result of section 9(1), the local authority could not apply for a specific issue order with respect to the issue of vaccination. Also, given the gravity of the issue in dispute, it was not appropriate for the local authority to give its consent to immunisation pursuant to the provisions of section 33(3), on the basis of its shared parental responsibility for the child under the interim care order. Instead, there was a need to make an application for relief under the inherent jurisdiction of the High Court, and to seek leave to invoke the jurisdiction in the first instance, pursuant to section 100(4). Having said that, there have been significant developments in this area over the last few years. In particular, in the case of *Re C (Looked After Child) (Covid-19 Vaccination)* [2021] EWHC 2993 (Fam), Poole J referred to the Court of Appeal decision in *Re H* [2020] EWCA Civ 664, and decided that a local authority with a care order had the right under section 33 of the CA 1989 to exercise parental responsibility by arranging for, and consenting to, vaccinations for the child for Covid-19 and/or the winter flu virus notwithstanding parental objection. At [21], His Lordship said that in the absence of any factors of substance that might realistically call into question whether the vaccinations are in an individual child's best interests, decisions for the child to undergo standard or routine vaccinations that are part of national vaccination programmes are not to be regarded as 'grave' decisions having profound or enduring consequences for the child. Furthermore, as referred to at para 3.1, in *A Local Authority v WSP & Others (A Child) (Vaccination: Religious Objection)* [2023] EWHC 2622 (Fam), the local authority was able to exercise its parental responsibility under section 33(3) of the CA 1989, to arrange for the child to receive routine childhood vaccinations. The mother had objected to the vaccinations on the grounds of her religious beliefs, but on the facts, there was a lack of any cogent and credible evidence of contraindication on health or welfare grounds in the child's case to prevent the local authority from consenting to the vaccinations on the basis they were in the best interests of the child's welfare.

3.1.3   What if there is no one with parental responsibility?

Where immediate action is needed for the welfare of the child and no one with parental responsibility is available, section 3(5) of the CA 1989 provides that:

> A person who:
>
> > (a) does not have parental responsibility for a particular child; but
> >
> > (b) has care of the child,
>
> may do what is reasonable in all the circumstances of the case for the purpose of safeguarding or promoting the child's welfare.

This could apply to child minders, foster carers, neighbours and others looking after children who may need to take a child quickly to the GP or dentist, etc. This section, however, is not intended to cover consent for major medical issues.

In this context, it is worth noting the comments made by Lady Hale in *Williams & Another v London Borough of Hackney* [2018] UKSC 37, whereby at [44], Her Ladyship stated that section 20(8) of the CA 1989 makes it absolutely clear that a parent with parental responsibility may remove the child from accommodation provided or arranged by a local authority at any time. There is no need to give notice, in writing or otherwise. The only caveat, as Munby J said in *R (G) v Nottingham City Council* [2008] EWHC 152 (Admin), was the right of anyone to take necessary steps to protect a person, including a child, from being physically harmed by another: for example, if a parent turned up drunk demanding to drive the child home. In such circumstances, the people caring for the child would have the power (under section 3(5) of the CA 1989) to do what is reasonable in all the circumstances for the purpose of safeguarding or promoting the child's welfare.

3.2 Legal position of child's birth mother

Parental responsibility always belongs to a mother in relation to the children to whom she has given birth. It does not matter whether or not she is married to the father of the child (or to anyone else). Nothing can remove that parental responsibility from her save death, adoption of the child or a parental order. For surrogacy arrangements, see paras 3.5.6 and 3.5.7.

3.3 Legal position of child's father

3.3.1 Married fathers and those who are civil partners

Under section 2(1) of the CA 1989, a father automatically has parental responsibility for his child if he was married to (or the civil partner of) the child's mother at the time of the child's birth. This concept includes marriage/civil partnership at the time of the child's conception. See *Re Overbury (Deceased)* [1954] 3 All ER 308. The man must be the biological father. Section 1(2)–(4) of the Family Law Reform Act 1987 includes in the meaning of section 2(1) children who are legitimated by statute. This enables a child's father to gain parental responsibility if he subsequently marries (or enters into a civil partnership with) the child's mother after conception or the birth of the child.

The authors are told by clients that many arguments by married couples have ended with '… and anyway she is not your child!'. The parents of a legitimate child have parental responsibility for that child. The test of legitimacy is that the child is born to parents who are married to, or the civil partner of, each other at the time of the child's birth. Section 1(2) and (3) of the Family Law Reform Act 1987 includes children who are legitimated by their parents' subsequent marriage/civil partnership. A child's legitimacy may be rebutted by cogent evidence, for example, a DNA paternity test showing that the husband is not the father of the child.

Children born to a married couple or civil partners as a result of artificial insemination will, however, be regarded as the child of the husband or civil partner provided that the conditions set out in the Human Fertilisation and Embryology Act 2008 (HFEA 2008) are met.

Note that a man who becomes a step-parent on marriage or civil partnership does not automatically acquire parental responsibility for his spouse's or civil partner's children, see para 3.5.2.

3.3.2   Unmarried fathers

A father who is not married to, nor a civil partner of, the mother of his child has no parental responsibility at the time of birth, but he can acquire it in a number of ways. These are set out below.

3.4   Acquisition and loss of parental responsibility by child's birth father

3.4.1   Parental responsibility order

A father may apply under section 4(1)(a) of the CA 1989 for a parental responsibility order.

Applicant

The father without parental responsibility (section 4(1) of the CA 1989). Also, the spouse or civil partner who has parental responsibility for the child (section 4A), as well as the second female legal parent pursuant to section 43 of the HFEA 2008 (no one else can apply).

Attendance

All parties shall attend, unless otherwise directed (rule 12.14(2)(a) of the FPR 2010). The Rules make an exception that proceedings shall take place in the absence of any party (including the child if he is represented by a children's guardian or solicitor, and it is in the child's interests having regard to the issues or evidence (rule 12.14(3))).

Issues for the court

Degree of attachment between father and child; commitment shown by father to child; the reasons for the application (not improper or wrong). CA 1989 principles – welfare of child paramount, no delay and no order unless it is in best interests of child to make it.

Relevant cases: *Re G (Minor) (Parental Responsibility Order)* [1994] 1 FLR 504, *Re T (Minor) (Parental Responsibility)* [1993] 2 FLR 450, *Re S (Parental Responsibility)* [1995] 2 FLR 648, *Re M (Contact: Family Assistance: McKenzie Friend)* [1999] 1 FLR 75 and *Re J (Parental Responsibility)* [1999] 1 FLR 784.

Also, see later case law, which has considered the concept of 'parenthood' in disputes surrounding parental responsibility. In particular, consider *Re D (Contact and PR: Lesbian Mothers and Known Father) (No 2)* [2006] EWHC 2 (Fam), [2006] 1 FCR 556 in which Black J made use of 'recitals' in applications for parental responsibility by the father. Contrast this case, however, with the case of *R v E and F (Female Parents: Known Father)* [2010] EWHC 417 (Fam), [2010] 2 FLR 383, in which Bennett J decided that the father of the child had a key role to play in the child's life, but was not on an 'equal footing' with the mother and her partner on the facts. In the case of *JB v KS (A Child)* [2015] EWHC 180 (Fam), the court was satisfied that the father, in applying for a parental responsibility order, would not use the order in any way to undermine the mother. He shared so many of the mother's objectives. He ultimately sought the order so that his status as a father could be properly reflected in law.

In the context of private children law applications, note the introduction of the concept of 'parental involvement' by section 11 of the CFA 2014, which came into force on 22 October 2014. The effect of section 11(1) of the CFA 2014 is that section 1 of the CA 1989, in relation to the welfare of the child, is amended so that section 1(2A) of the CA 1989 has the effect that in certain situations, unless the contrary is shown, the court is to presume that the involvement of that parent in the life of the child concerned will further the child's welfare. In terms of what a 'parent' is, for the purposes of this concept of parental involvement, section 11(3) of the CFA 2014 defines a 'parent' as a parent of the child concerned. This is provided for within section 1(6) of the CA 1989.

Notice

Local authority providing accommodation for the child. Also, person(s) with whom the child is living at time of application, and those providing a refuge need to be served with FPR 2010 PD 12C, Form C6A, paragraph 3.1.

Parties / respondents

All those with parental responsibility (or if a care order is in force, those who had parental responsibility immediately prior to that order) (rule 12.3 of the FPR 2010).

On a discharge application, all parties to the original proceedings will be respondents, as well as the respondent to the parental responsibility application (rule 12.3 of the FPR 2010).

Procedural notes

Family proceedings under the CA 1989. Application on Form C1. Also, Form FM1 is to be sent to court (pursuant to FPR 2010 PD 3A and section 10 of the CFA 2014). Form C1A is also to be sent to court if it is alleged that the child who is subject to the application has suffered, or is at risk of suffering, significant harm, in the form of domestic abuse, violence, abduction or other behaviour.

Service at least 14 days before date of directions/hearing (FPR 2010 PD 12C, paragraph 2.1). Respondents are served with notice in Form C6, and non-parties are to be served with Form C6A, which gives them notice of the proceedings (FPR 2010 PD 12C, paragraph 3.1). Individuals can be joined to the application for parental responsibility by applying on Form C2 (rule 12.3(3) of the FPR 2010). The court can also join people using its general case management powers in making the order for joinder of its own initiative, pursuant to rule 4.3 of the FPR 2010. The remaining procedure is the same as for section 8 applications, see Chapter 13, and see, in particular, FPR 2010 PD 12B and the subsequent pilot programmes.

Status of child

With leave, a child of sufficient age and understanding can oppose the application or apply to set aside the order.

3.4.2   Parental responsibility agreement with the mother

The mother and father may agree that the father shall have parental responsibility for the child. The agreement must be made in accordance with the Children (Parental Responsibility Agreement) Regulations 1991 (SI 1991/1478) (as amended by the Parental Responsibility Agreement (Amendment) Regulations 1994 (SI 1994/3157), the Parental Responsibility Agreement (Amendment) Regulations 2005 (SI 2005/2808) and the Parental Responsibility Agreement (Amendment) Regulations 2009 (SI 2009/2026)). Note that the latter statutory instrument amends the previous Regulations, so as to provide for the acquisition of parental responsibility by a second female parent. This involves completion of Form C (PRA3).

The prescribed Form C (PRA1) for use by the mother of the child and the father is straightforward and must be completed, signed by the mother and father and witnessed by a magistrate, justices' clerk or a court officer. The child's birth certificate should be produced, together with proof of identity incorporating a signature and photograph, for example a photo card driving licence, official pass or passport.

Note that, under section 4A of the CA 1989, a step-parent who is the married partner of, or (following the implementation of the Civil Partnership Act 2004) civil partner to, a parent with parental responsibility for a child, may enter into a parental responsibility agreement with the parent(s) of the child. In this case, the parental responsibility agreement will be on Form C (PRA2) and the same proofs of identity will be required. In addition, proof of the marriage or civil registration will be necessary. The completed and witnessed Form C (PRA2) then has to be registered with the Central Family Court, at First Avenue House, 42–49 High Holborn, London WC1V 6NP, and will take effect once it is registered. A copy is sent to each parent. Form C (PRA3), referred to above, will be used for the second female legal parent.

Precedents for all three forms are set out in the Schedule to the Parental Responsibility Agreement (Amendment) Regulations 2009 (SI 2009/2026), available at www.legislation.gov.uk.

3.4.3 Joint registration of the birth by father and mother

The effect of section 4(1)(a) of the CA 1989 is that where a child's father and mother were not married to (or civil partners of) each other at the time of his birth, the father shall acquire parental responsibility for the child if he becomes registered as the child's father under any of the enactments specified in subsection (1A) of the CA 1989. This was a provision brought in by the Adoption and Children Act 2002 and it applies only to registrations of birth made on or after 1 December 2003. The mother must agree to the inclusion of the father at the registration of the birth. Registration can unilaterally be applied for where there is a court order in force for parental responsibility or financial relief, or a parental responsibility agreement is in force.

3.4.4 Child arrangements order, specifying living with, and parental responsibility

A child's father may acquire a child arrangements order, specifying living with, under section 8 of the CA 1989. This may be granted on application or of the court's own initiative in the course of family proceedings, see Chapter 13.

The court has power to award parental responsibility with a child arrangements order, specifying living with, which subsists while the order remains in force. Pursuant to section 37 of the Children and Young Persons Act 2008 (CYPA 2008), section 8 of the CA 1989 was amended so that the age at which a child arrangements order, specifying living with, automatically ends, was raised from 16 to 18 years of age, unless the court decides otherwise.

There are special provisions in the CA 1989 when the father or the female legal parent acquires a child arrangements order, specifying living with. These were brought in as a result of the CFA 2014. First, the effect of section 12(1) of the CA 1989 is that where the court makes a child arrangements order with respect to a child, and the father of a child or a woman who is a parent of the child by virtue of section 43 of the HFEA 2008 is named in the order as a person with whom the child is to live, and the father or the woman would not otherwise have parental responsibility for the child, the court must also make an order under section 4, giving the father, or under section 4ZA, giving the woman, that responsibility. Secondly, the effect of section 12(1A) of the CA 1989 is that when the court makes a child arrangements order, and the father of the child or a woman who is a parent under section 43 of the HFEA 2008 is named in the order as a person with whom the child is to spend time, or otherwise have contact, but is not named in the order as a person with whom the child is to live, and the father or the woman would not otherwise have parental responsibility, the court must then decide whether it would be appropriate, in view of the provision made in the order, for him or her to have parental responsibility for the child. If it decides that it would be appropriate, the court must then make an order under section 4 or section 4ZA giving that responsibility.

In specific circumstances, the father of a child who does not have parental responsibility may also acquire it (in the same way as another relative or non-relative might), through one or more of the ways outlined in para 3.5, where an application is open to him; for example, where appropriate, he may apply for guardianship.

In exceptional cases, a father's parental responsibility may be removed by a court order, where this is in the child's best interests (*D v E (Termination of Parental Responsibility)* [2021] EWFC 37) but only where the father was not married to, or a civil partner of, the child's mother (*Re A (Parental Responsibility)* [2023] EWCA Civ 689). More recently, in *Re EMP (A Child) (Re Section 8 of the Children Act 1989)* [2024] EWFC 12, the court decided that it was necessary to revoke the parental responsibility of the father given he had caused significant harm to the mother, and he had failed to acknowledge the court's findings. His continued involvement in the child's life would affect the mother and, in turn, the child.

3.5   Acquisition of parental responsibility by others

3.5.1   Relatives

Relatives can obtain parental responsibility for a child along with a child arrangements order, specifying living with, under sections 8 and 12(2) of the CA 1989. Relatives could also seek an appointment under section 5 as guardian of the child, which automatically gives them parental responsibility until the child reaches 18 or the court orders otherwise. Also, note the effect of section 12(2A) of the CA 1989. This provision, introduced by the CFA 2014, has the effect that when the court makes a child arrangements order, and the person who is not the parent or the guardian of the child is named in the order as a person with whom the child is to spend time or otherwise have contact, but the person is not named in the order as a person with whom the child is to live, the court may provide in the order for the person to have parental responsibility for the child, whilst the paragraphs relating to spending time with or otherwise having contact with continue to be met in that person's case. An authority which had considered this point, and which led to the making of an order under section 12(2A) of the CA 1989, is *A v B and C (by her Children's Guardian)* [2018] EWHC 3834 (Fam). A relative could also apply to adopt a child, which will grant them exclusive parental responsibility for the child. As a result of adoption leading to a total severance of all legal ties with existing parents, the court may not regard it appropriate for a relative to adopt the child in situations where this may then complicate family relationships and dynamics. Having said that, in specific circumstances, adoption by relatives may be considered appropriate.

It is important to note that, in relation to applications under the CA 1989, a civil partner is treated in law in the same way as a married spouse. For example, a civil partner of a parent with parental responsibility can enter into a parental responsibility agreement with that child's parent(s), subject to certain conditions, see para 3.4.

3.5.2   Step-parents

Step-parents do not acquire parental responsibility for the children of their partners automatically on marriage. Currently, they can only acquire parental responsibility alongside a child arrangements order, specifying living with, through adoption, a parental responsibility agreement or a parental responsibility order.

A step-parent who is married to, or a civil partner of, a parent with parental responsibility of the child can acquire parental responsibility for the child by entering into a parental responsibility agreement with the parent(s) of the child under section 4 of the CA 1989. Details of how to do this are set out in para 3.4.2.

The mother of a child (who always has parental responsibility herself) may develop a terminal illness or she may die whilst in the relationship with a man who is not the father of her child. The child may be very attached to him, and he may be committed to the care of the child. If the child's mother dies in this situation, there are three possible scenarios:

(a)   The child's biological father is alive, but has no parental responsibility. The child will then legally have no one with parental responsibility.

What are the remedies?

- before the mother's death, the stepfather obtains a child arrangements order, specifying living with, alone or shared with the mother;

- the mother appoints the stepfather as a guardian under section 5 of the CA 1989;

- if the mother has died, the stepfather may obtain a child arrangements order, specifying living with, or a guardianship order under section 5(1)(a) of the CA 1989. Guardianship automatically gives him parental responsibility until the child reaches 18 or the court orders otherwise;

- the step-parent may apply for a special guardianship order under section 14A of the CA 1989, which will enable him to have parental responsibility for the child, and create stronger legal ties with the child, but this is less final than adoption, which would sever legal links with the child's birth family. Under a special guardianship order, links with the child's birth family are retained.

(b)   The child's biological father is alive and has parental responsibility.

- The biological father will then automatically hold the legal responsibility for the child. The stepfather can seek a child arrangements order, specifying living with. If he has been appointed as guardian by the mother before her death, this will only be effective immediately if she had a child arrangements order, specifying living with, in her favour before her death (section 5(7)(b) of the CA 1989). He could seek guardianship under section 5(1)(b) if the deceased mother had a child arrangements order, specifying living with, in her favour. In either case, he would have to share parental responsibility with the biological father, and resolve disputes by seeking an appropriate section 8 order. See Chapter 13 for discussion of section 8 orders. The stepfather may also be advised about the possibility of a parental responsibility order.

(c)   The biological father has died, meaning there is no one with parental responsibility for this child.

- The stepfather can seek a child arrangements order, specifying living with, under section 8, or guardianship under section 5(1)(a) of the CA 1989. Guardianship automatically gives him parental responsibility until the child reaches 18 or the court orders otherwise.

- The stepmother of a child, living with the child's father, would face similar problems on his death. The child's mother would have parental responsibility. She would have a legal right to the care of the child unless otherwise agreed or ordered by the court. The stepmother could seek a child arrangements order, specifying living with, or guardianship, if the father had a child arrangements order, specifying living with, in force in his favour at the time of his death.

3.5.3   Non-relatives

Non-relatives may acquire parental responsibility with a child arrangements order, specifying living with, or through guardianship, special guardianship, or adoption.

A local authority obtains parental responsibility for a child under section 31 of the CA 1989 when a care order is made, sharing parental responsibility with the child's mother and anyone else who has it. The exercise by others of their parental responsibility in relation to the child may be limited by the local authority under the care order, but there should be partnership and co-operation. The local authority does not acquire parental responsibility when looking after children in voluntary arrangements.

3.5.4   Guardianship

The court may appoint a guardian for a child under section 5 of the CA 1989 where:

- there is no person with parental responsibility for the child; or

- a child arrangements order, specifying living with, has been made in favour of a parent or guardian who died whilst the order was in force.

This parental responsibility subsists until the child reaches 18, unless ended earlier by the court.

A parent who has parental responsibility for his child may appoint another individual to be the child's guardian in the event of his death (section 5(3) of the CA 1989). If the parent dies, and there is no other parent alive with parental responsibility, the appointed guardian will act. However, if there is a parent with parental responsibility still alive, then the guardian will only be able to act after the death of the other parent with parental responsibility. Also note that if a parent with a child arrangements order, specifying living with, in her favour appoints a guardian, then the guardian will act on the death of the appointer, in conjunction with any other parent remaining alive, who has parental responsibility. There are similar provisions relating to appointments by guardians and special guardians. Therefore, pursuant to section 5(4) of the CA 1989, a guardian of a child may appoint another individual to take his place as the child's guardian in the event of his death, and a special guardian of a child may appoint another individual to be the child's guardian in the event of his death.

3.5.5   Special guardianship order

Special guardianship is an order created by the Adoption and Children Act 2002 and imported into the CA 1989 as section 14A. The court can make this order in public or private law proceedings.

The effects of a special guardianship order are that:

• the special guardian has parental responsibility for the child until the child reaches 18;

• special guardians can exercise their parental responsibility to the exclusion of others who have it (other than another special guardian, section 14C(1)(b) of the CA 1989);

• the child's parents are specifically excluded from application.

The persons who can apply are set out in section 14A(5)(a)–(e) of the CA 1989. They include (in relation to that child):

• any guardian of the child;

• people with a child arrangements order, specifying living with, in their favour;

• anyone listed under section 10(5)(b) or (c) of the CA 1989;

- a relative (defined under section 105(1) of the CA 1989) with whom the child has lived for a period of at least one year immediately before they make the application (section 14(5)(e) of the CA 1989). This provision came into effect as a result of section 38 of the CYPA 2008, in September 2009;

- a local authority foster carer with whom the child has lived for at least one year immediately before he or she applies.

For the purposes of section 10(5)(b) and (c) of the CA 1989, a simplified summary of the list of people included are:

  (b) any person with whom the child has lived for a period of at least three years;

  (c) any person who—

    (i) in any case where a child arrangements order, specifying living with, is in force with respect to the child, has the consent of each of the persons in whose favour the order was made;

    (ii) in any case where the child is in the care of a local authority, has the consent of that authority; or

    (iii) in any other case, has the consent of each of those (if any) who have parental responsibility for the child.

The court can make this order of its own initiative in family proceedings (section 14A(6)(b) of the CA 1989).

Local authorities must make special guardianship services available (including counselling, mediation and resources which may include cash assistance) under section 14F of the CA 1989 and regulation 3 of the Special Guardianship Regulations 2005 (SI 2005/1109).

For the distinction between the effects of special guardianship and a child arrangements order, specifying living with, see *Birmingham City Council v R* [2006] EWCA Civ 1748, [2007] 1 FLR 564, and for a contrast with adoption, see *Re S (Adoption Order or Special Guardianship Order)* [2007] EWCA Civ 54, [2007] 1 FLR 819. In the later case of *Re T (A Child: Adoption or Special Guardianship)* [2017] EWCA Civ 1797, in handing down the leading judgment, Peter Jackson LJ emphasised at [13] that the lower court had recognised that special guardianship could, just like adoption, also offer children security and stability, but described it as a less secure form of permanency than adoption.

A special guardianship order can be discharged on the application of the birth parents, but is not to be discharged unless there is a significant change of circumstances since the order was made (section 14(D)(5) of the CA 1989), see *Re M (Special Guardianship Order: Leave to Apply to Discharge)* [2021] EWCA Civ 442. In this case, the Court of Appeal emphasised that when a court is considering an application for leave to apply to discharge a special guardianship order, it must first consider whether the applicant has shown, by means of credible evidence, that there has been a significant change of circumstances since the order was made. If there has not been, the application will fail. If there has, the court will decide whether leave should be granted, based on a realistic evaluation of the applicant's prospects of success in the context of the effect on the child's welfare of the application being heard or not heard. The prospects of success must be real, and the child's welfare is an important factor, but it is not the paramount consideration. Furthermore, the degree of any change in circumstances is likely to be intertwined with the prospects of success, and the greater the prospects of success, the more likely it is that leave will be granted.

It is also worth noting that, similar to orders under section 8 of the CA 1989, the court can make section 91(14) directions alongside the special guardianship order. Therefore, in *K (Children) v Sheffield City Council* [2011] EWCA Civ 635, the Court of Appeal provided for a special guardianship order to be made, with a section 91(14) direction for 3 years attached, to prevent the parents continuing to make multiple applications.

Furthermore, the case of *Re F and G (Discharge of Special Guardianship Order)* [2021] EWCA Civ 622 shows that, in appropriate cases, a care order and special guardianship order may co-exist. It was the case that the drafting of the amendments to the CA 1989 by which special guardianship was introduced allowed for a special guardianship order to continue after the making of a care order, be it an interim care order under section 38 or a final care order under section 31 of the CA 1989. Like adoption, special guardianship is a relationship which provides long-term support for the child, and the court stated that there was no reason for the sense of security, continuity, commitment, identity and belonging to come to an end when the child moves away.

In relation to an application for a special guardianship order applied for during care proceedings, the child may have the benefit of the existing children's guardian. If the child is already subject to a care order, then the child may have the benefit of the previous children's guardian. The court can appoint a children's guardian if the court considers that it is in the child's interests (rule 16.2 of the FPR 2010). If so, the guardian will be appointed under rule 16.4.

3.5.6   Parental responsibility, surrogacy and the Human Fertilisation and Embryology Act 2008

This is a complex area and has developed further with the HFEA 2008.

Some of the key provisions surrounding 'parenthood' are set out at para 3.5.7 and cover the situation when the surrogate mother is the child's genetic mother, or was impregnated with an embryo, or eggs.

The effect of section 42 of the HFEA 2008 is that if the child's mother was in a civil partnership with, or married to, another woman, at the time of her having had an embryo, sperm and eggs placed in her, or at the time of her undergoing artificial insemination, if her partner has agreed to this procedure, that partner will then be treated as the child's second parent (this is subject to the provisions relating to the legitimacy of the child, or if the child is, through adoption, not treated as the women's child, see section 45(2) and (4)).

The combined effect of sections 43 and 44 of the HFEA 2008 is that there is provision for situations where the child's mother is in a relationship with another woman, and the two women are *not* civil partners, *nor* married to each other at the time of the procedure. These sections provide that if the child is born as a result of the provision of licensed treatment services in the United Kingdom, then if both women consent to the procedure (and subject to section 45(2) and (4) – see above), the non-biological mother is regarded in law as the child's second parent.

Section 2(1A) of the CA 1989 has the effect that where a child has a parent under either section 42 or section 43 of the HFEA 2008, to whom section 1(3) of the Family Law Reform Act 1987 applies, then the child's biological mother and the other parent shall both have parental responsibility for the child.

What if the man is not the child's genetic father? Can he be treated as the child's father under the law? Under section 35(1) of the HFEA 2008, if the mother was married to her husband or in a civil partnership with a man (who does not provide the sperm) at the time when the mother has placed into her the embryo, or sperm and eggs, or she undergoes artificial insemination, then provided that her husband or civil partner consented to this process, he is treated as the child's father.

Consider section 36 of the HFEA 2008 – this has the effect that if the woman has had the child born to her through the same process as referred to above under section 35, but the man and woman have given written notice to the effect that they consent to the man being treated as the child's father, then provided the process occurs in the United Kingdom, through a licensed provider, the man will be treated as the child's father, even though he had not provided his sperm. This, however, is subject to the presumption of legitimacy, and if the child, by virtue of adoption, is not treated as that man's child.

3.5.7   Parental orders under section 54 of the Human Fertilisation and Embryology Act 2008

The HFEA 2008 allows a couple who have agreed with a surrogate mother to commission the birth of a child to apply under section 54 of the HFEA 2008 for a parental order that they be treated in law as the parents of that child.

The conditions on the making of a parental order include that:

- the applicants are aged 18 or over, and they must be domiciled in the United Kingdom, the Channel Islands or the Isle of Man at the time of the application;

- the surrogate mother who carried the child must not be one of the applicants;

- the gametes of at least one of the applicants must have been used, so as to bring about the creation of the embryo;

- the applicants must be married or civil partners, or living in an enduring family relationship, and are not within the prohibited degrees of relationship to each other;

- the application must normally be made within 6 months of the birth of the child (subject to section 54(11) of the HFEA 2008);

- the birth mother was a surrogate mother, and that the agreement by her is ineffective if it is given less than 6 weeks after the child's birth. The court can dispense with agreement in specified circumstances;

- the child was living with the applicants at the time of the application;

- unless authorised by the court, no money or benefit has been handed over save for reasonable expenses incurred;

- any other person who is a parent of the child (but who is not one of the applicants) agreed to the making of the order, unless they cannot be traced.

There has been a lot of case law surrounding the position with the applicant seeking a declaration as to parentage, pursuant to section 55A of the Family Law Act 1986, on the premise that the correct procedure had not been followed. For example, consider *In the Matter of the Human*

Fertilisation and Embryology Act 2008 (Cases AD, AE, AF, AG and AH) (No 2) [2017] EWHC 1782 (Fam). These cases involved treatment provided by fertility clinics. Each of the clinics was regulated by the Human Fertilisation and Embryology Authority. The applicant sought a declaration pursuant to section 55A that he or she was, in accordance with sections 36 and 37 or, as the case may be, sections 43 and 44 of the HFEA 2008, the legal parent of the child. In each case, the mother consented, in situations in which the forms had been incorrectly completed, in one way or another. The then President of the Family Division, Sir James Munby, made the declarations in the terms sought by the applicant(s). A later case where such a declaration was made is *Re AL (HFEA 2008)* [2018] EWHC 1300 (Fam), in which the President stated that this case was the 38th of these cases in which judgment had been given. The court granted the declaration as to parentage. The clinic had discovered its error, and agreed to pay the applicant's reasonable costs.

There has also been a breadth of case law over the years surrounding the position with the payments made, the timescale within which to apply, and the issue of consent when seeking parental orders. In particular, in *Re A, B and C (UK Surrogacy Expenses)* [2016] EWFC 33, the court emphasised that the statements of the applicants in support of the parental order should have set out fully and frankly the sums paid. The amounts paid for expenses reasonably incurred should have been set out in detail, and each expense identified, with documentary evidence in support of the amounts paid exhibited to the statements. The case of *A & Another v C & Another* [2016] EWFC 4 emphasises that it is vital that the application for a parental order is made as soon the applicant(s) become aware of the need to do so. Each case sits on its own facts, so that in the decision of *Re A (Surrogacy: s 54 Criteria)* [2020] EWHC 1426 (Fam), Keehan J decided, at [54], that a failure to adhere to the 6-month time limit to make an application for a parental order is not fatal to the making of the order. Furthermore, the existence of family life is not defined, nor is its existence constrained, by legal, societal or religious conventions.

Also note the Human Fertilisation and Embryology (Parental Orders) Regulations 2018 (SI 2018/1412), which were made as a result of the introduction of section 54A to the HFEA 2008 by the Human Fertilisation and Embryology Act 2008 (Remedial) Order 2018 (SI 2018/1413), so as to allow for granting of parental orders to one applicant only.

More recently, in *Re X, Y and Z (Children: Parental Orders: Time Limit)* [2022] EWHC 198 (Fam), the application for the parental order was received by the court outside the period of 6 months from birth within which a parental order application should be made. Nonetheless, the court was satisfied that the applicants had been careful and organised in the arrangements they had made with respect to all aspects of the surrogacy arrangements entered into. They received legal advice in the USA as to the way in which they could acquire legal parentage in that jurisdiction and had understood that advice would be recognised in other jurisdictions. They had acted in good faith and were unaware of the necessity to apply for a parental order in this jurisdiction. It was a reasonable oversight given that they lived outside this jurisdiction at the time and had not had any advice from a UK-based solicitor. As soon as they received advice to make the application they did so. Accordingly, the court granted the orders.

3.6   Public funding in children cases

For those practitioners who provide public funding through their firms, there are various levels and schemes available. See *Lord Chancellor's Guidance on Determining Financial Eligibility for Certificated Work* (August 2023), at https://assets.publishing.service.gov.uk/media/64f1cf309ee0f2000fb7bd a7/Lord_Chancellor_s_guide_to_determining_financial_eligibility_for_ certificated_work__August_2023_.pdf.

When considering public funding for children proceedings, it should be noted that following the implementation of the Legal Aid, Sentencing and Punishment of Offenders Act 2012 (LASPO), the scope of services funded as part of civil legal aid had changed. In the case of many public law proceedings and the representation of children, these remained in scope under Schedule 1, Part 1 to LASPO. However, although most of the private family law cases involving children or finance remained in scope, there had been added the need to show gateway evidence of domestic violence/abuse or child abuse.

Considering private children law cases first, the effect of LASPO, as from 1 April 2013, has been that it brought in significant changes, principally concerning the 'merits' test. Chapter 13 discusses private children law orders in particular. In terms of eligibility for public funding to cover private children law applications, there is a requirement to satisfy both the 'means' and 'merits' tests. As for the means test, it is necessary for the applicant to demonstrate that he or she is on certain prescribed benefits or is within a certain financial limit. There is a requirement to consider not only the applicant's income, but also his or her capital, so as to ensure that these are within the financial limits. In terms of the merits test, one has to show the 'gateway evidence' of 'domestic violence' or 'child abuse', as defined within the regulations. The original regulations only permitted such evidence to be provided for the previous 2 years, although following various changes to the regulations, there is now no restriction as to the age of the evidence that can be relied upon. Therefore, the Civil Legal Aid (Procedure) (Amendment) (No 2) Regulations 2017 (SI 2017/1237), as from 8 January 2018, had the effect of removing the time limitation as to the evidence of 'domestic violence' or 'child abuse' that is relied upon.

The funding in public children law matters is very different to that in private children law. In the case of 'Special Children Act Proceedings' under Parts 4 and 5 of the CA 1989, and which will include care orders, supervision orders, child assessment orders and emergency protection orders, the funding is available on a non-means/merits basis for the child who is the subject of the order and parents/parties with parental responsibility for the subject child. For other parties, such as an extended family member who may be joined as a party to the proceedings, unless that person has parental responsibility for the child, he or she will need to satisfy both the means and merits tests.

For those persons who are eligible, the non-means/merits funding will cover funding for the duration of the proceedings and therefore in care proceedings, even where there may be interim orders in place. The funding is also available where there has been written notice of intention from the local authority to issue care proceedings. In relation to 'Special Children Act Proceedings' under Parts 4 and 5 of the CA 1989, care and supervision orders are covered in Chapter 7 and emergency protection orders are covered in Chapter 5. As for child assessment orders, these are discussed in Chapter 6.

For other orders under Parts 4 and 5 of the CA 1989, which will include, for example, applications for contact with a child in care, appeals in public law cases or the discharge/variation of a care/supervision order, the funding is means and merits tested for all parties. Discharge and variation of care/supervision orders and appeals are covered in Chapters 7 and 17.

As regards to orders under the inherent jurisdiction of the High Court in relation to children, and wardship, the funding is means and merits tested for all parties. This will cover, in particular, applications for DoL orders. These orders, as well as secure accommodation orders, are covered in Chapter 8.

Subject to the changes set out in para 3.6.1, if there are related proceedings, such as an application for a placement order or a recovery order, if these are heard together with proceedings relating, for example, to 'Special Children Act Proceedings' under Parts 4 and 5 of the CA 1989, then the funding is non-means/merits tested in such cases.

In terms of the funding for the various areas of work referred to above, the funding may cover not just legal fees, but also certain disbursements. However, there are various disbursements that cannot be incurred on the public funding certificates. In particular, the cost of, or expenses in relation to, treatment, therapy, training or other interventions of an educational or rehabilitating venture may not be charged as a disbursement to the Legal Aid Agency. Since October 2007, the cost of residential assessments, including pre-assessments or viability assessments (whether residential or not) undertaken to consider whether a residential assessment is appropriate, is removed from the scope of legal aid funding.

In terms of advocacy, there are fee arrangements for certificates as from 9 May 2011. The Family Advocacy Scheme creates a single graduated fee scheme, covering payments to advocates across all levels, for public and private children law cases. There are also certain 'bolt on' payments available as appropriate, such as if a client has difficulty in giving instructions or understanding advice, or if there is representation of a client who is facing allegations that they have caused significant harm to a child, and such allegations are a live issue in the proceedings. Additional payments can also be paid for preparation of a court bundle, according to the size of the court bundle for the hearing. The advocacy fee is paid in terms of units and the fee covers preparation, the hearing itself, travelling, waiting and negotiations at court. There are various family advocacy units payable, which are Unit 1 (for advocacy finishing 60 minutes or less from the time that the hearing is listed) and Unit 2 (for advocacy of more than 60 minutes but less than 2.5 hours). Further Unit 2s are payable for any additional 2.5 hours, and there is also, if appropriate, a final hearing fee. The fixed advocacy fees do not apply to those relating to final appeals, child abduction and inherent jurisdiction and wardship matters.

3.6.1   Public funding changes

Recently, there have been changes to public funding principally in public law cases and also in some private children law matters. Note the effect of the Legal Aid, Sentencing and Punishment of Offenders Act 2012 (Legal Aid: Family and Domestic Abuse) (Miscellaneous Amendments) Order 2023 (SI 2023/150). This has brought about amendments to the Civil Legal Aid (Merits Criteria) Regulations 2013 (SI 2013/104) and the Civil Legal Aid (Financial Resources and Payment for Services) Regulations 2013 (SI 2013/480). A summary of the changes is that for children and family practitioners, as from 1 May 2023, non-means testing has become available to cover the costs of providing legal assistance not only to parents, but also to other people with parental responsibility for the child, in cases where there is an application for a special guardianship order, a placement order or an adoption order. Note that these various applications do need to be running outside care proceedings. Therefore, this could be relevant where there is a freestanding special guardianship application, such as in a private children law case. In relation to public children law cases, the changes have the effect that, for example, once the care and placement proceedings have been concluded, if a child has been placed for adoption, and there is an adoption application lodged, non-means testing funding would be available. This funding is therefore available, and on a non-means basis, not only for the parents involved in the application, but also for other persons who may have parental responsibility for the child at that stage. This is particularly useful therefore to assist a parent who may be able to get much needed non-means tested funding to be represented on a leave to oppose the making of an adoption order application.

These regulations also brought about changes to the evidence requirements to obtain public funding, provided for in the Civil Legal Aid (Procedure) Regulations 2012 (SI 2012/3098). Therefore, they provide for domestic abuse protection notices and orders (introduced by the Domestic Abuse Act 2021, and to be piloted in 2024) as an acceptable form of supporting evidence for applications for civil legal aid falling within Schedule 1, Part 1, paragraph 12. Also, in terms of getting 'gateway' evidence of domestic abuse from a health professional (such as a GP), the regulations provide for the examination by the health professional to take place over the telephone or by video conference, as an alternative to examination in person, for the purposes of providing a report or letter as supporting evidence of domestic abuse.

4 *Every Child Matters*: Child Protection Procedures in Health and Social Work

Current child protection procedures are formed to operate within the framework of the CA 1989 and the Children Act 2004, underpinning the *Every Child Matters: Change for Children* (DfES, 2004) (*Every Child Matters*) programme, which included the provisions for the establishment of Local Safeguarding Children Boards (LSCBs).

The CA 1989 and the Children Act 2004 apply to both England and Wales, but *Every Child Matters* was a policy applicable only in England, and there are some variations in Wales. For example, the *Working Together* guidance referred to below does not apply in Wales, which has its own statutory guidance, *Working Together to Safeguard People. Volume 5 – Handling Individual Cases to Protect Children at Risk* (Welsh Government, 2018) and the non-statutory Wales Safeguarding Procedures: Children and Young People at Risk of Harm (https://safeguarding.wales/en/). In Wales, the statutory guidance is contained in the Codes of Practice issued pursuant to section 145 of the SSW(W)A 2014. These Codes contain a mixture of both statutory and non-statutory guidance. In relation to assessments, there was previously the *Framework for Assessment of Children in Need and their Families* tool of 2001. Since April 2016, this tool for assessing children and families is now included in *Social Services and Well-being (Wales) Act 2014 – Part 3 Code of Practice (assessing the needs of individuals)* (Welsh Government, 2015) (*Part 3 Code of Practice*).

The child protection procedures for England are set out in a number of publications. The main publication is *Working Together to Safeguard Children 2023: A guide to multi-agency working to help, protect and promote the welfare of children* (DfE, 2023) (*Working Together*), which was last updated in December 2023 and is available at the Department for Education website, www.gov.uk/government/organisations/department-for-education. The website has very useful information and is worth visiting at regular intervals to see the new publications added.

Some of the key updates include a new chapter on 'a shared responsibility', so as to bring together new and existing guidance to emphasise that successful outcomes for children depend on strong multi-agency partnership working. Chapter 2 of *Working Together* relates to changes brought about to strengthen how local multi-agency safeguarding arrangements (local authorities, integrated care boards and the police) work to safeguard and protect children locally, including with relevant agencies. In particular, there is useful information on clarifying the roles and responsibilities of safeguarding partners, distinguishing between lead safeguarding partners and delegated safeguarding partners.

Chapter 3 of the updated *Working Together* guidance relates to providing help, support and protection, so that it emphasises the use of 'early help', safeguarding and promoting the welfare of children, as well as child protection.

Given changes to the duties owed to care leavers, Chapter 5 of *Working Together* covers learning from serious child safeguarding incidents. It sets out the requirements for 'keeping in touch' with care leavers over the age of 21, and the non-mandatory reporting of care leaver deaths up to the age of 25 to improve learning and outcomes. Furthermore, Chapter 6 of the guidance covers child death reviews and refers, specifically, to the Domestic Abuse Act 2021, and it clarifies the child safeguarding practice review process, and the process for submitting serious incidents notifications.

Various other very useful publications include the following:

- *Care of unaccompanied migrant children and child victims of modern slavery* (DfE, 2017).

- *Child sexual exploitation: definition and guide for practitioners* (DfE, 2017).

- *Children Act 1989: care planning, placement and case review* (DfE, 2021).

- *Keeping children safe in education* (DfE, 2023).

- *Promoting and supporting mental health and wellbeing in schools and colleges* (DfE, 2024).

- *Safeguarding children who may have been trafficked* (DfE and Home Office, 2011).

- *Safeguarding strategy – unaccompanied asylum seeking and refugee children* (DfE, 2017).

- *Sexual violence and sexual harassment between children in schools and colleges* (DfE, 2021).

- *Statutory guidance on children who run away or go missing from home or care* (DfE, 2014).

- *What to do if you're worried a child is being abused: advice for practitioners* (DfE, 2015).

The Department for Education website also contains guidance issued by other government departments and agencies, such as the following:

- *Achieving Best Evidence in Criminal Proceedings: Guidance on interviewing victims and witnesses, and guidance on using special measures* (Ministry of Justice, 2023).
- *Advice to parents and carers on gangs* (Home Office, 2014).
- *Advice to schools and colleges on gangs and youth violence* (Home Office, 2013).
- *Guidance for health professionals on domestic violence* (Department of Health and Social Care, 2013).
- *Handling cases of forced marriage: multi-agency practice guidelines* (HM Government, 2014).
- *How to protect, advise and support victims of forced marriage, including information and practice guidelines for professionals* (Home Office and Foreign & Commonwealth Office, Foreign, Commonwealth & Development Office, 2023).
- *Modern slavery: how to identify and support victims* (Home Office, 2024).
- *Multi-agency statutory guidance for dealing with forced marriage and multi-agency practice guidelines: Handling cases of forced marriage* (Home Office and Foreign, Commonwealth & Development Office, 2023).
- *Multi-agency statutory guidance on female genital mutilation* (Department for Education, Home Office & Department of Health and Social Care, 2020).
- *Sudden unexpected death in infancy and childhood: multi-agency guidelines for care and investigation* (Royal College of Pathologists, 2016).

The CA 1989 has been clarified and explained by the various volumes of *The Children Act 1989 Guidance and Regulations* (DCSF, 2008), which have been updated through new publications, at the Department for Education website, www.gov.uk/government/organisations/department-for-education. These volumes of guidance are all mandatory guidelines issued under section 7 of the Local Authority Social Services Act 1970. Local authorities must follow that guidance, unless local circumstances indicate exceptional reasons that justify a variation, and any departure from it must be justified in respect of any complaints procedure or judicial review. The volumes of *The Children Act 1989 Guidance and Regulations* are:

- *Volume 1: court orders* (DfE, 2014).
- *Volume 2: care planning, placement and case review* (DfE, 2021).
- *Volume 3: planning transition to adulthood for care leavers* (DfE, 2022).
- *Volume 4: fostering services* (DfE, 2015).
- *Volume 5: children's homes regulations, including quality standards: guide* (DfE, 2015).

Working Together is issued under various statutory provisions, such as under section 7 of the Local Authority Social Services Act 1970 referred to above. This statutory guidance should be read and followed by leaders, managers and frontline practitioners of all organisations and agencies.

The guidance provides that it is essential that these arrangements are strongly led and promoted at a local level, specifically by elected local area leaders, including lead members of children's services, mayors, police and crime commissioners, and through the commitment of chief officers in all organisations and agencies, particularly those representing the three safeguarding partners. These are local authority chief executives, chief constables of police and chief executives of integrated care boards. Other senior leaders within organisations and agencies that commission and provide services for children and families, and in education settings, also have a key role to play in safeguarding and providing help and support to children in their local area. Members of the Child Safeguarding Practice Review Panel should also read and follow this guidance.

4.1   Safeguarding partners, child safeguarding practice reviews, child death review partners and child practice reviews

4.1.1   Safeguarding partners and child safeguarding practice reviews

Following the inquiry into the death of Victoria Climbié, the Children Act 2004 required all local authorities across England and Wales to set up an LSCB. The task of the LSCB was to safeguard and promote the welfare of children and young people in their area. Subsequently, as a result of the Children and Social Work Act 2017, LSCBs were replaced in England by 'safeguarding partners', which are made up of three safeguarding partners, namely: local authorities, chief officers of police, and clinical commissioning groups. All three partners are required to make arrangements to work together with relevant agencies, so as to then safeguard and protect the welfare of children in the area. There is an expectation to have a local safeguarding arrangement in place. The safeguarding partners must set out in their published arrangements which organisations and agencies they will be working with to safeguard and promote the welfare of children, and this will change over time. A list of relevant agencies is set out in the Child Safeguarding Practice Review and Relevant Agency (England) Regulations 2018 (SI 2018/789). The updated *Working Together* guidance (paragraphs 320–322) refers to the need for 'Child Safeguarding Practice Reviews', the purpose of which (both at a

person or organisation, they must inform them. In addition, child death review partners must, in particular, and as appropriate, prepare and publish reports on what they have done as a result of the child death review arrangements in their area and how effective the arrangements have been in practice.

In this context, also note the guidance set out by the then President of the Family Division covering the role of the judiciary in Serious Case Reviews (SCRs), as they were referred to previously. This guidance should be noted in the context of child safeguarding practice reviews (see *President of the Family Division's Guidance covering the role of the judiciary in serious case reviews*, 2 May 2017).

4.1.3   Child practice reviews

In Wales, before the introduction of Safeguarding Children Boards, LSCBs were responsible for carrying out safeguarding functions. Subsequently, the Safeguarding Boards (Functions and Procedures) (Wales) Regulations 2015 (SI 2015/1466) provided for the functions and procedures of Safeguarding Children Boards and Safeguarding Adults Boards (Safeguarding Boards), which were established under section 134 of the SSW(W)A 2014. Regulation 4 of these regulations provides that the Safeguarding Board must undertake a practice review, the purpose of which is to identify any steps that can be taken by Safeguarding Board partners or other bodies to achieve improvements in multi-agency child and adult protection practice. In relation to children, the Board must undertake a concise practice review in any of the situations where, within the area of the Board, abuse or neglect of a child is known or suspected and the child has died; or sustained potentially life threatening injury; or sustained serious and permanent impairment of health or development; and the child was neither on the child protection register nor a looked after child on any date during the 6 months preceding the date of the event referred to above or the date on which a local authority or relevant partner identifies that a child has sustained serious and permanent impairment of health and development.

Regulation 5 sets out the procedures of the Safeguarding Boards. There is specific guidance set out in the *Social Services and Well-being (Wales) Act 2014 – Working Together to Safeguard People, Volume 2 – Child Practice Reviews* (Welsh Government, 2016). Chapters 1–7 of this guidance are issued under section 139 of the SSW(W)A 2014. Paragraph 3.5 of this guidance provides that the purpose of the concise child practice review is to identify learning for future practice. It involves practitioners, managers and senior officers in exploring the detail and context of agencies' work with a child and family. There is also reference to the conducting of an extended review. This would be required when, within the area of the Board, abuse or neglect of a child is known or suspected and the child has died; or sustained potentially life threatening injury; or sustained serious and permanent impairment of health or development; and the child was on the child protection register and/or was a looked after child (including a care leaver under the age of 18) on any date during the 6 months preceding the date of the event referred to above; or the date on which a local authority or relevant partner identifies that a child has sustained serious and permanent impairment of health and development. The output of a review is intended to generate professional and organisational learning and promote improvement in future inter-agency child protection practice.

4.2   Hierarchy within social services departments

Each social services department will use terminology that is likely to vary geographically. The head of social services may be called the director of social services, supported by one or more assistant directors, each of whom usually has an administrative responsibility related either to an area of work, or to a geographical area. The *Statutory Guidance on the roles and responsibilities of the Director of Children's Services and the Lead Member for Children's Services* (DfE, 2013) covers the legislative basis for the two appointments, roles and responsibilities of the post holders, and how this relates to government expectations about the role of local authorities in education and children and young people's services. It is available at www.gov.uk/government/publications/directors-of-childrens-services-roles-and-responsibilities.

The local authority children's social care department deals with child protection. Social services departments are generally divided into task-related divisions, for example, child care and services, adult care and services, and community care and services, etc. One assistant director may have the responsibility for child care, which may or may not include adoption.

Out in the field, the frontline work may be divided into geographical areas, and then sub-divided into specific tasks, headed by a person in a managerial role, perhaps called the divisional manager or district manager. The work is usually carried out by social work teams.

4.3   Referral procedures and preliminary investigations

For detailed guidance on referral procedures, see *Working Together*, Chapter 3, section 2 ('safeguarding and promoting the welfare of children'), and see also Figure 4.1.

At paragraphs 149–150 of *Working Together* it is provided that the local authority children's social care department has the responsibility for clarifying the process for referrals in its area. As well as protocols for practitioners working with children and families, contact details should be signposted clearly so that children, parents, other family members and community partners are aware of who they can contact if they wish to make a referral, or require advice or support. It is set out that anyone who has concerns about a child's welfare should consider whether a referral needs to be made to the local authority children's social care department and should do so immediately if there is a concern that the child is suffering significant harm or is likely to do so.

Practitioners will be aware that a member of the public concerned about a child may contact the police, the local authority children's social care department or the NSPCC. The police will usually either use their powers under section 46 of the CA 1989 in an emergency or refer the matter to the local authority social care department.

The local authority social care department in each area will have a system of taking and dealing with referrals. The person taking the referral will note the information given, ask further details to establish the name, whereabouts and circumstances of the child, and request information about the person making the referral if appropriate.

The *Working Together* guidance (at paragraph 153) provides that within one working day of a referral being received, a local authority social worker should acknowledge receipt to the referrer, and then make a decision about the next steps and the type of response required. This will include in particular deciding on whether the child requires immediate protection and whether urgent action is required; or whether the child is in need, and should be assessed under section 17 of the CA 1989; or whether there is reasonable cause to suspect that the child is suffering or likely to suffer significant harm, and whether enquires must be made and the child assessed under section 47.

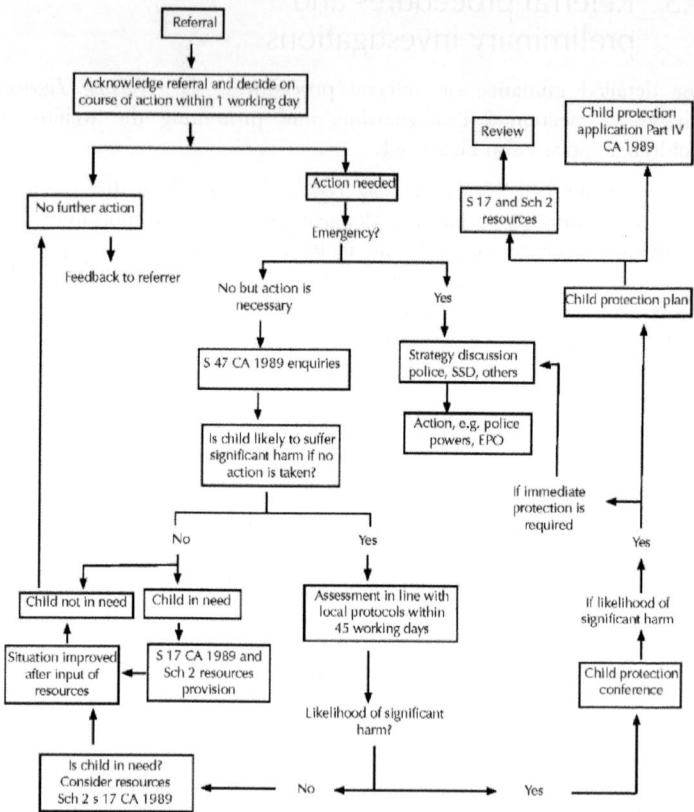

Figure 4.1   Local authority referral procedures and steps taken

Key

SSD = social services department; EPO = emergency protection order.

Other steps could include the social worker deciding as to whether any services are required by the child and family, and to then determine the type of service, as well as consideration of any specialist assessments, as well as deciding whether to see the child as soon as possible if the decision is taken that the referral requires further assessment.

The important role of the IRO should be emphasised here. The IRO is appointed by the local authority to regularly review the implementation of the care plan for all children in local authority care, bearing in mind the needs and welfare of the child. The IRO takes on the independent monitoring and oversight role. It is therefore important that this is borne in mind and that the children's guardian considers whether he or she needs to feed back to or liaise with the IRO before closing his or her files. A child at risk of significant harm is, by definition, a child in need. In most cases, a child in need would remain at home, helped by the provision of appropriate services, resources and advice for the family. However, some children need greater levels of protection. There will be situations when children are in need of immediate protection, and in such situations, action must be taken by the social worker, or the police or the NSPCC if removal is required, as soon as possible after the referral has been made to the local authority children's social care department. It is important to note that the maximum timeframe for the assessment to conclude, such that it is possible to reach a decision on next steps, should be no longer than 45 working days from the point of referral. As sometimes happens, following discussion with a child and his family and other practitioners, an assessment exceeds 45 working days. In such cases, the social worker should record the reasons for exceeding the time limit. The local authority may carry out an initial assessment and decide quickly whether it is necessary to seek emergency protection, child assessment or any other CA 1989 order. See Chapter 16 for details of the assessment process.

4.3.1   Involving the child

Working Together sets out that social worker should see the child within a timescale that is appropriate to the nature of the concerns expressed at referral, according to an agreed plan, and conduct interviews with the child and family members, separately and together, as appropriate. The initial discussions with the child should be conducted in a way that minimises distress to the child and maximises the likelihood that the child will provide accurate and complete information, avoiding leading or suggestive questions (*Working Together*, page 89). Also, in relation to section 47 enquiries, *Working Together* continues in emphasising that the social worker should carry out enquiries in a way that minimises distress for the child and family, and also the social worker should see the child to ascertain his wishes and feelings, as well as to assess his understanding of his situation, and to assess his relationships and circumstances more broadly. Furthermore, the social worker should interview parents/carers and determine the wider social and environmental factors that might impact on them and their child (*Working Together*, page 89).

The child's welfare should be kept sharply in focus in all work with the child and family. The significance of seeing and observing the child cannot be overstated. The child should be spoken and listened to, and his wishes and feelings ascertained, taken into account (having regard to his age and understanding) and recorded when making decisions about the provision of services. Some of the worst failures of the system have occurred when professionals have lost sight of the child and concentrated too heavily on the adults. It should also be noted that special provision should be put in place to support dialogue with children who may, for example, have communication difficulties, or are unaccompanied children or refugees, as well as those children who are victims of modern slavery and/or trafficking and those who do not speak English, or for whom English is not their first language (*Working Together*, paragraph 14).

4.3.2   Involving families and information sharing

Working Together (paragraph 18) sets out that in the context of a child-centred approach, all practitioners should work in partnership with parents and carers as far as possible. Working collaboratively will mean parents and carers have the best chance of making changes, and practitioners can make fair and accurate decisions about how to support children and keep them safe. The importance of developing a co-operative working relationship is emphasised, so that parents or caregivers feel respected and informed; believe staff are being open and honest with them; and, in turn, are confident about providing vital information about their child, themselves and their circumstances.

In terms of information sharing, practitioners should be proactive in sharing information as early as possible to help identify, assess and respond to risks or concerns about the safety and welfare of children. This may be when problems are first emerging (e.g. persistent school absences) or where a child is already known to the local authority children's social care department. Sharing information about any adults with whom that child has contact, which may impact the child's safety or welfare, is also critical (*Working Together*, paragraph 29).

All practitioners should aim to gain consent to share information but should be mindful of situations where to do so would place a child at increased risk of harm. Information may be shared without consent if a practitioner believes that there is good reason to do so, and that the sharing of information will enhance the safeguarding of a child. When decisions are made to share or withhold information, practitioners should record who has been given the information and why.

Given the changes that have been brought into play during 2018 with the UK General Data Protection Regulation (UK GDPR), *Working Together* specifically provides that practitioners must have due regard to the relevant data protection principles which allow them to share personal information, as provided for in the Data Protection Act 2018 and the UK GDPR. It sets out that the processing conditions under the Data Protection Act 2018 and the UK GDPR allow the storing and sharing of information for safeguarding purposes, including information which is sensitive and personal, and that this should be treated as special category personal data. Where practitioners need to share special category personal data, the Data Protection Act 2018 contains 'safeguarding of children and individuals at risk' as a processing condition that allows practitioners to share information. This includes allowing practitioners to share information without consent, if it is not possible to gain consent, it cannot be reasonably expected that a practitioner gains consent, or if to gain consent would place a child at risk (*Working Together*, page 20, paragraph 32). Possible outcomes, following the receipt of a referral are:

(a)   no further local authority social care involvement at this stage needs to be taken;

(b)   protection can be achieved by working in co-operation with the parents and provision of services, etc;

(c)   assessment is required under section 17 or section 47 of the CA 1989, which may lead to further assessment work;

(d)   child protection conference is required;

(e)   urgent court proceedings are necessary.

4.4   Child protection conferences

Child protection conferences bring together the child and his or her family members with those professionals most involved with them. *Working Together* provides detailed guidance for child protection conferences, reviews and decision-making processes (*Working Together*, pages 91–103). See Figure 4.2 for the child protection conference process.

4.4.1   Purpose

The purpose of the child protection conference is to:

*   bring together the family, child and professionals most involved and analyse evidence about the needs of the child and the parents' or carers' capacity to respond to the child's needs;

*   ensure the child's safety and promote the child's health and development in the context of his or her wider family and environment. If the child is at continuing risk of significant harm, the conference must decide what future action is required to safeguard and promote the welfare of the child.

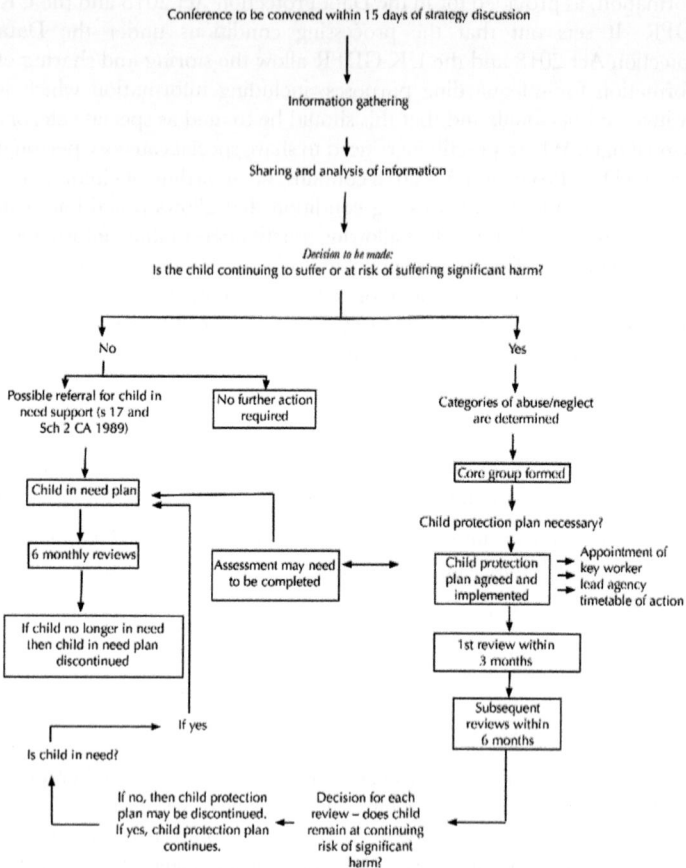

Figure 4.2   Process of child protection conference

4.4.2   Who should be invited to a child protection conference?

The parents, carers and child (if of sufficient age and maturity) should be invited. The professionals invited should include all those who can make a significant contribution to the discussion. Those who are invited but cannot attend should be invited to submit a written report.

In practice, the person(s) invited to conference will include (although not always) the following:

- the child (subject to age and understanding) or his or her representative;
- family members (including wider family where appropriate);
- local authority children's social care department staff involved with the child and family;
- foster carers, residential care staff;
- professionals involved with the child and family (medical, support, education, etc);
- those involved in investigations (e.g. the police);
- experts, if appropriate;
- legal services;
- representative of the NSPCC, where relevant.

4.4.3 Documents

The child protection conference will often have information before it, including:

- a local authority written report, including any information obtained from the safeguarding checks;
- a chronology of significant events and professional contact with the family;
- information on the capacity of the parents/carers to meet the child's needs and provide protection;
- the expressed views, wishes and feelings of the child, parents and family members;
- an analysis of the implications of the information gained.

Working Together provides that the lead practitioners should prepare a report for the conference on the child and family which sets out and analyses what is known about the child and family and the local authority's recommendation (*Working Together*, page 94). It is important to ensure that the child and parents should be provided with a copy of the local authority report before the conference and the contents explained appropriately. They should be helped to think about and convey what they want to say to the conference.

4.4.4   Decisions to be made and actions to be taken

(a)   Is the child at continuing risk of significant harm?

The test is one of the following:

  (i)   the child can be shown to have suffered ill-treatment or impairment of health or development as a result of physical, emotional or sexual abuse or neglect, and professional judgment is that further ill-treatment or impairment is likely; or

  (ii)   professional judgment, substantiated by the findings of enquiries in this individual case or by research evidence, is that the child is likely to suffer ill-treatment or the impairment of health or development as a result of physical, emotional or sexual abuse; or

  (iii)   neglect.

(b)   The child may be a child in need (but not subject to a child protection plan) and a child in need plan can be drawn up and reviewed.

(c)   If the child is at continuing risk of significant harm, then inter-agency help will be required, delivered through a child protection plan (in Wales, through registration on the Child Protection Register).

(d)   If a child protection plan is required, there should be a determination as to the category (or categories) of abuse (physical, sexual, emotional or neglect).

(e)   The child protection plan must be agreed in detail.

(f)   The conference must agree on the appointment of a key lead practitioner and establish the core group of professionals and family members who will implement the plan.

(g)   The responsibilities of the core group members and family must be agreed upon.

(h)   The provision of resources for child/family by the agencies must be agreed upon.

In relation to the core group, *Working Together* sets out that it should meet within 10 working days from the initial child protection conference if the child is the subject of a child protection plan, and one key role of the core group is to implement the child protection plan and take joint responsibility for carrying out the agreed tasks, as well as monitoring progress and outcomes (*Working Together*, page 97).

As for the conference chair, he or she is accountable to the Director of Children's Services; where possible, the same person should chair subsequent child protection reviews. The chair should be a practitioner, independent of operational and/or line management responsibilities for the case.

Attendance at child protection conferences is by invitation, which should include all professionals involved with the family, the parents and carers of the child and the child, if of sufficient age and understanding. The chair should ensure that invitees are made welcome and comfortable, with refreshments, toilet facilities and other necessities being provided. Minutes should be taken, and decisions recorded. Exclusions should be by the conference chair, and only when justified, in an adversarial role.

The Law Society Practice Note, *Attendance of solicitors at local authority Children Act meetings* (7 May 2021), provides essential guidance to those legal representatives attending local authority meetings, which will encompass, amongst other meetings, attending child protection conferences. In particular, paragraph 3.1 provides that if a local authority solicitor attends, he should offer expert advice to the conference on any legal issues which may arise, but should not be a full participant. Also, he should not address substantive questions about the matter under consideration directly to parents, as this could well mean asking questions of another solicitor's client without that solicitor's permission; nor should he ask questions of a lay participant, which should more appropriately be asked in court proceedings, without his solicitor's consent. Legal advice to the local authority on its agency in care planning and on commencing court proceedings should be given outside the conference. The solicitor can, in particular, assist in the decision as to whether the criteria are fulfilled for making a child the subject of a child protection plan, and advise the local authority that it should consider commencing court proceedings, but any decision actually to initiate or pursue court proceedings should be made by the local authority outside the conference. Paragraph 3.2 provides that representatives accompanying parents or children to a conference should be able to assist their clients to express their views and participate in the meeting, and should (with the chair's permission) be allowed to speak on their behalf. For representatives of children, paragraph 3.3 sets out that in advance of any local authority meeting, they should discuss with the children's guardian, and with the child if appropriate, who should attend the meeting. When representing the parents or persons with parental responsibility, paragraph 3.2 provides that if the person cannot attend in person, and instead sends a representative of the firm, he must ensure that the representative is knowledgeable in child care law and procedures, and is fully informed of the circumstances of the case. See the Practice Note for full details and essential practical guidance.

A review of the child protection plan should regularly follow a child protection conference. The first should take place within 3 months of the conference. The following reviews should take place at no more than 6-monthly intervals. Extra reviews may be convened at the request of other professionals.

The provision of resources under section 17 of, and Schedule 2 to, the CA 1989 is a statutory duty for a child in need (see para 4.7) and should not depend on registration. Note the equivalent provisions in Wales, which have substituted Schedule 2 to the CA 1989, namely the Social Services and Well-being (Wales) Act 2014 (Consequential Amendments) Regulations 2016 (SI 2016/413) (W 131).

4.4.5   Categories of abuse

Working Together defines the various categories of abuse (Appendix A: Glossary, at page 158). The four categories of abuse are set out below.

Emotional abuse

The persistent emotional maltreatment of a child so as to cause severe and persistent adverse effects on the child's emotional development. It may involve conveying to a child that he is worthless or unloved, inadequate or valued only insofar as he meets the needs of another person. It may include not giving the child opportunities to express his views, deliberately silencing him, or making fun of what he says or how he communicates. It may feature age or developmentally inappropriate expectations being imposed on children. These may include interactions that are beyond a child's developmental capability, as well as over-protection and limitation of exploration and learning, or preventing the child participating in normal social interaction. It may involve seeing or hearing the ill-treatment of another. It may involve serious bullying (including cyber bullying), causing children frequently to feel frightened or in danger, or the exploitation or corruption of children. Some level of emotional abuse is involved in all types of maltreatment of a child, though it may occur alone.

Neglect

The persistent failure to meet a child's basic physical and/or psychological needs, likely to result in the serious impairment of the child's health or development. Neglect may occur during pregnancy as a result of maternal substance abuse. Once a child is born, neglect may involve a parent or carer failing: to provide adequate food, clothing and shelter (including exclusion from home or abandonment); to protect a child from physical and emotional harm or danger; to ensure adequate supervision (including the use of inadequate caregivers); to ensure access to appropriate medical care or treatment; or to provide suitable education. It may also include neglect of, or unresponsiveness to, a child's basic emotional needs.

Physical injury

A form of abuse which may involve hitting, shaking, throwing, poisoning, burning, scalding, drowning or suffocating, or otherwise causing physical harm to a child. Physical harm may also be caused when a parent or carer fabricates the symptoms of, or deliberately induces, illness in a child.

Sexual abuse

Involves forcing or enticing a child or young person to take part in sexual activities, not necessarily involving a high level of violence, whether or not the child is aware of what is happening. The activities may involve physical contact, including assault by penetration (e.g. rape or oral sex) or non-penetrative acts, such as masturbation, kissing, rubbing and touching outside clothing. They may also include non-contact activities, such as involving children in looking at, or in the production of, sexual images, watching sexual activities, encouraging children to behave in sexually inappropriate ways or grooming a child in preparation for abuse. Sexual abuse can take place online, and technology can be used to facilitate offline abuse. Sexual abuse is not solely perpetrated by adult males. Women can also commit acts of sexual abuse, as can other children.

4.4.6 Criteria for discontinuance of the child protection plan

- No longer a continuing risk of significant harm requiring safeguarding.

- Child and/or family moved permanently to another area.

- Requirement that the new area local authority takes over the responsibility for future management of the case within 15 working days. Only after this event should the initial local authority discontinue its child protection plan.

- Child reaches 18, dies, or has permanently left the United Kingdom.

4.5 Assessment of risk

Local authorities, on referral, assess the likelihood of significant harm to a child, i.e. evaluation of the potential risk to the child should he or she remain within the family or the risk to the child if removed from home. After registration, there should follow a carefully planned and structured comprehensive assessment within the child protection plan, to gain a better understanding of the child's situation.

Comprehensive assessments require co-operation of agencies and professionals involved with the family. Professionals involved should be asked about how long they will need, the venue, timing and personnel to carry out the assessment – all must be clearly agreed.

4.6   Child protection plan

Child protection plans should not be confused with the care plans which are required in care proceedings; see Chapters 7 and 16.

As set out above, *Working Together* addresses the formulation and implementation of child protection plans made between family and professionals. Once the plan is agreed, each person should take responsibility to implement his or her part of it and to communicate with the others involved, with contingency provisions for crises and regular review. Parents and sufficiently competent children should have a copy of the plan, be informed of the nature and purposes of the interventions offered, and confirm that they agree with the plan and are willing to work with it. If the family has particular preferences about the protection work that are not accepted by the professionals, then the professionals' reasons should be explained to the family, together with the right of the family to complain or to make representations.

The child protection plan should:

- be in writing, in clear language, setting out the expectations and responsibilities of each party;

- describe the identifiable needs of the child and what therapeutic services are required;

- include specific, achievable, child-focused outcomes intended to safeguard and promote the welfare of the child;

- include realistic strategies and specific actions to achieve the planned outcomes;

- include a contingency plan to be followed if circumstances change significantly and require prompt action;

- clearly identify roles and responsibilities of professionals and family members, including the nature and frequency of contact by professionals with children and family members;

- lay down points at which progress will be reviewed, and the means by which progress will be judged; and

- set out clearly the roles and responsibilities of those professionals with routine contact with the child – e.g. health visitors, GPs and teachers – as well as those professionals providing specialist or targeted support to the child and family.

4.7   Child and Family Court Advisory Support Service

Following a consultation paper in 1998, the government made radical changes to the Family Court advisory system, unifying the Children's Guardian and Reporting Officer Service, the Family Court Welfare Service and the Children's Branch of the Official Solicitor's Department to form the Children and Family Court Advisory and Support Service (Cafcass), with the motto 'children first'.

Information can be obtained from the Cafcass government website, www.cafcass.gov.uk and at the website of NAGALRO (Professional Association for Children's Guardians, Family Court Advisers and Independent Social Workers), www.nagalro.com. Cafcass's functions are as follows:

- to safeguard and promote the welfare of children who are the subject of family proceedings;

- to give advice to any court about any application made to it in such proceedings;

- to make provision for children to be represented in such proceedings;

- to provide information, advice and other support for children and their families.

The Cafcass officer is appointed by the court and can be referred to by this general title. The Welsh equivalent is the Welsh Family Proceedings Officer, and further information can be obtained from the Cafcass Cymru website, www.gov.wales/cafcass-cymru.

Cafcass officers have different roles in private and public law proceedings:

- children's guardians, who are appointed to safeguard the interests of a child who is the subject of specified proceedings under the CA 1989 or who is the subject of adoption and related proceedings;

- reporting officers, where it appears that a parent or guardian of the child is willing to consent to the placing of the child for adoption and/or to the making of an adoption order;

- parental order reporters, who are appointed to investigate and report to the court on circumstances relevant under the HFEA 2008;

- children and family reporters, who prepare welfare reports for the court in relation to private law proceedings (this will include principally applications under section 8 of the CA 1989). Increasingly, they also work with families at the stage of their initial application to the court;

- Cafcass officers can also be appointed to provide support under a family assistance order under section 16 of the CA 1989. (Local authority officers can also be appointed for this purpose.)

Where a Cafcass officer has been appointed under section 41 of the CA 1989, he has a statutory right to access and take copies of local authority records relating to the child concerned and any application under the CA 1989. That power also extends to other records that relate to the child and the wider functions of the local authority or records held by an authorised body (e.g. the NSPCC) that relate to that child. The effect of rule 16.3(1) of the FPR 2010 is that unless it is satisfied that it is not necessary to do so to safeguard the interests of the child, the court must appoint a children's guardian for a child who is the subject of, and a party to, proceedings, which are specified proceedings, or to which Part 14 applies. Furthermore, rule 16.3(4) sets out that when appointing a children's guardian, the court will consider the appointment of anyone who has previously acted as a children's guardian of the same child.

Where a Cafcass officer has been appointed by the court as children's guardian and the matter before the court relates to specified proceedings (specified proceedings include various forms of public law proceedings, as well as certain types of applications that relate to section 8 of the CA 1989), the officer should be invited to all formal planning meetings convened by the local authority in respect of the child. This includes statutory reviews of children who are accommodated or looked after and child protection conferences. The conference chair should ensure that all those attending such meetings, including the child and any family members, understand the role of the Cafcass officer.

It should be noted that the independence of the children's guardian from Cafcass was clarified by the then President of the Family Division, Sir Nicholas Wall, in 2011, in *A County Council v K & Others* [2011] EWHC 1672 (Fam). The President stressed the independence of the children's guardian and the personal nature of the appointment as enshrined in section 41 of the CA 1989. He went on to set out guidance as to what should happen in care proceedings when there is an irrevocable disagreement between Cafcass and the individual guardian appointed by the court under section 41. Furthermore, in the Court of Appeal decision of *Re B (Children) (Remote Hearing: Interim Care Order)* [2020] EWCA Civ 584, the President of the Family Division (at [22]) emphasised that once a guardian has been appointed, he or she needs to exercise professional judgment, whatever the circumstances of the appointment. The court relies on guardians to be independent in promoting and protecting the interests of the children in the litigation, and they may take, and not infrequently do take, a different position to that of the local authority.

4.8   Local authority duty to promote welfare of children in its area

In England, section 17 of, and Schedule 2 to, the CA 1989 impose on local authorities a duty to promote the welfare of children in their area, with special provision for 'children in need'. Schedule 2 provides a list of the services and resources that may be provided. In particular, the local authority needs to publish information about services provided by it under sections 17, 18, 20 and 23D, where it considers it appropriate, and to take such steps as are reasonably practicable to ensure that those who might benefit from the services receive the information relevant to them. There are various provisions setting out the provision of services within Schedule 2. For example, local authorities shall provide family centres as appropriate for children in their area with counselling advice or guidance, occupational, cultural, social or recreational activities (Schedule 2, paragraph 9). Also, the local authority shall take reasonable steps, through the provision of services under Part III to prevent children within its area suffering ill-treatment or neglect (Schedule 2, paragraph 4). It is also notable to mention Schedule 2, paragraph 7, which places a positive duty on the local authority to take reasonable steps in reducing particularly the need to bring proceedings for care or supervision orders with respect to children within its area, or any other proceedings which might lead to them being placed in the authority's care.

4.8.1   Duty to investigate potential or actual harm to child

Section 47 of the CA 1989 requires a local authority, when informed that a child who lives or is found in its area is subject to emergency or police protection, or has reasonable cause to suspect that the child is suffering, or is likely to suffer significant harm, to 'make such enquiries as they consider necessary to enable them to decide whether they should take any action to safeguard or promote the child's welfare'. See *Working Together*, page 91.

The enquiries are intended to establish whether the authority should make any application to the court or exercise its powers under the CA 1989. The authority should consider providing accommodation for a child subject to an emergency protection order if it is not already doing so (section 47(3)(b)); and, if the child is in police protection, then the authority should consider applying for an emergency protection order (section 47(3)(c)). Enquiries may be made with the child's school, carers and others. Refusal of access to the child or denial of information may justify an application for an emergency protection order. The local authority is under a duty to consider and timetable a review, if no present action is required. If action is necessary, then the authority is under a duty to take it (section 47(8)).

4.8.2   Local authority duty to children in need

Section 17(1) of the CA 1989 imposes on local authorities a twofold duty:

  (a) to safeguard and promote the welfare of children within their area who are in need; and

  (b) so far as is consistent with that duty, to promote the upbringing of such children by their families,

  by providing a range and level of services appropriate to those children's needs.

Under section 17 of the CA 1989, those services are free to families on certain prescribed benefits, but otherwise may be subject to means-related contributions.

Section 17(10) of the CA 1989 defines a child being in need if:

  (a) he is unlikely to achieve or maintain, or to have the opportunity of achieving or maintaining, a reasonable standard of health or development without the provision for him of services by a local authority ... ;

  (b) his health or development is likely to be significantly impaired, or further impaired, without the provision for him of such services; or

  (c) he is disabled.

The services can be provided to the child direct or to the family for the benefit of the child. Local authorities should publish information about the services in their area. Services are listed in Schedule 2 to the CA 1989.

'Health', 'development' and 'disabled' are all defined in the CA 1989. Under section 17(6), the services provided by the local authority may include providing accommodation and giving assistance in kind or in cash.

4.8.3   Services for children and their families

Schedule 2, paragraph 8 to the CA 1989 lists services which local authorities should provide for children living with their families:

(a)   advice, guidance and counselling;

(b)   occupational, social, cultural or recreational activities;

(c)   home help (which may include laundry facilities);

(d)   facilities for, or assistance with, travelling to and from home for the purpose of taking advantage of any other service provided under this Act or similar service; and

(e)   assistance to enable the child concerned and his family to have a holiday.

However, the section 17 duty is a general duty and does not create an entitlement for an individual child to receive specific services. Children with disabilities may be entitled to direct support under section 2 of the Chronically Sick and Disabled Persons Act 1970. In Wales, this legislation has been replaced by provisions in the SSW(W)A 2014.

4.8.4   Duty to children aged under 5

There is power under section 18 of the CA 1989 to provide day care for children under school age. Day care is defined as any form of care or supervised activity provided for children during the day (whether or not it is provided on a regular basis). There is also the provision to provide for children in need, who are attending any school, such care or supervised activities as appropriate outside school hours, or during school holidays.

4.8.5   Compliance with court order to investigate child's circumstances, section 37 of the Children Act 1989

Under section 37 of the CA 1989, in any 'family proceedings' in which a question arises as to the welfare of any child, if it appears to the court that it may be appropriate for a care or supervision order to be made, the court may order the local authority to investigate the child's circumstances. The local authority then has to consider whether it should apply for a care or supervision order, provide services for the family or take any other action with respect to the child (section 37(2)). If the local authority decides not to seek an order, its reasons must be reported to the court within 8 weeks, as must the services provided or to be provided, and any other action taken or proposed with respect to the child (section 37(3) and (4)). The local authority may also need to review the situation and set a date for such a review (section 37(6)).

4.8.6   Looked after children: responsibility of the local authority

Local authorities may provide accommodation for certain children in need, whether voluntarily at the request of the child's parents or carers; under a care order or for assessment purposes, or otherwise by order of the court, for example where the child is required to live in secure accommodation.

There is strict regulation of the standards of care for children who are accommodated or looked after by local authorities – this includes children who are provided with accommodation by the local authority on a voluntary basis under section 20 of the CA 1989 (or the Welsh equivalent under section 76 of the SSW(W)A 2014).

Some children are provided with accommodation under section 59 of the CA 1989 by voluntary organisations. The local authorities are also responsible for oversight of the standards of this care.

For all looked after children, care plans and regular reviews must be made under the Care Planning, Placement and Case Review (England) Regulations 2010 (SI 2010/959) (the 2010 Regulations) (or the Welsh equivalent, namely the Care Planning, Placement and Case Review (Wales) Regulations 2015 (SI 2015/1818) (W 261) (the 2015 Regulations)), and an independent reporting officer appointed to oversee the welfare of the child.

5 Emergency Protection Orders

Emergency protection orders are available under section 44 of the CA 1989 (as amended by section 52 of, and Schedule 6, paragraph 3 to, the Family Law Act 1996). They are designed for situations when a child needs urgent removal to a safe place or to be retained in a safe place, such as a hospital. These orders may also be used to obtain access to a child in danger, when urgent action is necessary and/or to exclude a named person from a dwelling house or defined area in which the child lives, and they may include a power of arrest. An order may be made in respect of any child under 18 years of age living or found within the jurisdiction of the court.

5.1 Effects of order

The order gives parental responsibility for the child to the applicant (section 44(4)(c) of the CA 1989). It authorises the applicant to remove or retain the child (section 44(4)(b)); and it operates as a direction to anyone in a position to do so, to produce the child (section 44(4)(a)). Under section 44(15) it is a criminal offence to obstruct the applicant in the exercise of his powers under the order.

The order has wide powers, and may contain any or all of these directions:

- authorisation for a doctor, nurse or registered midwife to accompany the applicant to carry out the order (section 45(12) of the CA 1989);

- for a child to have contact with any named person (section 44(6)(a));

- for medical or psychiatric examination of the child (section 44(6)(b));

- requirement to disclose information concerning the whereabouts of the child (section 48(1));

- authorisation to enter premises and search for the child (section 48(3));

- authorisation to search for another child in the same premises (section 48(4));

- issue of a warrant to a police officer to assist the applicant (section 48(9));

- authorisation for a nurse, doctor or registered midwife to accompany police (section 48(11));

- an exclusion requirement under section 44(A)(2) requiring a named person to leave and remain away from the dwelling house or area in which the child lives;

- an undertaking in respect of an exclusion requirement (section 44B); and

- power of arrest in relation to an exclusion requirement (section 44A(5) and (8)).

5.2   Duration

Emergency protection orders last initially for up to 8 days, renewable for up to a further 7 days (section 45(1) and (5) of the CA 1989).

There are some exceptions to this general rule, including the following:

- if the order would expire on a public holiday – the first order goes to noon on the next day (section 45(2) of the CA 1989);

- if the child was in police protection (duration 72 hours maximum) before the emergency protection order, and the designated police officer is the applicant on behalf of the local authority, the emergency protection order commences from the beginning of police protection (section 45(3)).

5.3   Grounds for application

The grounds to be proved depend upon who the applicant is.

With the first ground, anyone can apply for this order. This is that if the intention is to remove the child to a safe place, the applicant must satisfy the court that there is reasonable cause to believe that the child will suffer significant harm if not removed to accommodation provided by him (section 44(1)(a)(i) of the CA 1989).

If the applicant intends to retain the child in a safe place, then it must be proved that there is reasonable cause to believe that the child is likely to suffer significant harm unless retained in a safe place (section 44(1)(a)(ii) of the CA 1989). The grounds can be established on the existence of present harm or a prognosis indicating a future risk to the child. For the definition of 'significant harm', see Chapter 7, paras 7.2–7.3.

A local authority applicant has an additional ground. It can satisfy the court that during enquiries made under section 47 of the CA 1989 about a child in its area, access to the child requested by a person authorised to seek it is being refused unreasonably, and that the access is required as a matter of urgency (section 44(1)(b)(i) and (ii)). The question of reasonable refusal is a matter for the court. If the application is made by an authorised officer of the local authority or an 'authorised person' (currently only the NSPCC), there is either the general ground, or an additional ground, that the applicant has reasonable cause to suspect that the child is suffering or is likely to suffer significant harm, that the applicant is making enquiries as to the child's welfare, that access to the child is being unreasonably refused, and access is urgently needed (section 44(1)(c)).

The CA 1989 principles of the paramountcy of the welfare of the child, avoidance of delay and no order unless necessary for the welfare of the child apply. However, the application is not 'family proceedings' within the meaning of section 8(4) of the CA 1989 and so the 'welfare checklist' does not strictly apply.

5.4 Practice and procedure

5.4.1 Application

Emergency protection orders may be sought by any person. Usually, however, the applicant will be an 'authorised officer' of the local authority or, less commonly, applications may be made by an 'authorised person' (currently only the NSPCC) or 'a designated officer' of the police.

The application should be made to the Family Court, through His Majesty's Courts and Tribunals Service's MyHMCTS online case management system. Application is made electronically on online version of Form C110A. See FPR 2010 PD 41D and, in particular, paragraph 4.1, which provides that the online system allows for specified applications and stages in the proceedings specified in paragraph 1.3(a) of this Practice Direction to be dealt with online.

Emergency protection orders are classified as 'specified proceedings' for the purposes of section 41 of the CA 1989, and these orders appear in Part V of the CA 1989. The procedure of these orders is governed by the FPR 2010, and in particular Part 12, as well as PD 12C. Applications for extensions should be made to the court that made the original order.

In relation to allocation, this is governed by the *President's Guidance on Allocation and Gatekeeping for Care, Supervision and other Proceedings under Part IV of the Children Act 1989 (Public Law)* (22 April 2014) (as amended in 2020), issued in accordance with rule 21 of the Family Court (Composition and Distribution of Business) Rules 2014 (SI 2014/840) (as amended in 2021). The Family Court (Composition and Distribution of Business) (Amendment) Rules 2021 (SI 2021/505) amend the Family Court (Composition and Distribution of Business) Rules 2014.

The application should name the child and, if this is not possible, it should give a description of the child for identification purposes.

A children's guardian will be appointed by the court to oversee the welfare of the child and to advise the court on the child's best interests (sections 41–42 of the CA 1989), see Chapter 15, para 15.1.

As discussed at para 3.6, for the purposes of public funding, emergency protection orders come within the definition of 'Special Children Act Proceedings' under Parts 4 and 5 of the CA 1989. Therefore, funding in relation to these applications is available on a non-means/merits basis for the child who is the subject of the order and for parents of, or parties with parental responsibility for, the subject child.

5.4.2   Respondents

The forms of notice on Form C6 plus a copy of the application, with the hearing date endorsed on it, must be served on respondents, together with notice of the date and place of the hearing.

Those listed below are automatically considered respondents to the application (rule 12.3 of the FPR 2010):

- everyone with parental responsibility for the child;
- if there is a care order, all those who had parental responsibility immediately prior to the care order;
- the child, if of sufficient age and understanding.

Others may be joined as respondents, and respondents may be removed by direction of the court (rules 4.3 and 12.3(3)).

5.4.3   Applications made without notice (previously referred to as *ex parte* applications)

Reference is to be made to the 'interpretation section' in Part 2 of the FPR 2010 in terms of usage of terms such as '*ex parte*' and 'leave'. An application for an emergency protection order may be made 'without notice', in appropriate cases. Any order that is made would be expected to be served upon each respondent within 48 hours of the order being made (rule 12.16(5) of the FPR 2010 and PD 12E), although, in practice, it will usually be served on the same day that it was granted.

5.4.4   Notice

If an application is made on notice, Form C6A, and the date, time and venue of the application, must be given within one day of the hearing to (FPR 2010 PD 12C, paragraph 2.1):

- parents of the child without parental responsibility;
- any person caring for the child or with whom the child is living when the proceedings are commenced;
- a local authority providing accommodation for the child;
- a person providing a refuge under section 51 of the CA 1989, in which the child lives.

5.4.5 Service

Service must be effected one day before the directions or application hearing, FPR 2010 PD 12C, paragraph 2.1. It is important to note that in some cases of urgency, for example, where the local authority needs to seek an emergency protection order on the day a child is born, and to do so 'on notice', it may seek to apply to abridge time for service to less than a day. Such a direction can be made pursuant to rule 4.1(3)(a).

5.4.6 Attendance

By rule 4.1(d) of the FPR 2010, the court can direct that the parties and/or their legal representatives must attend directions appointments and hearings unless otherwise directed by the court. If respondents fail to appear, the court may proceed in their absence. If applicants fail to attend, the court may refuse their application. Rule 4.3(1) provides that except where an enactment provides otherwise, the court may exercise its powers on an application, or of its own initiative.

5.5 Contact, accommodation and the rights of the child

5.5.1 Contact

The child must be allowed reasonable contact with:

- parents;
- those with parental responsibility for the child;
- anyone with whom the child was living before the order;
- any person named in a child arrangements order as a person with whom the child is to spend time with, or otherwise have contact with;
- any person who has contact under an order under section 34 of the CA 1989;
- any person acting on behalf of any of the above (section 44(13)).

The court can control the contact by directions within the emergency protection order (section 44(6)(a) of the CA 1989).

In relation to contact between parents and babies/infants, see the practice points set out in cases such as *Re M (Care Proceedings: Judicial Review)* [2003] EWHC 850 (Admin), [2003] 2 FLR 171, and *Kirklees Metropolitan Borough Council v S (Contact to New Born Babies)* [2006] 1 FLR 333. Also, see the useful research by J Kenrick, 'Concurrent Planning: A Retrospective Study of the Continuity and Discontinuity of Care and their Impact on the Development of Infant and Young Children placed for Adoption by the Coram Concurrent Planning Project' (2009) 33(4) *Adoption & Fostering* 5–18. There has also been other research of a similar nature undertaken in Australia by C Humphreys and M Kiraly, 'High-Frequency Family Contact: A Road to Nowhere for Infants' (2011) 16(1) *Child & Family Social Work* 1–11.

5.5.2   Accommodation

The child has the right to accommodation provided, funded or arranged by the local authority, see in particular the amendments to section 23 of the CA 1989, brought about by sections 8–9 of the CYPA 2008. Section 22 of the CA 1989 requires the local authority to provide accommodation, services and education for the child whom it is looking after. Section 22G of the CA 1989 requires the local authority to ensure that there is secure accommodation available where necessary for looked after children.

5.5.3   Rights of the child

The child has the right to be returned to his home once the danger has passed and the grounds for the order no longer subsist (section 44(10) of the CA 1989).

A child of sufficient age and understanding has the right to be consulted and informed about events that are happening. In particular, section 25B of the CA 1989 (inserted by section 10 of the CYPA 2008) should be considered, which requires the IRO to ensure that the ascertainable wishes and feelings of the child are given appropriate consideration by the local authority.

The emergency protection order may include a direction about medical or psychiatric assessment of the child (section 44(6)(b) of the CA 1989). The directions can order or prohibit examinations, either completely or without permission of the court. Directions for examination/assessment can include venue, personnel to be present and nomination of the person(s) to whom results should be given. A child of sufficient age and understanding has the right to make an informed refusal of medical or psychiatric assessment. A '*Gillick*-competent' child, or a young person over 16, may consent to or refuse medical treatment, see Chapter 12, paras 12.1 and 12.2.

5.6   Variation and discharge

There is no right of appeal against an emergency protection order, perhaps because of its short duration (section 45(10) of the CA 1989). It can be challenged by an application to vary or to discharge the order.

The child, the child's parents, those with parental responsibility for the child, and anyone with whom the child was living when the order was made, can make an application for variation or discharge (section 45(8) of the CA 1989).

Note that, previously, it was the case that there had to be a time lapse of 72 hours after the order 'without notice' before there could be a hearing of an application for discharge (section 45(9) of the CA 1989). However, this provision was revoked in April 2009 by section 30 of the CYPA 2008, so that it is possible to apply for discharge of the order even on the same day it was made.

The rules provide, however, that if a person has had notice of the original application for the emergency protection order and has attended and opposed the application at the hearing, then there is no right to seek a discharge (section 45(11) of the CA 1989).

5.7   Exclusion requirement under emergency protection order

The local authority may wish to make arrangements for the removal of an alleged abuser as an alternative to an emergency removal of the child. Under Schedule 2, paragraph 5 to the CA 1989, the local authority has power to assist the alleged abuser in finding alternative accommodation.

A summary of the effect of section 44A(1)–(2) of the CA 1989 is that the court can make an exclusion requirement where:

(a)   there is reasonable cause to believe that if a person is excluded from the dwelling in which the child lives, the child will cease to suffer or cease to be likely to suffer, significant harm; and

(b)   another person living in the dwelling house (whether a parent of the child or some other person):

(i)   is able and willing to give to the child the care which it would be reasonable to expect a parent to give him, and

(ii)   consents to the inclusion of the exclusion requirement.

The consent can be given at court, orally or in writing.

A power of arrest can be attached to the exclusion requirement, under section 44A(5) of the CA 1989. Note that, as set out in FPR 2010 PD 12K, paragraph 3, any order of committal made otherwise than in public, or in a courtroom open to the public, shall be announced in open court at the earliest opportunity. This may be either on the same day when the court proceeds to hear cases in open court, or where there is no further business in open court on that day, at the next listed sitting of the court. The announcement shall state: (a) the name of the person committed; (b) in general terms the nature of the contempt of the court in respect of which the order of committal has been made; and (c) the length of the period of committal.

5.7.1   Two notes of caution

*   An undertaking from the person required to leave the dwelling house can be accepted instead of an exclusion order, but no power of arrest can then be attached (section 44B(2) of the CA 1989).

*   If the child is removed from the house to which an exclusion order or undertaking applies for a continuous period of more than 24 hours, the order or undertaking will cease to apply (section 44A(10) of the CA 1989). If an exclusion order is in force and the child is to be absent from the house for more than 24 hours for any reason which is known in advance, it would be wise to notify the court, and to seek appropriate directions.

5.8   How do 'without notice' orders and Article 6 of the ECHR fit together?

There are various procedural safeguards to ensure that these orders are compliant with the ECHR. In particular, the fact that magistrates need to provide 'reasons' for making the order, and the appointment of a guardian, would ensure that this would balance the right of a parent to a fair trial, against the need of the child to be protected in an emergency. Where an order is made without notice, the parent(s) must be given a full record of the proceedings as soon as possible after the order has taken effect (and see para 5.4.3).

Cases such as *P, C and S v UK* (Application No 56547/00) [2002] ECHR 604, [2002] 2 FLR 631, *X Council v B & Others* [2004] EWHC 2015 (Fam), [2005] 1 FLR 341 and *Re X (Emergency Protection Orders)* [2006] EWHC 510 (Fam), [2006] 2 FLR 701 should be considered. In the latter case, *Re X (Emergency Protection Orders)*, McFarlane J (as he then was) stressed that an emergency protection order is a Draconian and extremely harsh measure, requiring exceptional justification and extraordinarily compelling reasons. One needs to establish 'imminent danger'. Also, the order should be made for no longer than is absolutely necessary in order to protect the child. When an order is made, the local authority is authorised to remove the child only if this is still the proportionate action to protect him or her. Furthermore, cases of emotional abuse will rarely, if ever, warrant an emergency protection order, let alone an application 'without notice'. Cases of sexual abuse where the allegations are inchoate and non-specific, and where there is no evidence of the immediate risk of harm to the child, will rarely warrant an emergency protection order.

Normally, an application to protect a child cannot be made until the child is born. However, there are limited exceptions where the courts have endorsed the plan to remove at birth without giving notice to the parent in advance. Furthermore, the evidence in support of an application for an emergency protection order must be full, detailed, precise and compelling. More recently, in *A Local Authority v Mrs X (A Mother), Mr X (A Father), [Children] (by their children's guardian)* [2023] EWFC 69, the court was concerned that neither the written emergency protection order application itself nor the notes from either of the advocates present during the hearing drew the court's attention to the guidance contained in *X Council v B & Others* [2004] EWHC 2015 (Fam), [2005] 1 FLR 341 or *Re X (Emergency Protection Orders)* [2006] EWHC 510 (Fam).

5.9 Emergency applications and newborn children

Consider the case of *Nottingham City Council v LW & Others* [2016] EWHC 11 (Fam), in which Keehan J emphasised a number of important steps to take when lodging proceedings on newborn children. In particular, His Lordship emphasised, at [30], that that the following should always be borne in mind:

(a) a hospital may not detain a baby in hospital against the wishes of the mother or a father with parental responsibility;

(b) the capability of a maternity unit or a hospital to accommodate a healthy newborn child may change within hours, whatever the good intentions of the unit or hospital, depending upon the challenging demands with which it may be presented;

(c) the ability to invite the police to exercise police protection, or for a local authority to apply for an emergency protection order, are available as emergency remedies, but such procedures do not afford the parents, nor, most importantly, the child, with the degree of participation, representation and protection as an on notice interim care order application;

(d)   the indication of a maternity unit as to the date of discharge of a newborn baby should never, save in the most extraordinary of circumstances, set or lead the time for an application for an interim care order in respect of a newborn child.

Furthermore, at [31], His Lordship stated that where the pre-birth plan provides for an application to be made for the removal of a child at or shortly after birth, it is neither 'usual' nor 'ideal' practice for an application for an interim care order to be made on the day of the child's birth, rather it is essential and best practice for this to occur.

In this context, consider the Final Report of the Public Law Working Group (chaired by Mr Justice Keehan), *Recommendations to achieve best practice in the child protection and family justice systems* (March 2021). This report is available at www.judiciary.uk/wp-content/uploads/2021/03/March-2021-report-final_clickable.pdf. In terms of applications to the court, recommendation 15 of the Best Practice guidance in this report (at paragraph 134) provides that there should be the sharing of existing protocols/local agreements with health services to promote similar arrangements on a national basis. The long-term recommendation (at paragraph 147) surrounding newborn babies is in relation to the role of Cafcass pre-proceedings, so that the Working Group recommended that consideration be given to the means by which planning for newborns can be improved, including the potential role of Cafcass pre-birth.

5.9.1   Out-of-hours emergency protection order applications

Following the creation of the single Family Court in April 2014, the then President of the Family Division, Sir James Munby, introduced changes to the way in which 'out-of-hours', emergency protection orders were to be dealt with. These are to be managed by Urgent Court Business Officers under the Urgent Court Business Scheme. If there is no judge available, then the Urgent Court Business Officer can be contacted. In relation to applications made outside normal working hours, also note the provisions set out in FPR 2010 PD 20A, paragraph 4.5, as well as PD 12E, which relates to urgent business. The out-of-hours hearing will often take place remotely. In this context, given the onset of the Covid-19 pandemic in March 2020, all courts needed to move swiftly onto greater use of technology to accommodate court business, and consequently, remote hearings, which were previously mainly used for out-of-hours hearings, became more widely used during office hours. Even though we have transitioned through the recovery period of the pandemic, there are still many uses and benefits of remote hearings across England and Wales at the time of writing in 2024.

6 Child Assessment Orders

6.1 Effects of order

Child assessment orders were created by section 43 of the CA 1989. They enable the local authority to discover sufficient information about the child to plan appropriate action in the child's interests. In this context, note the Department for Education publication, *Court Orders and Pre-Proceedings for Local Authorities* (DfE, April 2014). This guidance replaced the 2008 guidance, *The Children Act 1989 Guidance and Regulations: Volume 1: court orders*. At paragraph 5, Chapter 4 of this guidance, it is suggested that the use of child assessment orders is most relevant in circumstances where the child is not thought to be at immediate risk, to the extent that removal from his parents' care is required, but where parents have refused to co-operate with attempts to assess the child. This may be where the suspected harm to the child appears to be longer term and cumulative, rather than sudden and severe. Paragraph 8 of this guidance states that, if possible, before an application is made, the child should have been seen by someone who is competent to form a judgment about the child's welfare and development. When considering an application for any order, the court will expect to be given details of the enquiries made including, in particular, details of the extent to which, if at all, the enquiries have been frustrated by the failure or refusal of the parents to co-operate. The order can stipulate the nature of the assessment sought, the venue and duration, the person(s) to whom the results are to be given, and the contact between the child and others during the subsistence of the order.

In practice, it has been found that child assessment orders are rarely made, probably because in a situation where parents do not co-operate when the local authority has concerns about a child's welfare, an application for a care order may prove necessary.

One notable example of where the order was made was in the case of *Re I (Children: Child Assessment Order)* [2020] EWCA Civ 281. Here, the court emphasised (at [35]) that a child assessment order allowed for a brief, focussed assessment of the state of a child's health or development, or the way in which he or she had been treated, where that was required to enable the local authority to determine whether or not the child was suffering, or was likely to suffer, significant harm and to establish whether there was a need and justification for any further action. The purpose of the assessment was to provide a range of information, identifying not only whether harm may exist, but also describing its nature and extent. It was the least interventionist of the court's child protection powers and was designed to enable information that could not be obtained by other means to be gathered without the need to remove the child from home. It was not an emergency power, and it may be particularly apt where the suspected harm to the child may be longer term and cumulative rather than sudden and severe. On the facts, the order would allow an assessment of the children by an 'intervention provider' in relation to concerns over radicalisation of the children.

6.2   Grounds for application

The court may, by section 43(1) of the CA 1989, make the order only if it is satisfied that:

- the applicant has reasonable cause to suspect that the child is suffering, or is likely to suffer, significant harm;

- an assessment of the child's state of health or development, or of the way in which he is being treated, is required to enable the applicant to determine whether or not the child is suffering or is likely to suffer significant harm; and

- it is unlikely that such an assessment will be made, or be satisfactory, in the absence of an order under this section.

6.3   Practice and procedure

6.3.1   Application

An application can only be made by a local authority or authorised officer (this category currently only includes the NSPCC) (sections 43(1) and (13) and 31(9) of the CA 1989, and rule 12.3 of the FPR 2010). The application is covered by Part V of the CA 1989, and the application should be on Form C1, together with supplemental Form C16. FPR 2010 PD 41D, paragraph 4.1 provides that the online system (HMCTS's MyHMCTS online case management system) allows for certain public law applications and stages in the proceedings specified in paragraph 1.3(a) of this Practice Direction to be dealt with online. Child assessment order applications are classed as 'public law proceedings' for the purposes of the online system (rule 12.2 of the FPR 2010) and therefore such an application is made electronically.

The application must be determined at a full court hearing. Under section 91(15), no further applications may be made without leave in a 6-month period following disposal of the first application.

As discussed at para 3.6, for the purposes of public funding, child assessment orders come within the definition of 'Special Children Act Proceedings' under Parts 4 and 5 of the CA 1989. Therefore, funding in relation to these applications is available on a non-means/merits basis for the child who is the subject of the order and parents of/parties with parental responsibility for the subject child.

6.3.2 Venue

Consider the *President's Guidance: Jurisdiction of the Family Court: Allocation of Cases within the Family Court to High Court Judge Level and Transfer of Cases from the Family Court to the High Court* (24 May 2021). Paragraph 18 of this guidance provides that, except as specified in the Schedule to the guidance, every family matter must be commenced in the Family Court, and not in the High Court. The child assessment order application does not come within the schedule to this guidance, and hence, must be made to the Family Court.

6.3.3 Respondents

Rule 12.3 of the FPR 2010 provides that notice, plus a copy of the application with the date, time and place of hearing, must be served on those listed below who are automatically regarded as respondents to the application.

These include:

(a)   everyone with parental responsibility for the child;

(b)   the child;

(c)   where there is a care order, everyone with parental responsibility before the making of the care order;

(d)   in the case of an application to extend, vary or discharge the order, the parties to the proceedings leading to the order which it is sought to have extended, varied or discharged; in the case of specified proceedings.

Others may be joined as respondents, and automatic respondents may be removed by order of the court (rule 12.3(3)(a)–(b) of the FPR 2010).

6.3.4   Notice

Notice of the proceedings on Form C6A and the date, time and venue of the application must be given to those entitled, including (section 43(11) of the CA 1989, rule 12.3 of the FPR 2010 and PD 12C, paragraph 3.1):

(a)   parents;

(b)   those with parental responsibility for the child;

(c)   any person caring for the child or with whom the child is living;

(d)   any person named in a child arrangements order as a person with whom the child is to spend time or otherwise have contact;

(d)   anyone entitled to contact with the child under section 34 of the CA 1989;

(e)   the child.

6.3.5   Service

Child assessment orders are regarded as public law proceedings. Service must be at least 7 days before the directions or application hearing (FPR 2010 PD 12C, paragraph 2.1). However, under rule 4.1(3)(a) of the FPR 2010, the court may extend or shorten the time period for service. Rule 12.5(2) provides that insofar as practicable in public law proceedings, the court will set a date for the case management hearing (CMH).

6.3.6   Generally

The principles in section 1 of the CA 1989 apply to section 43 applications, save that the welfare checklist does not apply. The order does not confer on the local authority, parental responsibility for the child. Section 8(3)–(4) of the CA 1989 defines 'family proceedings', and within these proceedings the court has power to make other orders of its own initiative. Section 43 orders are not, however, 'family proceedings' as they are covered by Part V. This means that the court can only make or refuse the order sought, or treat the application as one for an emergency protection order instead (section 43(3)). The court must not make a child assessment order if in all the circumstances of the case the court considers an emergency protection order more appropriate (section 43(4)).

The duration of the order is limited to 7 days from the date specified for commencement (section 43(5) of the CA 1989). The CA 1989 does not state that the 7 days must be consecutive, but there seems no other practicable interpretation. It cannot be extended and, unless the court grants permission, it cannot be renewed until a 6-month period has elapsed (section 91(15)).

6.3.7   Discharge of order

On an application for discharge of a child assessment order, the case will be listed. The procedure is the same as an application for an original order.

6.4   Contact, accommodation and the rights of the child

6.4.1   Contact

If the child is going to be kept away from the family home, then the order shall contain such directions as the court thinks fit in relation to the contact that the child must be allowed to have with other people whilst away from the home (section 43(10) of the CA 1989).

Note the operation of Article 8 of the ECHR (right to respect for privacy and family life) as it may affect a child's right to contact with family and siblings.

6.4.2   Accommodation

If the child is removed from the family home and accommodated by the local authority, it is submitted that this would be pursuant to section 20(4) of the CA 1989, or the Welsh equivalent in sections 75 and 76 of the SSW(W)A 2014.

In relation to looked after children, the local authority needs to ensure that the placement of the child is in accordance with the 2010 Regulations or the Welsh equivalent, as set out in the 2015 Regulations.

One of the key provisions under the CA 1989 is that, pursuant to section 22(4) of the CA 1989, in determining the child's placement, the local authority needs, insofar as is reasonably practicable, to ascertain the views of, amongst others, the child (if of sufficient age and understanding) and the child's parents.

6.4.3   Rights of the child

The child assessment order will usually include a direction about medical or psychiatric assessment of the child. Examinations can be ordered or prohibited. Directions can include venue, personnel to be present and nomination of the person(s) to whom results of assessments, etc should be given. A child of sufficient age and understanding has the right to make an informed refusal of medical or psychiatric assessment (section 43(8) of the CA 1989). A '*Gillick*-competent' child, or a young person over 16, may consent to or refuse medical treatment. See Chapter 12.

A child should only be kept away from home where it is necessary for assessment purposes, and in accordance with directions in the order, for such period or periods as may be specified in the order (section 43(9)(a)–(c) of the CA 1989).

6.5   Appeals, variation and discharge

Part 30 of the FPR 2010 covers appeals. Rule 30.1 provides that the rules in Part 30 apply to appeals to: (a) the High Court; and (b) the Family Court. Also, PD 30A, paragraph 2.1 sets out a table, providing for which court or judge an appeal is to be made (subject to obtaining any necessary permission) from decisions of the Family Court. This is coupled with the Access to Justice Act 1999 (Destination of Appeals) (Family Proceedings) Order 2014 (SI 2014/602), which sets out the appeal route from certain judges and office holders to the Family Court, instead of the appeal lying to the Court of Appeal. There are also the amendments to the 2014 Order (made by the Access to Justice Act 1999 (Destination of Appeals) (Family Proceedings) (Amendment) Order 2016 (SI 2016/891)), which route certain appeals from circuit judges or recorders to the High Court, instead of needing to go to the Court of Appeal. See Chapter 17 for more detail on appeals and the specific provisions within Part 30 of the FPR 2010. Applications to vary or discharge the order (under section 43(12) of the CA 1989) may be made with 7 days' notice, to the court which made the original order. See FPR 2010 PD 12C, paragraphs 1.1 and 2.1.

Contraventions of the ECHR may be dealt with by complaint, judicial review or appeal against a court order.

7 Care and Supervision Proceedings

7.1 Care order – definitions

'Care orders' are those orders made under section 31 of the CA 1989, placing a child into the care of a designated local authority. The 'designated local authority' is the local authority for the area in which the child resides, or within whose area any circumstances arose in consequence of which the care order is being made.

A 'child' is a person under the age of 18 (section 105(1) of the CA 1989). The term 'care order' includes an 'interim care order' made under section 38 as well as an order made under section 31. Reference to a 'child in the care of the local authority' is defined by section 105(1) to mean a child subject to a care order (and not therefore a child who is accommodated by a local authority under a section 20 voluntary care arrangement), although children who are in the care of the local authority are also looked after and the same planning and review regime applies as for accommodated children.

7.2 Grounds for application for a care or supervision order

A care order cannot be made in respect of a child aged 17 years or older, or 16 if married (section 31(3) of the CA 1989). It should be noted that as a result of the Marriage and Civil Partnership (Minimum Age) Act 2022, the minimum age at which a person may marry or enter into a civil partnership was raised to 18 as from 27 February 2023.

Under the CA 1989 there is only one route into statutory care. The court must be satisfied that the criteria set out in section 31 are met and also that an order is necessary for the welfare of the child.

The underlying principles in section 1(1), (2) and (5) of the CA 1989 – the paramountcy of the welfare of the child, avoidance of delay and no order unless necessary – all apply. The court must have regard to the welfare checklist in section 1(3), see Chapter 2.

Care orders and supervision orders are mutually exclusive, but the grounds in section 31 for the application for both are the same. On hearing an application for a care order, if the threshold criteria are met, the court may instead order supervision, or vice versa. Where a care order is in force, the court may, at any time during it, substitute supervision, but the making of the supervision order will discharge the existing care order.

Section 31(2) of the CA 1989 specifies the grounds for application for a care or supervision order:

(a) that the child concerned is suffering, or likely to suffer, significant harm; and

(b) that the harm; or likelihood of harm, is attributable to:

(i) the care given to the child, or likely to be given to him if an order were not made, not being what it would be reasonable to expect a parent to give to him; or

(ii) the child's being beyond parental control.

The following definitions are taken from section 31(9) of the CA 1989.

Development

Physical, intellectual, emotional, social or behavioural development.

Harm

Ill treatment or the impairment of health or development, including, for example, impairment suffered from seeing or hearing the ill treatment of another.

Health

Includes physical or mental health.

Ill treatment

Includes sexual abuse and forms of ill treatment which are not physical.

7.3   Significant harm

The difficult part for practitioners in care and supervision proceedings is often the definition and proof of 'significant harm'. Section 31(9) of the CA 1989 gives the definitions (see above). It is also provided in section 31(10) that: 'Where the question of whether harm suffered by a child is significant turns upon the child's health or development, his health or development shall be compared with that which could reasonably be expected of a similar child'. The court will therefore have to compare this particular child with a notional similar child, of similar background, age, ethnicity, culture, race, religion and physique. See Figure 7.1.

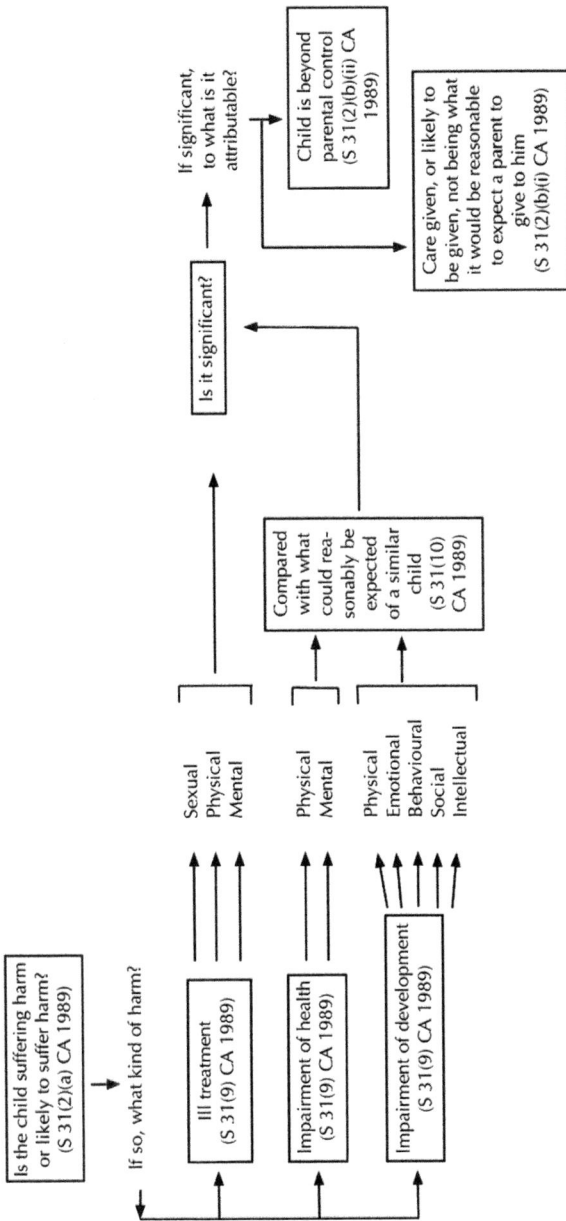

Figure 7.1   Significant harm flowchart

Significant harm must be attributable to parental care falling below a reasonable standard, or the child being beyond parental control. The test is objective, measured against a reasonable standard of parenting. However, the definition became problematic in *Re MA (Care Threshold)* [2009] EWCA Civ 853.

Subsequently, in *Re B (A Child)* [2013] UKSC 33, there were important points made surrounding threshold and the terms 'significant' and 'likelihood of harm'. Lord Wilson stated the word 'significant' involves comparing what that child has suffered, with what can be reasonably expected of a similar child. Also, that the court should avoid attempting to explain the word 'significant'. His Lordship stated at [25]:

> The first matter is the meaning of the word 'significant'. In this regard Parliament chose to help the court to a limited extent by providing in section 31(10) as follows:
>
>> 'Where the question of whether harm suffered by a child is significant turns on the child's health or development, his health or development shall be compared with that which could reasonably be expected of a similar child.'
>
> When we read this subsection together with the definition of 'harm' in the preceding subsection, we conclude that, whereas the concept of 'ill-treatment' is absolute, the concept of 'impairment of health or development' is relative to the health or development which could reasonably be expected of a similar child. This is helpful but little more than common sense.

As to the concept of 'likelihood of harm', Lord Wilson described it in the following way (at [24]):

> ... It is common ground that, as recently reaffirmed by this court in *In re J (Children) (Care Proceedings: Threshold Criteria)* [2013] UKSC 9, [2013] 2 WLR 649, a likelihood of significant harm means no more than a real possibility that it will occur but a conclusion to that effect must be based upon a fact or facts established on a balance of probabilities. In the context of the present case it is also noteworthy that, by section 31(9), 'harm' means 'ill-treatment or the impairment of health or development ...' and 'development' includes 'emotional ... development'. Beyond this, however, the debate surrounds two matters.

In *Re M (Minor) (Care Order: Threshold Conditions)* [1994] 2 AC 424, the House of Lords held that 'is suffering' means at the date of the hearing, or at the moment when the child protection was initiated, provided that the protection is uninterrupted until the date of the hearing. A careful reading of this judgment is recommended. Whilst the court may find the grounds proved, it may also take account of the circumstances prevailing at the hearing date in considering whether it is necessary to make an order, and which order would be most appropriate.

7.3.1   Standard of proof

The threshold criteria for proceedings under section 31 of the CA 1989 must be established on a 'simple balance of probabilities', i.e. significant harm (unlike the 'likelihood' element mentioned at para 7.3) must be established on a balance of probabilities. The House of Lords put it very clearly as '... a real possibility, a possibility that cannot be sensibly ignored, having regard to the nature and gravity of the feared harm in the particular case ...'. See *Re H & Others (Child Sexual Abuse: Standard of Proof)* [1996] 1 FLR 80, a section 31 application in respect of four children based on an allegation that the father had sexually abused the oldest child, and positing a likelihood of significant harm to the younger three. The court found that the section 31(2) criteria were not met in the case of the oldest child, leaving no power to go on and even consider the likelihood of harm to the younger three children.

Difficulties in reaching the standard of proof occurred in subsequent cases because of *dicta* in *Re H & Others* (above) suggesting that the more serious the allegation, the greater the level of proof needed. However, in *Re B (Children) (Sexual Abuse: Standard of proof)* [2008] UKHL 35, [2008] 2 FCR 339, Baroness Hale clarified that the standard of proof necessary to establish threshold under section 31 is the 'simple balance of probabilities, nothing more nor less'.

7.3.2   Linking harm or likelihood of harm to the facts and test for separation

Under section 31 of the CA 1989, the local authority must also prove that the harm was attributable to the parents' care (or lack of care). This can cause difficulties in the case of 'uncertain perpetrators' when it is not known which parent or carer was responsible for an injury. In *Re O and N (Children) (Non-accidental injury)* [2003] UKHL 18, the House of Lords held that where an injury could be attributed to the parents but neither would say who was responsible, the court should proceed to the welfare stage on the basis that each is a possible perpetrator.

Subsequently, in *Re A (A Child)* [2015] EWFC 11 at [7], the then President of the Family Division, Sir James Munby, set out three key aspects surrounding threshold. The first is that it is the local authority which has to prove, on the balance of probabilities, the facts upon which it relies. The court stated that findings of fact must be based on evidence, not suspicion or speculation. The allegations that are put, such as 'he appears to have' or 'other people that stated, or reported' or 'there is an allegation' should not be used. The allegation should not be 'he appears to have lied', instead it should be 'he lied'. The second fundamental point is the need to link the facts relied upon by the local authority with its case on threshold, and therefore, the need to demonstrate why the facts asserted justify the conclusion that the child has suffered, or is at risk of suffering, significant harm. Thirdly, at [14] of the judgment, His Lordship emphasised that society must be willing to tolerate very diverse standards of parenting, and that children will have very different experiences of parenting. Also, note the case of *Re BR (Proof of Facts)* [2015] EWFC 41, in which Jackson J (as he then was) stated that the court acts on evidence, not speculation or assumption. It acts on facts, not worries or concerns. Also, evidence comes in many forms. It can be live, written, direct, hearsay, electronic, photographic, circumstantial, factual, or by way of expert opinion. The burden of proving a fact rests on the person who asserts it.

Also, in terms of demonstrating the causal link between the threshold for the purposes of section 31(2) of the CA 1989 and the welfare stage, the case of *WBC v A* [2016] EWFC B70 emphasises the point that if the threshold criteria are met, then a second stage must be considered. In this case, the court referred to the court's investigative responsibility in care proceedings where the parties were agreed as to the outcome, as considered in *Re G (A Minor) (Care Order: Threshold Conditions)* [1995] Fam 16, and also *A County Council v DP, RS & BS* [2005] EWHC 1593 (Fam). These cases showed that even where all parties agree that threshold conditions are met, the court has a duty to satisfy itself about welfare. The court therefore needs to apply the overriding objective under Part 1 of the FPR 2010, and the duty to manage cases under Part 2 of the FPR 2010 applies, so that the court has a duty to deal with cases expeditiously, and fairly, as well as dealing with them in ways which are proportionate to the nature of the case. It is also worth noting the later decision in *Re G (Children: Fair Hearing)* [2019] EWCA Civ 126, which emphasises the care that the court needs to take in ensuring that a party is not deprived of a meaningful opportunity to oppose the making of an interim care order.

As referred to at para 7.2, there is also the second limb under section 31(2) of the CA 1989, namely 'beyond parental control'. In practice, a local authority would rely upon this in circumstances where it is necessary to protect children who are at risk of significant harm due to the inability of a parent to meet the child's needs, but due to no fault on the part of the parent. This may sometimes be relevant where the child has a disability and is suffering significant harm because, despite parental care, the parent is unable to meet the child's needs.

The issue of threshold was considered in the decision of *West Sussex County Council v K* [2022] EWFC 170. The court had to consider whether the threshold should be met in any case in which a parent became incapacitated. The court stated that in a situation where the parent cannot provide any safe care for a child, where the parent cannot exercise any parental responsibility, on a practical level, where no alternative family carers are available, and where parties are agreed that a child requires accommodating because of the parent's inability to provide care, it would be wholly proper for section 31 of the CA 1989 to be brought into play.

Note that during the currency of the care or supervision order application proceedings, the local authority may invite the court to grant an interim care or interim supervision order, often for the duration of the proceedings. If so, section 38(2) of the CA 1989 is relevant and needs to be met, so as to satisfy the *interim* threshold. Section 38(2) provides that the court may only make an interim care or supervision order if satisfied that there are *reasonable grounds* to believe that the child concerned is suffering, or is likely to suffer, significant harm, and that harm, or likelihood of harm, is attributable to: (a) the care given to the child, or likely to be given to him if the order were not made, not being what it would be reasonable to expect a parent to give to him; or (b) the child is beyond parental control.

Assuming that the threshold is met for an interim order (pursuant to section 38(2) of the CA 1989), if the local authority seeks separation of the child from the parent, the court would need to be satisfied that the child's safety demands immediate or continued separation. In the Court of Appeal decision of *Re C (A Child) (Interim Separation)* [2019] EWCA Civ 1998, Jackson LJ set out some significant guidance in this regard. In particular, His Lordship set out (at [2]) that:

(1) An interim order is inevitably made at a stage when the evidence is incomplete. It should therefore only be made in order to regulate matters that cannot await the final hearing and it is not intended to place any party to the proceedings at an advantage or a disadvantage.

(2) The removal of a child from a parent is an interference with their right to respect for family life under Art. 8. Removal at an interim stage is a particularly sharp interference, which is compounded in the case of a baby when removal will affect the formation and development of the parent–child bond.

(3) Accordingly, in all cases an order for separation under an interim care order will only be justified where it is both necessary and proportionate. The lower ('reasonable grounds') threshold for an interim care order is not an invitation to make an order that does not satisfy these exacting criteria.

(4) A plan for immediate separation is therefore only to be sanctioned by the court where the child's physical safety or psychological or emotional welfare demands it and where the length and likely consequences of the separation are a proportionate response to the risks that would arise if it did not occur.

(5) The high standard of justification that must be shown by a local authority seeking an order for separation requires it to inform the court of all available resources that might remove the need for separation.

The need for the court to be satisfied that the child's safety demands immediate or continued separation was recently once again emphasised in *Re J, K and L (Children: Interim Removal)* [2023] EWCA Civ 1266, whereby, the court, at [25], stated that the authority of *Re C (A Child) (Interim Separation)* [2019] EWCA Civ 1998 was very properly identified in the case summary prepared on behalf of the local authority for the hearing, and the key passage from [2] (4) of the judgment (set out above) expressly cited. However, it was not mentioned in the judgment and, at one point, the judge referred to 'the immediate risk of serious harm' which, as the court made clear in *Re L-A (Children)* [2009] EWCA Civ 822, was not the test. It is also of note that in *Re D (Children: Interim Care Order: Hair Strand Testing)* [2024] EWCA Civ 498, the Court of Appeal has stated that although *Re C* (set out above) refers to removal of a child 'from a parent', it had rightly been acknowledged in this appeal that such principles were also applicable to a proposed removal from a grandmother or other primary family care-giver.

7.4   Practice and procedure

7.4.1   Applicants and public funding

Only a local authority or an authorised person may apply for a care order (section 31(1) of the CA 1989). An 'authorised person' at the moment is an officer of the NSPCC (section 31(9)), although at the time of writing, no record could be found of the NSPCC using this provision.

The court has no power to make a care order without an application, but under section 38(1) of the CA 1989 it may make an interim care or supervision order on adjourning an application for a full order; or alongside making a direction to the local authority to investigate the child's circumstances under section 37.

Under rule 29.4(2) of the FPR 2010, any application relating to care proceedings cannot be withdrawn without the permission of the court. This was emphasised in the case of *WBC v A* [2016] EWFC B70.

As discussed at para 3.6, for the purposes of public funding, care and supervision orders come within the definition of 'Special Children Act Proceedings' under Parts 4 and 5 of the CA 1989. Therefore, funding in relation to these applications is available on a non-means/merits basis for the child who is the subject of the order and parents of, or parties with parental responsibility for, the subject child. Therefore, if for example, an aunt was joined as a party in the care proceedings, then unless she had parental responsibility for the child, in terms of public funding, she would need to satisfy both the means and merits tests for the purposes of eligibility. For those persons who are eligible, the non-means/merits funding will cover funding for the duration of the proceedings and therefore in care proceedings, even where there may be interim orders in place. The funding is also available where there has been written notice of intention from the local authority to issue care proceedings.

7.4.2   Venue

To understand the position with venue, it is necessary to consider the set-up of the Family Court. The effect of section 17(3) of the Crime and Courts Act 2013 was to create the single Family Court, as from 22 April 2014. It merged the FPCs, the family jurisdiction of the various county courts, and also the various aspects of the High Court's family work, into a single Family Court. Therefore, the FPCs, and the county court function covering family jurisdiction, no longer exist. The inherent jurisdiction of the High Court remains, and therefore the work that remains in the Family Division of the High Court is mainly that involving the inherent jurisdiction, and international cases, often involving those relating to various conventions, such as the Hague Convention on the Civil Aspects of International Child Abduction 1980 (the 1980 Hague Convention), the Hague Convention on Jurisdiction, Applicable Law, Recognition, Enforcement and Co-operation in Respect of Parental Responsibility and Measures for the Protection of Children 1996 (the 1996 Hague Convention) and, for matters prior to the UK's exit from the EU, the Brussels II Regulation (Council Regulation (EC) 2201/2003 of 27 November 2003 concerning jurisdiction and the recognition and enforcement of judgments in matrimonial matters and the matters of parental responsibility (BIIR)).

A Joint Statement by the then President of the Family Division, Sir James Munby, and the HMCTS Family Business Authority of April 2013 set out that the various geographical areas across England and Wales would be split into designated family centres. All new applications were to be lodged at the designated family centre, and therefore there was to be a 'single point of entry', through which there would be centralised gate-keeping and allocation teams. The allocation teams deal with allocation, so as to ensure that they are handled by the appropriate person(s), who are best placed to deal with that matter, based upon the type of matter it is, and the type of experience it requires. In public children law cases, the guidance is set out in the *President's Guidance on Allocation and Gatekeeping for Care, Supervision and other Proceedings under Part IV of the Children Act 1989 (Public Law)* (22 April 2014) (as amended in 2020), issued in accordance with rule 21 of the Family Court (Composition and Distribution of Business) Rules 2014 (as amended in 2021), together with the Allocation Schedule.

Insofar as allocation is concerned, paragraph 5 of the *President's Guidance on Allocation and Gatekeeping for Care, Supervision and other Proceedings under Part IV of the Children Act 1989 (Public Law)* states that local authority applicants are to complete the Allocation Proposal section of the C110A application form when issuing proceedings. The Allocation Proposal section is to be used by the gatekeepers to record their allocation decision.

Paragraph 7 of the guidance goes on to provide that when the allocation decision has been made, the case management judge or case manager will issue the Standard Directions on Issue and Allocation, in accordance with FPR 2010 PD 12A, together with any appropriate Notice of Hearing.

It is important that when a local authority is completing Form C110A, now being completed electronically, through the MyHMCTS portal, in relation to allocation, it should make specific reference to the relevant part of the schedule(s) accompanying this guidance, so as to assist the court in its allocation decision. For example, paragraphs 20 and 21 of the *President's Guidance on Allocation and Gatekeeping for Care, Supervision and other Proceedings under Part IV of the Children Act 1989 (Public Law)* stipulate that it is expected that proceedings described in column 1 of the schedule to this Guidance will be allocated to a judge of district judge level, and that it is expected that proceedings described in column 2 of the schedule to this Guidance will be allocated to a judge of circuit judge level or a judge of High Court Judge level and will not be allocated to a judge of district judge level unless specifically released by the Designated Family Judge or one of his nominated deputies.

The corresponding allocation guidance in the case of private children law cases, is the *President's Guidance on Allocation and Gatekeeping for Proceedings under Part II of the Children Act 1989 (Private Law)* (22 April 2014) (as amended in 2020), issued in accordance with rule 21 of the Family Court (Composition and Distribution of Business) Rules 2014 (as amended in 2021), together with the Allocation Schedule. Insofar as private children law is concerned, allocation decisions must be made in accordance with the Family Court (Composition and Distribution of Business) Rules 2014. Paragraph 25 of the guidance is of particular note, which provides that when considering specifically the complexity of a case, it is envisaged that proceedings described in Part 1 of the Schedule to the guidance will be allocated to a district judge, or a district judge (magistrates' court). If it appears to the district judge that the particular circumstances of the individual case justify allocation to a circuit judge, the district judge shall so allocate it.

In terms of which court matters are commenced in, be it Family Court or High Court, the *Jurisdiction of the Family Court: Allocation of Cases within the Family Court to High Court Judge Level and Transfer of Cases from the Family Court to the High Court* (24 May 2021) is particularly relevant here. This has replaced the *President's Guidance: Jurisdiction of the Family Court: Allocation of Cases within the Family Court to High Court Judge Level and Transfer of Cases from the Family Court to the High Court* (28 February 2018) and is considered in more detail in Chapter 14.

7.4.3   Form

The application is in Form C110A and is to be completed electronically. This application form incorporates all applications for care, supervision and other Part 4 applications. It also incorporates emergency protection order applications. Therefore, it is be possible to lodge both an emergency protection order application, and also a care/supervision order application on the same form. Various documents must be annexed to the application form: the genogram, social work chronology, social work statement, care plan, current assessment(s) relating to the child or family, or friends, and which the social work statement refers to, and which the local authority relies upon. An index of checklist documents must also be provided. Note that it is only the index of the checklist documents that needs to be filed, not the actual documents themselves, unless the court asks for any of them to be filed. Checklist documents are those that already appear on the local authority files.

In many local authority areas in England, a completed Social Worker Evidence Template (SWET) form is submitted. This document can be used to provide the information in a self-contained format, so as to replace the need for a separate genogram, social work chronology and social work statement. In some geographical areas, the SWET also incorporates the initial and final care plan.

7.4.4   Respondents

FPR 2010 PD 12C, paragraph 1.1 provides that the application in Form C110A, Form C6 (Notice of proceedings) and such of the documents specified in the Annex to Form C110A as are available, are to be served on the respondents to the application, as well as on Cafcass or Cafcass Cymru.

These must therefore be served before the hearing on those listed below who are automatically considered respondents to the application, namely:

(a)   everyone whom the local authority believes has parental responsibility for the child;

(b)   the child, if of sufficient age and understanding.

See rule 12.3 of the FPR 2010 regarding parties, and Part 6 regarding service. Others may be joined as respondents and automatic respondents may be removed by direction of the court. Under rule 12.3(2) any person who has parental responsibility who has not already been made a respondent will be joined by the court on that person's request.

7.4.5   Notice and court actions on issue

When the proceedings are issued, the court will consider allocation of the case and the appropriate level of judicial officer.

Form C110A should set out whether there is a need for an urgent hearing, to consider an interim care order application, or for the purposes of holding a preliminary CMH.

Note that on 16 January 2023, the President of the Family Division re-launched the PLO (see *Re-Launch of the Public Law Outline (PLO)*, at www.judiciary.uk/courts-and-tribunals/family-law-courts/re-launch-of-the-public-law-outline-plo/). In this document, the President set out that only those very rare cases that are truly urgent should be the subject of an 'urgent' first hearing and that, too often, an 'urgent' hearing is sought as a matter of course. Urgently fixed hearings are seldom fully effective and a further hearing or hearings will normally be required.

FPR 2010 PD 12A, paragraph 2 relates to the flexible powers of the court. Paragraph 2.4 provides that if a party has requested an urgent hearing, the court would need to consider making immediate directions, or to facilitate any case management issues which are to be considered at the CMH, or to decide whether an interim care order is necessary. Paragraph 2.4 provides that it is anticipated that the urgent preliminary hearing will only be necessary to consider issues relating to, for example, jurisdiction, parentage, party status, capacity to litigate, disclosure, and whether there should be a request to a central authority or other competent authority in the foreign state or counsellor authority in England and Wales, in an international case.

On day one, the court officer will issue the application, and will provide standard directions on issue. The local authority will need to serve the application form, as well as the annex documents and evidential checklist documents on the parties, together with the notice of proceedings, which will set out the date and time of the CMH, and any urgent hearing. FPR 2010 PD 12A, paragraph 3.1 provides that the CMH is to be held not before day 12, but no later than day 18 of issue. This is once again emphasised in the *Re-Launch of the Public Law Outline (PLO)*, so that the President has stated that the first hearing should be the CMH, held 'not before Day 12 and no later than Day 18'; and an advocates meeting is to be held no later than 2 days before the CMH.

Under FPR 2010 PD 12C, paragraph 3.1, notice must be given to any of the following non-parties on Form 6A:

• a local authority looking after the child;

• a person caring for the child when the proceedings commence;

• if the child is staying in a refuge, the provider of that refuge service;

- every person the applicant believes to be a party in pending relevant proceedings;

- every person whom the applicant believes to be a parent of the child who does not have parental responsibility.

7.4.6 Service

Part 6 of the FPR 2010 and PD 6A deal with service of documents on respondents. The court can dispense with the requirements of service under rules 6.36 and 7.1 of the FPR 2010 in appropriate cases.

7.4.7 Attendance

Proceedings may take place in the child's absence if the court considers this to be in his interests, having regard to the matters to be discussed or the evidence likely to be given, and if he is represented by a solicitor (rule 12.14(3) of the FPR 2010).

The other parties and/or their legal representatives have to attend the hearings unless otherwise directed by the court. If respondents fail to appear, the court may proceed in their absence. If applicants fail to attend, the court may refuse their application (rule 12.14(5)–(7) of the FPR 2010). For discussion of case preparation, see Chapter 11.

7.5 Interim orders

As discussed at para 7.3.2, on adjourning a care or supervision application, the court has the power to make an interim order when satisfied that there are reasonable grounds for believing the circumstances justifying a care order exist (section 38(2) of the CA 1989).

Section 14(4) of the CFA 2014 changed the position with the length of interim orders. That is, in relation to section 38 of the CA 1989 (interim care and supervision orders), changes were brought about in April 2014, so as to bring in an amended section 38(4) of the CA 1989. These changes are that unlike previously (where there were limits to an interim order being made for a period of up to 28 days on each occasion in most cases), the position now is that the court is able to set the length of interim orders for a period which is considered appropriate in the circumstances of the case. However, no interim order can endure beyond the cessation of the proceedings themselves. In practice, it is quite common for the court to make an interim order for the duration of the proceedings.

On making an interim order, directions may require medical or psychiatric examination or assessment of the child, which a child of sufficient understanding may refuse (section 38(6) of the CA 1989). (See Chapter 12 for the rights of children.) Directions may prevent the abuse of children by repeated examinations (section 38(7)). Directions may also govern the time and venue of the examination, who shall be present and to whom the results will be given.

Directions for assessment under section 38 of the CA 1989 can include assessments of the parents' capacity, for example, as part of a residential parent and child assessment (*Re C (A Minor) (Interim Care Order) (Residential Assessment)* [1997] AC 489), but not to provide treatment or therapy for parents (*Re G (A Minor) (Interim Care Order) (Residential Assessments)* [2005] UKHL 68). In *Re Y (A Child) (s.38(6) Assessment)* [2018] EWCA Civ 992, the court determined that in deciding an application under section 38(6), one must consider whether the proposal falls within the terms of section 38(6). If so, one has to ask as to whether the assessment is necessary to assist the court to resolve the proceedings justly, as required by section 38(7A) of the CA 1989, having regard to the matters in section 38(7B).

In relation to applications through section 38(6) of the CA 1989, HHJ Moradifar, in *Re K and R (Unregulated Placement: Authorisation Pursuant to the Court's Inherent Jurisdiction: Prohibition)* [2022] EWHC 1890 (Fam), was asked to sanction the placements in exercising the inherent jurisdiction of the High Court, or alternatively by directing the assessment of each child, pursuant to section 38(6) of the CA 1989. His Honour was satisfied that the placements sought were a residential placement, whose function in assessing the children was fulfilled in part and in other parts was ancillary to the fulfilment of the assessment of each of these children. Therefore, it fell well within the ambit of section 38(6).

7.6   Effects of care order

7.6.1   Duration

A care order subsists until the child reaches 18, unless brought to an end earlier by the court (section 91(12) of the CA 1989).

A care order will cease on the making of:

(a)   an adoption order under section 46(2)(b) of the Adoption and Children Act 2002;

(b)   a placement order, see section 29(1) of the Adoption and Children Act 2002. The care order will therefore not take effect whilst the placement order is in force;

(c)　a special guardianship order (section 91(5)(a) of the CA 1989);

(d)　a child arrangements order, specifying living with (section 91(1) of the CA 1989);

(e)　a supervision order made in substitution for a care order (section 39(4) of the CA 1989);

(f)　an order for discharge of care (section 39(1) of the CA 1989).

A care order will also cease:

(g)　when a child goes to live in Northern Ireland, the Isle of Man or the Channel Islands, provided the relevant regulations are satisfied (section 101(4) of the CA 1989) (it should be noted that at the time of writing, the regulations about this have not yet been made under section 101(4)).

7.6.2　Parental responsibility and care plans

The local authority acquires parental responsibility under a care order, sharing it with those who already have it. The local authority may, however, limit the exercise of parental responsibility by others whilst the care order subsists (section 33(3) of the CA 1989). There are limits on the powers of the local authority during a care order. The local authority may not change a child's religion, consent to his adoption or appoint a guardian for the child (section 33(6)). The parental responsibility which others had when the care order was made still subsists, but it cannot be exercised in a way which conflicts with a court order (section 2(6) and (8)). The child's name may not be changed or the child removed from the United Kingdom without written consent of all with parental responsibility or leave of the court (section 33(7)). The local authority may remove the child from the jurisdiction of the court for up to one month and, in England, under Schedule 2, paragraph 19 to the CA 1989, can make arrangements for a child to live abroad, with certain restrictions. The equivalent provision in Wales is section 124 of the SSW(W)A 2014. See *Re E (A Child)* [2017] EWHC B11 (Fam), which considered an application by the local authority for removal out of the jurisdiction.

For care plans, see Local Authority Circular LAC (99)29, *Care Plans and Care Proceedings under the Children Act 1989* and, subsequently, the amended section 31A of the CA 1989, which provides that where an application is made on which a care order might be made with respect to a child, the appropriate local authority must, within such time as the court may direct, prepare a care plan for the future care of the child, and whilst the application is pending, the authority must keep under review any care plan it prepares. If the authority is of the opinion some change is required, it must revise the plan, or make a new plan, accordingly. The appropriate local authority is the one in respect of which a care order might be made. Note that section 31A(5) provides that in this section, references to a care order do not include an interim care order.

As for the aspects of the section 31A care plan that the court needs to consider before making a care order, changes brought about by the CFA 2014 were such that the amended section 31(3A) of the CA 1989 provided for the court to consider the permanence provisions of the section 31A plan for the child concerned, but it was not required to consider the remainder of the section 31A plan, subject to section 34(11). The significance of this is that it enables the court to focus its consideration on the provisions of the care plan that set out the long-term plan for the upbringing of the child. Specifically, this provided that the court is to consider whether the local authority care plan is for the child to live with a parent or any member or friend of the child's family, or whether the child is to be adopted or placed in other long-term care. These are referred to as the 'permanence provisions' of the section 31A plan. The court is not required to consider the remainder of the section 31A plan (subject to section 34(11)), which requires the court to consider the contact arrangements for the child), although the amendments do not prevent the court from doing so. Further amendments brought about in October 2017 by section 8 of the Children and Social Work Act 2017 were that, in addition to considering the matters included in section 31(3B) of the CA 1989, the court was also required to consider such provisions of the child's care plan that set out the impact on the child concerned of any harm he has suffered (or was likely to have suffered), the child's current and future needs (including needs arising from that impact), and the way in which the long-term plan for the child's upbringing would meet those current and future needs. Therefore, it is important for the local authority to ensure that it provides for these additional matters as part of the child's care plan. The court has no authority to make 'starred care plans' as set out in the House of Lords' decisions of *Re S (Minors) (Care Order: Implementation of Care Plan), Re W (Minors) (Care Order: Adequacy of Care Plan)* [2002] UKHL 10, [2002] 1 FLR 815.

Lastly, it is important to note that in line with the least interventionist principle, a child's needs, both short term and long term, may be met whilst placed voluntarily, as opposed to under the auspices of an interim care/care order. This was emphasised by the Court of Appeal in the decision of *Re S (A Child) and Re W (A Child) (s 20 Accommodation)* [2023] EWCA Civ 1, where the court found that the first instance judge fell into error into thinking that section 20 of the CA 1989 could only be used as a short-term measure.

7.6.3 Proportionality, kinship care and local authority accommodation of the child

Hale LJ expressed the purpose of the CA 1989 as follows, 'The principle has to be that the local authority works to support, and eventually reunite, the family, unless the risks are so high that the child's welfare requires alternative family care', see *Re C and B (Care Order: Future Harm)* [2000] EWCA Civ 3040, [2001] 1 FLR 611.

Proportionality is therefore vital to comply with Article 8 of the ECHR.

In England, the Department for Education publication, *The Children Act 1989 Guidance and Regulations: Volume 2: care planning, placement and case review* (July 2021) governs the placements of children in residential and foster care and placements with their immediate family or in the 'kinship care' of wider family and friends. The guidance emphasises the duty on the local authority to consider the placement of children with their birth family if possible, consistent with their welfare, and the importance of maintaining family links.

In this context, note the local authority duty under section 22C(2) of the CA 1989, whereby, insofar as is reasonably practicable, the local authority needs to make arrangements for the child to live with, in the first instance, the parent of the child; secondly, somebody who is not the parent, but has parental responsibility for the child; and, thirdly, in the case where the child is in the care of the local authority and there was a child arrangements order in force with respect to the child immediately before the care order was made, the person was a person named in the child arrangements order as a person with whom the child was to live. Furthermore, if the local authority is unable to make such arrangements, then under section 22C(5), it needs to make arrangements for the child to be placed in the most 'appropriate' placement. The CA 1989 refers to this as, first, placement with an individual who is a relative, friend or other person connected with the child, and who is also a local authority foster parent; and, secondly, placement with a local authority foster parent who does not fall within this definition.

If the child needs to live away from home, then under section 33(1) of the CA 1989, the local authority has a duty to receive the child into its care once the order is made.

During the period the child is subject to an interim care order (section 38 of the CA 1989) or care order (section 31), he or she is looked after by the local authority and therefore subject to the same planning and review regime in the *Guidance and Regulations* as children accommodated voluntarily under section 20.

7.6.4 Planning transition to adulthood

In England, the Department for Education publication, *Children Act 1989 Guidance and Regulations: Volume 3: planning transition to adulthood for care leavers* (February 2022) sets out the local authority's duties to assist the young person in care in transition into adulthood.

In Wales, note in particular the framework for assessing and meeting the care and support needs of children, and the support needs of their carers, particularly within Parts 3 and 4 of the SSW(W)A 2014. Also, note section 78(1), which provides that a local authority looking after any child, must: (a) safeguard and promote the child's well-being; and (b) make such use of services available for children cared for by their own parents as appears to the authority reasonable in the child's case. Under section 78(2), the duty of a local authority under subsection (1)(a) to safeguard and promote the well-being of a child looked after by it includes, for example: (a) a duty to promote the child's educational achievement; (b) a duty, (i) to assess from time to time whether the child has care and support needs which meet the eligibility criteria set under section 32, and (ii) if the child has needs which meet the eligibility criteria, to at least meet those needs.

Also, it is important to note that there are various provisions set out in the Children and Social Work Act 2017 relating to changes to local authority duties towards care leavers. These are set out specifically within sections 104–115 of the SSW(W)A 2014. In England, there is a requirement for the local authority to publish information about services which the local authority offers for care leavers as a result of its functions under the CA 1989, and also other services which the local authority offers that may assist care leavers in, or in preparing for, adulthood and independent living. Furthermore, the local authority is expected to provide the former relevant child with a personal adviser until the former relevant child reaches the age of 25 or, if earlier, informs the local authority that he or she no longer wants a personal adviser.

7.6.5 Contact with a child in care

Parents and others in financial or practical difficulty may receive help with travelling to contact sessions (Schedule 2, paragraph 16 to the CA 1989).

Contact with children in care is subject to the control of the court, if it cannot be agreed between the parents (or other persons with parental responsibility) and the local authority. This is different from contact in private law, where there is no legal presumption for or against contact.

The CA 1989 requires that children looked after by a local authority under a care order will be afforded 'reasonable contact' with those people listed in section 34(1). They are:

(a)   parents;

(b)   guardians;

(c)   anyone with a child arrangements order, specifying living with, in force immediately before the care order was made;

(d)   anyone with care of the child under a High Court order made under its inherent jurisdiction.

The court may, on the application of the children's guardian or the child, make whatever order it considers appropriate in respect of contact between the child and any named person. Where the child or the local authority is the applicant, the scope of the order is very wide. On the application of any person entitled to contact under section 34(1) of the CA 1989 (those listed above), or anyone else with leave of the court, a contact order may be made, pursuant to section 34(3).

When the court makes a care order, it may make a contact order if necessary in the interests of the child (section 34(5) of the CA 1989), even though no application for such an order has been made with respect to the child. The forms, those entitled to notice and respondents, are the same as for the care order.

In urgent cases, if necessary, a local authority may stop contact for up to 7 days (section 34(6) of the CA 1989). If it wishes to stop contact for longer, it must apply to the court for an order under section 34, authorising contact with a named person to be curtailed or to be refused. It may be argued that severe curtailment of contact is tantamount to a refusal within the meaning of section 34 since the section refers to 'reasonable contact' and the court is the ultimate arbiter of reasonableness. In *Re B (Minors) (Termination of Contact: Paramount Consideration)* [1993] Fam 301 at 311, Butler-Sloss LJ stated that contact must not be allowed to destabilise or endanger the arrangements for the child and that in many cases the local authority's plan will be decisive. She described the task of the court as having 'the greatest respect' for the local authority's plans to arrange contact in the best interests of the child, but also retaining the power to adjudicate these arrangements if they are not agreed between the local authority and those named in section 34(1).

Contact between looked after children and their parents and significant others, during care proceedings and beyond, is a fundamental component of proceedings and can often be the cause of conflict between the parties as to the right level and provision.

Within care proceedings, contact is invariably supervised by the local authority or its agent. The focus of the supervision is to ensure the safety of the child, protect him or her from being drawn into the court process by parents or visiting relatives, and to allow for regular observations of adult and child interactions, which feeds into the court process and the assessments of parenting and arrangements for future contact.

Within care proceedings the level of contact provided should not be pre-emptive of the issues resolution and/or final hearing, and should ensure that it is maintained at a sufficient level to keep the doors open to future reunification. Young babies will receive the highest levels of contact with birth parents, particularly where there is a possibility of reunification, placement in a residential assessment facility or a mother and baby foster placement. In the case of *Re M (Care Proceedings: Judicial Review)* [2003] EWHC 850 (Admin), [2003] 2 FLR 171, the court set out that, particularly when the mother is breastfeeding, contact needs to be led by the needs of family and not stunted by resources. However, it should be noted that resources are not a wholly irrelevant consideration. This was a matter that was considered in *Re D-S (Contact with Children in Care: Covid-19)* [2020] EWCA Civ 1031. Here, until the first Covid-19 pandemic lockdown in March 2020, the children had contact meetings with their mother three times a week, but as a result of the lockdown, the two contact centres closed. This led to the children then having only indirect contact by telephone and video call. Later that year the mother applied for a defined contact order on the basis that she challenged the requirement for social distancing, stating that she and her mother were willing to form a 'social bubble'. The Court of Appeal, in deciding on the application, stated that it did need information about the children's situation, the local authority's resources and the government guidance at the time.

There are occasions when it becomes evident that the quality of the contact and of the parent/child interactions are so poor that a reduction needs to be made before the conclusion of the proceedings in order to safeguard the welfare of the child. Such decisions are invariably contentious and often lead to contested interim hearings. There are occasions when it may become necessary for the local authority to suspend contact under section 34(6) of the CA 1989, for example if a child is harmed, abducted, or threatened with abduction, if there is violent behaviour or parents attending heavily under the influence of drugs or alcohol. As mentioned above, the local authority can suspend contact for 7 days before the matter needs to return to court for adjudication.

Care plans should detail the future proposals for contact, and they should be carefully considered by all parties to the proceedings. The arrangements for contact at the IRH and/or final hearing can sometimes cause greater conflict than the making of the care order and a recognition that a child will not return to the care of his or her parent(s). Contact is a complex area and the children's guardian and social worker will often be able to express an informed opinion on the current and future contact arrangements.

7.6.6 Rights of the child in care proceedings and under a care order

A child who is subject to an interim care order under section 38 of the CA 1989 or to a care order under section 31 has rights which are protected by the Human Rights Act 1998, the CA 1989 and also by the guidance issued under it. The child has a right to:

(a) refuse medical or psychiatric assessment ordered within an interim care order under section 38(6) of the CA 1989;

(b) contact with his or her family (see para 7.6.5);

(c) consultation: before making any decision with respect to a child being looked after by the local authority, the court must, so far as reasonably practicable, ascertain the wishes and feelings of the child, and give them due consideration, having regard to the child's age and understanding (section 22(4) and (5) of the CA 1989);

(d) participate in the care planning process, see section 22(4) of the CA 1989 and regulation 5a of the 2010 Regulations. This includes the permanence plan, health plan and personal education plan. The equivalent in Wales are regulations 4–10 of the 2015 Regulations;

(e) a review of the plan within 20 days of becoming looked after, then within 3 months and then every 6 months (regulation 33 of the 2010 Regulations; the Welsh equivalent is set out in regulation 39 of the 2015 Regulations);

(f) be allocated a named IRO whom the child will meet before each review. The IRO's role is set out in detail in the *IRO Handbook: Statutory guidance for independent reviewing officers and local authorities on their functions in relation to case management and review for looked after children* (DfE, 2010);

(g) be advised by the IRO, in accordance with the child's age and understanding, of his or her rights to make court applications or complaints and access to advocacy services and legal advice (regulation 45 of the 2010 Regulations);

(h) an independent visitor (regulations 28–31 of the 2010 Regulations);

(i) services to assist young people in the transition into adulthood. These are not covered in this book, but are found in sections inserted into the CA 1989 by the Children (Leaving Care) Act 2000. The provisions are set out principally within section 23A–D of the CA 1989. The equivalent services in Wales are set out within, principally, sections 103–118 of the SSW(W)A 2014.

7.6.7   Rights of parents of a child in care

Parents (with parental responsibility or not) and those with parental responsibility for a child in care, have the right to:

(a)   consultation and participation (section 22(4) of the CA 1989 and the 2010 Regulations);

(b)   information on where their child is being kept (Schedule 2, paragraph 15(2) to the CA 1989);

(c)   reasonable contact with their child (section 34 of the CA 1989);

(d)   receive, if appropriate, financial or practical assistance with travelling to see their child (Schedule 2, paragraph 16 to the CA 1989).

If the local authority departs from the care plan in breach of the child's ECHR rights, under sections 7 and 8 of the Human Rights Act 1998, the court may grant relief or remedy.

7.7   *Public Law Outline* – principles, 'fact-finding hearings', issues resolution, interim and final hearings

7.7.1   Main principles of the *Public Law Outline* (Practice Direction 12A)

Under FPR 2010 PD 12A the main principles underlying court case management in public law proceedings are:

(1)   timetable for the child (see paragraphs 5.1–6.6);

(2)   allocation: the court considers the initial allocation to a specified level of judge, in accordance with the *President's Guidance on Allocation and Gatekeeping for Care, Supervision and other Proceedings under Part IV of the Children Act 1989 (Public Law)* (22 April 2014) (as amended in 2020), issued in accordance with rule 21 of the Family Court (Composition and Distribution of Business) Rules 2014 (as amended in 2021), together with the Allocation Schedule. Where possible, FPR 2010 PD 12A requires judicial continuity;

(3)   main case management tools: each case will be managed by the court by using the appropriate main case management tools;

(4)   active case management: each case will be actively case managed by the court with a view at all times to furthering the overriding objective;

(5)   consistency: each case will, so far as compatible with the overriding objective, be managed in a consistent way and using the standardised steps.

The main case management tools are:

- The timetable for the child who is the subject of the proceedings. One has to set out all significant steps in the child's life that are likely to take place during the proceedings, to include legal, health care, social care, review and other steps.

- Insofar as the timetable for the proceedings is concerned, paragraph 5.1 provides that the court will draw up a timetable for the proceedings with a view to disposing of the application: (a) without delay; and (b) in any event, within 26 weeks, beginning with the day on which the application was issued in accordance with section 32(1)(a)(ii) of the CA 1989. Also, when the court is drawing up or revising a timetable, it needs to have particular regard to: (a) the impact which the timetable or any revised timetable would have on the welfare of the child to whom the application relates; and (b) the impact which the timetable or any revised timetable would have on the duration and conduct of the proceedings.

- Case management documentation which includes:

    - application form and annexed documents;

    - case analysis and recommendations provided by Cafcass or Cafcass Cymru;

    - local authority case summary;

    - parents' response.

- Case management record. This is the court's filing system under FPR 2010 PD 12A and will include:

    - case management documentation;

    - standard directions on issue and allocation;

    - case management orders approved by the court.

7.7.2   Various parts of Practice Direction 12A

- Pre-proceedings.
- Issue of application and allocation.

- CMH.

- IRH.

- Final hearing if necessary.

Often, cases present issues of fact which require identification, clarification or determination. The intention is that these should be narrowed to those still outstanding at the IRH stage by the use of directions at the CMH stage. Cases may be resolved at the IRH stage, thus dispensing with the need for a final hearing.

7.7.3   Fact-finding hearings/split hearings

Before FPR 2010 PD 12A came into force, the term 'split hearings' or 'fact-finding hearings' (meaning the separate hearings in which the process of fact finding, threshold criteria and subsequent disposal were decided in stages) was commonly used. 'Fact-finding' hearings are used to clarify and adjudicate on factual matters in dispute, for example, identification of the perpetrator in cases of sexual or physical abuse, and are split off from the final hearing of the case. Guidance has been given in a plethora of case law on the use of split hearings, for example in *Re P (Care Proceedings: Split Hearing)* [2007] EWCA Civ 1265, [2008] Fam Law 202 and *Re A (Children) (Split Hearings: Practice)* [2006] EWCA Civ 714. In the case of *Re S (A Child)* [2014] EWCA Civ 25, the Court of Appeal provided that there are essentially two situations in a public children law case, where there may be a need for a separate fact-finding hearing, These are, first, where there are 'single' issue cases, in that the threshold criteria could not be satisfied if a finding could not be made in that case; and, secondly, in the most complex medical causation cases, where death or very serious medical issues have arisen, and an accurate medical diagnosis is integral to the future care of the child.

If the court decides not to list the matter for a fact-finding hearing, then it may resolve the issues as to both threshold and welfare at a 'rolled up' hearing, often referred to as a 'composite hearing'. This is what occurred in the decision by Lieven J in *A Local Authority v CB and DE & Others* [2021] EWHC 2813 (Fam). The main issue was whether the court should list the matter for a 5-day composite final hearing covering both fact-finding and welfare issues, or whether the court should list the matter for a 20-day fact-finding hearing, but with the possibility that the time estimate may reduce closer to the hearing. On the facts, the court listed for the composite hearing, given the factual issues for determination were limited.

Will the court permit a further fact-finding hearing in situations where the threshold is met, but new allegations as to the threshold are raised? This was the issue raised in the recent Court of Appeal decision of *Re H-W (Care Proceedings: Further Fact-finding Hearing)* [2023] EWCA Civ 149. The proceedings related to an appeal by the local authority where the judge had refused to allow it a further fact-finding hearing in care proceedings, whereby findings had previously been made that the threshold criteria under section 31 of the CA 1989 were met. A child had made further allegations of sexual abuse against the father. At [24], Baker LJ stated that the principles to be applied by a judge when deciding whether to hold a fact-finding hearing are as set out by McFarlane J (as he then was) in *Oxfordshire County Council v DP, RS and BS* [2005] EWHC 1593 (Fam), as approved and developed by the Court of Appeal in in *Re H-D-H (Children), Re C (A Child)* [2021] EWCA Civ 1192. On the facts, the judge's decision to refuse the application for a further fact-finding hearing was plainly wrong. In particular, if these allegations were proved, the care plans for these children would be fundamentally different to what they were at present and therefore, there was a need for the further fact-finding hearing.

7.7.4 Practice Direction 12A checklists

Pre-proceedings checklist

For a detailed and authoritative explanation of FPR 2010 PD 12A, please refer to it in full. A summary of some key aspects of the various stages are set out below.

Annex documents to be attached to the application form:

- social work chronology;
- social work statement and genogram;
- current assessments relating to the child and/or the family and friends of the child to which the social work statement refers and on which the local authority relies;
- care plan;
- index of checklist documents.

It should be noted that in some geographical areas across England and Wales, rather than a separate social work chronology, statement, and genogram, a SWET is filed. This consists of an all-encompassing document, which has within it, in particular, the social work chronology, statement and analysis.

Checklist documents are those that are already existing on the local authority files, and are:

- Evidential documents including:
  - previous court orders, including foreign orders and judgments/ reasons;
  - any assessment materials relevant to the key issues, including capacity to litigate, section 7 and section 37 reports;
  - single, joint or inter-agency materials (e.g. health and education/ Home Office and Immigration Tribunal documents);
- Decision-making records including:
  - records of key discussions with the family;
  - key local authority minutes and records for the child;
  - pre-existing care plans (e.g. child in need plan, looked after child plan and child protection plan);
- Letters before proceedings.

Note that checklist documents are not to be filed with the court unless the court directs otherwise; and they should not be older than 2 years before the date of issue of the proceedings unless reliance is placed on the same in the local authority evidence.

At the time of writing, FPR 2010 PD 36ZF (Pilot Scheme: Public Law Outline: Checklists) has been introduced in some court centres, as from 2 January 2024. This pilot is running until 31 December 2024 and relates to piloted checklists to be used for readiness and expert assessment in public law children proceedings in certain courts. The aim is to reduce delay and also to improve communication between professionals in public law children proceedings.

STAGE 1 ISSUE AND ALLOCATION

Objectives: to ensure compliance with pre-proceedings checklist; to allocate proceedings; to obtain the information necessary for initial case management at the CMH.

On day 1 and day 2:

- local authority completes electronically the application form and uploads annex documents, and sends copies to Cafcass or Cafcass Cymru;
- local authority notifies the court of the need for an urgent preliminary CMH or an urgent contested interim care order hearing, where this is known or expected;

- court officer issues application;

- court considers jurisdiction in a case with an international element;

- court considers initial allocation to specified level of judge, in accordance with the *President's Guidance on Allocation and Gatekeeping for Care, Supervision and other Proceedings under Part IV of the Children Act 1989 (Public Law)* (22 April 2014) (as amended in 2020), issued in accordance with rule 21 of the Family Court (Composition and Distribution of Business) Rules 2014 (as amended in 2021), together with the Allocation Schedule;

- local authority serves the application form, annex documents and evidential checklist documents on the parties, together with the notice of date and time of CMH, and any urgent hearing;

- court gives standard directions on issue and allocation, including checking compliance with pre-proceedings checklist, and service of any missing annex documents. Some of the key directions on issue will include:

  - appointing children's guardian;

  - appointing solicitor for the child, only if necessary;

  - appointing, if the person to be appointed consents, a litigation friend for any protected party, or any non-subject child who is a party, including inviting the official solicitor, where appropriate;

  - identifying whether a request has been made or should be made to a central authority or other competent authority in a foreign state or a consular authority in England and Wales in a case with an international element;

  - filing and service of a local authority case summary;

  - filing and service of a case analysis by the children's guardian;

  - filing and serving the parents' response;

  - sending a request for disclosure to, e.g. the police or health service body;

  - filing and serving an application for permission relating to experts under Part 25 of the FPR 2010, on a date prior to the advocates meeting for the CMH;

  - directing the solicitor for the child to arrange an advocates meeting no later than 2 business days before the CMH;

  - listing the CMH.

STAGE 2 ADVOCATES MEETING AND CASE MANAGEMENT HEARING

Advocates meeting (including any litigants in person), no later than 2 business days before case management hearing (or further case management hearing if it is necessary)

Objectives: to prepare the draft case management order; to identify experts and draft questions for them.

Tasks:

- Consider information on the application form and annex documents, the local authority case summary, and the case analysis. Identify the parties' positions to be recited in the draft case management order.

- Identify the parties' positions about jurisdiction, in particular arising out of any international element.

- If necessary, identify proposed experts and draft questions in accordance with Part 25 of the FPR 2010 and PD 25C.

- Identify any disclosure that in the advocates' views is necessary.

- Immediately notify the court of the need for a contested interim care order hearing and any issue about allocation.

- Local authority advocate to file a draft case management order in prescribed form with court by 11 am on the business day before the CMH and/or further case management hearing (FCMH).

- Note that in the *Re-Launch of the Public Law Outline (PLO)* document, the President has stated that no other hearing should normally be listed after the CMH until the IRH.

Case management hearing

Not before day 12, and not later than day 18. An FCMH is to be held only if necessary, it is to be listed as soon as possible and in any event no later than day 25.

Objectives: to identify issue(s); to give full case management directions.

Tasks: court gives detailed case management directions, including:

- considering jurisdiction in a case with an international element, and confirming allocation;

- drawing up the timetable for the child and the proceedings, and considering if an extension is necessary;

- identifying additional parties, intervenors and representation (including confirming that Cafcass or Cafcass Cymru has allocated a children's guardian and that a litigation friend is appointed for any protected party or non-subject child);

- giving directions for the determination of any disputed issue about litigation capacity;

- identifying the evidence necessary to enable the court to resolve the key issues, and deciding whether there is a real issue about threshold;

- determining any application made under Part 25 of the FPR 2010, and identifying any necessary disclosure, and, if appropriate, giving directions;

- giving directions for any concurrent or proposed placement order proceedings, and ensuring compliance with the court's directions;

- if an FCMH is necessary, directing an advocates meeting and case analysis if required;

- directing filing of any threshold agreement, final evidence and care plan and responses to those documents for the IRH;

- directing a case analysis for the IRH and an advocates meeting for the IRH;

- listing (any FCMH) IRH, final hearing (including early final hearing);

- giving directions for participation directions and/or interpreters and intermediaries/lay advocates;

- issuing the case management order.

STAGE 3 ADVOCATES MEETING AND ISSUES RESOLUTION HEARING

Advocates meeting (including any litigants in person), no later than 7 business days before the IRH

Objective: to prepare or update the draft case management order.

Tasks:

- Review the evidence and the positions of the parties. It is necessary to identify the advocates' views of:

  - the remaining key issues and how the issues may be resolved or narrowed at the IRH, including by the making of final orders;

  - the further evidence which is required to be heard to enable the key issues to be resolved or narrowed at the IRH;

  - the evidence that is relevant and the witnesses that are required at the final hearing;

- the need for a contested hearing and/or time for oral evidence to be given at the IRH.

- The local authority advocate is to notify the court immediately of the outcome of the discussion at the meeting, and file a draft case management order with the court by 11 am on the business day before the IRH.

Issues resolution hearing

This is to be listed in accordance with the timetable for the proceedings.

Objectives: to resolve and narrow issue(s); to identify any remaining key issues.

Tasks:

- Court identifies the key issue(s) (if any) to be determined and the extent to which those issues can be resolved or narrowed at the IRH.

- Court considers whether the IRH can be used as a final hearing.

- Court resolves or narrows the issues by hearing evidence.

- Court identifies the evidence to be heard on the issues which remain to be resolved at the final hearing.

- Court gives final case management directions including:

  - any extension of the timetable for the proceedings which is necessary;

  - filing of the threshold agreement or a statement of facts/issues remaining to be determined;

  - filing of final evidence and care plan, case analysis for final hearing (if required), witness templates and skeleton arguments;

  - judicial reading list/reading time, including time estimate and an estimate for judgment writing time;

  - ensuring compliance with FPR 2010 PD 27A;

  - listing the final hearing.

- Court issues case management order.

STAGE 4 FINAL HEARING (IF NECESSARY)

Hearing set in accordance with the timetable for the child.

Objective: to determine remaining issues.

In the *Re-Launch of the Public Law Outline (PLO)* document, the President had also emphasised that robust case management by the court was required at all stages of the PLO. This would include, where necessary, regular 'compliance' hearings to deal with any failure by a party to meet dates. All parties would be expected to monitor compliance with the court timetable and, if needed, report any failures to the court. Furthermore, and in tune with the elements of the PLO, the President stated that there was a need to make cases 'smaller' by reducing the number of hearings per case and by making 'every hearing count'.

7.8   Assessments and care planning

Only when the threshold grounds (criteria in section 31 of the CA 1989) are established will the court go on to consider what, if any, order to make.

No care order may be made unless the court has first considered a care plan submitted by the local authority (section 31(3A) of the CA 1989).

The next task for the court, therefore, once the criteria in section 31 of the CA 1989 are satisfied, is to consider the circumstances of the child in the context of the underlying principles of the CA 1989, to consider the welfare checklist, to decide whether the making of an order is necessary in the best interests of the child and, if so, which order would be the most appropriate in all the circumstances of the case.

The courts subject the relevant aspects of the care plans to scrutiny. Evidence may be called in support of care plans, and known placement details made available to the court. Note that, once the care order is made, the court can no longer control events. In *Re S (Minors) (Care Order: Implementation of Care Plan), Re W (Minors) (Care Order: Adequacy of Care Plan)* [2002] UKHL 10, [2002] 1 FLR 815, the House of Lords affirmed the right of local authorities to discharge their responsibility under care orders without interference from the courts. However, since this case was heard, note the changes brought about to protect the interests of the child by section 118 of the Adoption and Children Act 2002, so as to bring about the revised section 26 of the CA 1989. This section covers reviews of cases and inquiries into representations. In this context, also note the provisions set out in regulation 32(2) of the 2010 Regulations, which provide that the local authority must not make any significant change to the child's care plan unless the proposed change has first been considered at a review of the child's case, unless this is not reasonably practicable. Schedule 7 to the 2010 Regulations sets out the factors to be considered in the child's review. The Welsh equivalents are set out in regulation 38 of, and Schedule 8 to, the 2015 Regulations.

If the threshold grounds are satisfied, the court's time will then be spent on considering proportionality, and assessment and discussion of the timetable and care plan, in order to make the best decision for the child's short- and long-term future. The *Family Justice Review Final Report* (Ministry of Justice, 2011) identified that detailed scrutiny of the care plan by the court was a cause of unnecessary delay, and recommended that the courts' scrutiny of care plans be curtailed. Consequently, there was introduced the provisions under section 31A of the CA 1989, in April 2014, by the CFA 2014, so as to limit the scrutiny of care plans to the permanence provisions and contact.

Recently, in the Court of Appeal decision of *Re JW (Child at Home under Care Order)* [2023] EWCA Civ 944, the President of the Family Division emphasised that there should be very limited situations where there should be a full care order made on the basis that the child is placed at home with the parent(s).

7.9 Effects of supervision order

The grounds for granting a supervision order are the same as for a care order under section 31 of the CA 1989, and will be granted if this is the proportionate order to make. It may initially be applied for, or made by the court when considering the range of its powers under section 1(3)(g).

A supervision order places the child under the supervision of a local authority or a probation officer. The duties and powers of the supervising officer are set out in section 35 of, and Schedule 3 to, the CA 1989, including a duty 'to advise, assist and befriend' the child. The supervising officer does not acquire parental responsibility for the child. The sanction for failure to co-operate with supervision is an application to discharge the order and to substitute something else, possibly a care order.

Directions may be made within supervision orders binding those responsible for the child and also the child to attend activities or live at specified places (see para 7.9.3). They subsist for the duration of the supervision order or such lesser period as the court may specify.

7.9.1   Interim orders

If a care or supervision order application is adjourned, the court can make an interim order (section 38(1) of the CA 1989). In the context of interim care or supervision orders, the court can make directions for medical or psychiatric assessment which a child of sufficient age and understanding may refuse (section 38(6) and (7)); and the court may also make an exclusion requirement under section 38A, ordering a named person to leave and/or excluding him or her from entering a dwelling house or defined geographical area in which the child lives. A power of arrest may be attached to the exclusion order, enforceable by the police (section 38A(5)–(9), rule 12.28 of the FPR 2010 and PD 12K).

Where the court has power to impose an exclusion requirement in an interim care order, undertakings may be accepted from the relevant person (section 38B of the CA 1989). However, undertakings, although they are enforceable as an order of the court, cannot be coupled with a power of arrest.

Section 38(3) of the CA 1989 provides that if there is an application for a care or supervision order, but the court decides to make a child arrangements order, specifying living with, instead of a care order, then the court must also make an interim supervision order unless it is satisfied that the child's welfare will be adequately safeguarded without one.

7.9.2　Duration of care and supervision

The effect of section 31(3) of the CA 1989 is that a care order can only be made in respect of a child under the age of 17, or 16 if the child is married, and that pursuant to section 91(12) of the CA 1989, unless the care order is brought to an end earlier, it will continue until the child is 18.

A supervision order may last for up to one year (Schedule 3, paragraph 6(1) to the CA 1989). It may be for shorter duration if so ordered by the court. A supervision order may also be extended by the court on a subsequent hearing for a further period or periods of up to a year, to a maximum of 3 years from the date it was first made (Schedule 3, paragraph 6(3) and (4)). Section 1 principles apply, see Chapter 2 and *Wakefield MDC UT* [2008] EWCA Civ 199, [2008] Fam Law 485.

No proceedings may normally be brought in relation to a child until after the child's birth, as set out in *Re F (In Utero) (Wardship)* [1988] Fam 122, but in the later case of *Bury Metropolitan Borough Council v D* [2009] EWHC 446 (Fam), the local authority had been granted a declaration to remove the child from mother's care immediately at birth, but without informing mother of its intentions. Such applications will of course be rare, given the direct conflict with Articles 6 and 8 of the ECHR.

7.9.3　Directions in supervision orders

Directions to the child

The court may embody in the order specific requirements with which the child is to comply; and/or a general term along the lines that 'the child must comply with the directions given from time to time by the supervisor'. The supervisor then has a certain amount of leeway about the directions given, provided they fall within the parameters set in Schedule 3, paragraph 2 to the CA 1989.

The parameters are:

(a)   to live at a place or places specified;

(b)   to present himself to a person or persons specified for a period or periods specified;

(c)   to participate in specified activities on dates and at times specified.

Directions to a 'responsible person'

A responsible person is defined in Schedule 3, paragraph 1 to the CA 1989 as 'a person who has parental responsibility for the child, and any other person with whom the child is living'.

Under Schedule 3 to the CA 1989, with the consent of the responsible person, the court can include in the order a number of requirements:

(a)   to take reasonable steps to ensure the child complies with the directions of the supervisor under Schedule 3, paragraph 2 (i.e. to live at a specified place, present himself to a person specified on a specific day and to participate in activities);

(b)   to take all reasonable steps to ensure the supervised child complies with directions regarding medical and psychiatric examinations (Schedule 3, paragraphs 3–5);

(c)   that he or she comply with the direction of the supervisor 'to attend at a place specified in the directions for the purpose of taking part in activities so specified'.

A supervision order may also direct the responsible person to keep the supervisor informed of change of address, and to allow the supervisor to visit the child at the place where he is living (Schedule 3, paragraph 8).

The responsible person may be directed to ensure the child complies with the supervisor's programme, giving the order a better chance of success. The adult may be asked to attend a treatment centre, to benefit the family and enable the child to remain at home.

The court has no jurisdiction to specify the activities in which the responsible person (with the court's consent) is to participate. This is for the supervisor to arrange.

The court may authorise medical or psychiatric examination, and also direct attendance by the child and/or carers for medical or psychiatric examination of the child, or, if necessary, inpatient or outpatient treatment, which a child of sufficient understanding has a right to refuse (see Chapter 12, and Schedule 3, paragraphs 4 and 5 to the CA 1989). Although the supervisor has the power to direct attendance by the child for medical or psychiatric examination or assessment, only the court can authorise medical or psychological examination. Before making these directions, the court must know that satisfactory arrangements have been, or can be, made for the treatment proposed. This implies that the practitioners concerned have indicated that they agree to carry it out. If the child has sufficient understanding, his or her consent is also required.

If a health practitioner is unwilling to continue treatment of the child, or the directions need altering because of any of the following circumstances:

(a)   the treatment should be extended beyond the period specified in the order;

(b)   different treatment is required;

(c)   the child is not susceptible to treatment; or

(d)   no further treatment is required;

he must submit a written report to the supervisor, who must then put that report back to the court for revision of the directions (Schedule 3, paragraph 5(6)–(7) to the CA 1989).

7.9.4   Enforcement

If there is a direction that the supervisor visits the child, and this is prevented, then the supervisor may bring the matter back to court for a warrant for a police officer to 'assist the supervisor to exercise these powers, using reasonable force if necessary' (section 102(1) of the CA 1989). Other conditions cannot specifically be enforced, but their breach can be justification for bringing the matter back before the court for an application to discharge the supervision order, to seek a care order or for a different order to be made.

The Court of Appeal has held that if a local authority wants to substitute care for supervision, it needs a specific application for a care order and the threshold criteria in section 31 of the CA 1989 must be proved in support of the care application, see *Re A (Minor) (Supervision Extension)* [1995] 2 FCR 114, CA.

The Public Law Working Group's supervision order sub-group published its final report in April 2023, entitled *Recommendations to achieve best practice in the child protection and family justice systems: Supervision orders*. This document sets out best practice guidance, and there are proposals for reform in relation to strengthening supervision orders. One of these is to consider reform in the longer term as to whether to replace supervision orders by a family support order (lasting up to 3 years). Furthermore, there are recommendations for an amendment to the CA 1989, so as to provide a statutory basis for supervision order support plans, and the possibility of introducing a statutory duty on a local authority to provide support and services under a supervision order.

7.9.5   Designated local authority

There are sometimes disputes at court over which local authority will be the designated authority for the purposes of the supervision order. There is provision to resolve this under Schedule 3, paragraph 9 to the CA 1989, which provides that a supervision order shall not designate a local authority as the supervisor unless: (a) the authority agree; or (b) the supervised child lives or will live within its area.

7.10   Removal of child from care

Local authorities have a duty to look after and maintain children subject to care orders while they are in force (section 33(1) of the CA 1989). A parent, or anyone else, may not remove a child from the care of the local authority without leave of the court. Removal of a child without permission of the local authority or leave of the court, keeping a child away from local authority care or inciting a child to run away or stay away are classed as the criminal offence of child abduction under section 49 of the CA 1989.

Note that if children are accommodated on a voluntary basis by a local authority (under section 20 of the CA 1989, or sections 75–76 of the SSW(W)A 2014), the situation is different in that they may be removed at any time by a person with parental responsibility for them (section 20(8) of the CA 1989, and section 76(5) of the SSW(W)A 2014). A local authority has no power to keep a child in voluntary accommodation where there is a person with parental responsibility ready and willing to look after the child (section 20(7) of the CA 1989, and section 76(4) of the SSW(W)A 2014). Also note the case of *Re N (Children)* [2015] EWCA Civ 1112, in which the then President of the Family Division, Sir James Munby, stated at [170] that the good practice in previous cases should be followed when seeking to voluntarily accommodate, so that wherever possible, the agreement of a parent to the accommodation of his child should be properly recorded in writing and evidenced by the parent's signature. Also, the written document should be clear and precise as to its terms, and drafted in simple and straightforward language that the particular parent can readily understand.

7.11 Variation, discharge and appeals

As set out above, care orders cease when the child reaches the age of 18, or earlier by order of the court (section 91(2) of the CA 1989).

Supervision orders cease when directed by the court or on effluxion of time.

7.11.1 Variation and discharge

Applicant

Pursuant to section 39 of the CA 1989, a care or supervision order may be varied or discharged on the application of:

(a)   any person with parental responsibility for the child;

(b)   the child (who does not need leave of the court);

(c)   in the case of supervision, the supervisor;

(d)   in the case of a care order, the local authority with the responsibility for the child.

The application needs to be on Form C110A given it is an application under Part IV of the CA 1989, and FPR 2010 PD 12A sets out the procedural aspects. The case will be allocated pursuant to the Family Court (Composition and Distribution of Business) Rules 2014, and the *President's Guidance on Allocation and Gatekeeping for Care, Supervision and other Proceedings under Part IV of the Children Act 1989 (Public Law)* (22 April 2014) (as amended in 2020), issued in accordance with rule 21 of the Family Court (Composition and Distribution of Business) Rules 2014 (as amended in 2021). Like other applications relating to care orders, once made, the application may only be withdrawn with leave of the court, see rule 29.4 of the FPR 2010.

If the court discharges a care order, it can order supervision, without having to re-prove the criteria in section 31(2) of the CA 1989 (section 39(4) and (5)).

Following an unsuccessful application to discharge a care order, one cannot make a further application without leave within 6 months (section 91(5) of the CA 1989). Under section 91(14), which can be used regarding any application under the CA 1989, the court can order no further applications without leave, but should use this power sparingly, see *Re A (A Child)* [2009] EWCA Civ 1548. Guidelines on the use of section 91(14) are set out in *Re P (A Child)* [1999] EWCA Civ 1323, and the new section 91A of the CA 1989 brought about by the Domestic Abuse Act 2021.

Notice

Applications for discharge should be made on notice. The applicant should serve each person entitled to notice with Form C6A, with the date and time of the hearing endorsed on it, at least 3 days before the first directions or hearing. See FPR 2010 PD 12C, paragraph 2.1. Those entitled to notice are the same as for the original application.

Respondents

All respondents are to be served with the application in Form C110A, and such of the documents specified in the Annex to Form C110A as are available. Notice needs to also be provided to Cafcass or Cafcass Cymru. Those who are entitled to be respondents should be served with a notice of the proceedings in Form C6, and the other documentation, at least 3 days before the hearing. See FPR 2010 PD 12C, paragraph 2.1. Those entitled to be respondents are those who were entitled to be, or were, respondents in the original application.

7.11.2   Appeals

Part 30 of the FPR 2010 covers appeals, as well as, in particular, PD 30A, which sets out a table, providing for which court or judge an appeal is to be made (subject to obtaining any necessary permission) from decisions of the Family Court. The Access to Justice Act 1999 (Destination of Appeals) (Family Proceedings) (Amendment) Order 2016 (SI 2016/891) also sets out the appeal route from certain judges and office holders to the Family Court, instead of the appeal lying to the Court of Appeal. See Chapter 17 for more detail on appeals.

On refusal to make a care order, or on discharge, the court has power to make a care order pending appeal (section 40(1) and (2) of the CA 1989); or to declare that the order appealed shall not take effect pending appeal (section 40(3)). If the court refuses to make a care order pending appeal, the appeal court may make an interim order under section 38.

7.12   Effects of the Human Rights Act 1998 on care and supervision proceedings

Public authorities must comply with the Human Rights Act 1998 and the ECHR. Any acts by public authorities incompatible with these may be challenged by complaint, appeal or judicial review.

Failure to act is a ground for complaint or challenge, see sections 6 and 7 of the Human Rights Act 1998. Section 22(4) of the Human Rights Act

1998 allows for the retrospective challenge of acts which occurred before the Human Rights Act 1998 came into force.

Article 6 (right to a fair trial) of the ECHR may provide an opportunity to encourage the involvement of children and families in decision making within care planning.

Article 8 of the ECHR gives the right to respect for family life, home and correspondence. It is therefore relevant to the interpretation of current law on contact, family involvement in care plans and care of children, post-adoption contact, and the rights of children and their parents in the context of residential care.

The European Court of Human Rights has made it clear that the state authority must make all efforts to reunite a child with his or her family. Under Article 8(2) of the ECHR, the right to family life can be interfered with to the extent of permanent separation only when the child's welfare demands this, see *KA v Finland* [2003] 1 FCR 230 and *R v Finland* [2006] 2 FCR 264.

In accordance with the right to freedom of expression under Article 10, the Family Court has become more open to the media and legal bloggers in recent years. Rule 27.11(2) of the FPR 2010 provides 'duly accredited representatives of news gathering and reporting organisations' and 'duly authorised lawyers' with a right to attend private hearings in family proceedings, although they can be excluded on specified grounds. However, journalists (and others) are normally not permitted to publish information they hear during the proceedings without permission of the court (section 12 of the Administration of Justice Act 1960), nor to identify a child in CA 1989 proceedings (section 97 of the CA 1989). Rule 27.11(1) expressly creates exceptions in relation to attendance by the media to: (a) hearings conducted for the purpose of judicially assisted conciliation or negotiation; (b) proceedings under, (i) Part 13 (proceedings under section 54 of the HFEA 2008), (ii) Part 14 (procedure for applications in adoption, placement and related proceedings), and (iii) any proceedings identified in a practice direction as being excepted from this rule. The extent of transparency and what can and cannot be reported from court proceedings is discussed in Chapter 11, para 11.8.

8 Secure Accommodation and Deprivation of Liberty Orders

Local authorities have a duty to provide accommodation for children in need in circumstances specified in section 20 of the CA 1989. The Welsh equivalent is section 76 of the SSW(W)A 2014. Secure accommodation is defined in section 25(1) of the CA 1989 as 'accommodation provided for the purpose of restricting liberty'. Section 119 of the SSW(W)A 2014 sets out the law surrounding the use of accommodation for restricting liberty in Wales. Currently, the law relating to secure accommodation is complex, and in need of clarification. Children can be placed in secure accommodation for a variety of reasons. They may have committed a criminal offence and need to have their liberty restricted for their own safety or that of others. Orders made in these circumstances are called 'secure orders', to distinguish them from the orders made in civil cases. Children being detained for certain grave crimes are not eligible for secure orders, see para 8.1.2.

A child who is looked after by a local authority, or subject to a care order, may be kept in secure accommodation by the power given by a court order under section 25 of the CA 1989, or section 119 of the SSW(W)A 2014. In certain circumstances, a child may be kept in secure accommodation by the consent of parents or those with parental responsibility.

In England, secure accommodation is currently governed by, in particular, section 25 of the CA 1989, the Children (Secure Accommodation) Regulations 1991 (SI 1991/1505) (Secure Accommodation Regulations 1991), the Children (Secure Accommodation) (No 2) Regulations 1991 (SI 1991/2034), the Children (Secure Accommodation) (Amendment) (England) Regulations 2015 (SI 2015/1883), and the *Guide to the Children's Homes Regulations, including the Quality Standards* (DfE, April 2015). Also of significance is Chapter 4 of *Court Orders and Pre-Proceedings for Local Authorities* (DfE, April 2014). In Wales, it is currently governed by section 119 of the SSW(W)A 2014, the Children (Secure Accommodation) (Wales) Regulations 2015 (SI 2015/1988) (W 298), the *Social Services and Well-being (Wales) Act 2014 – Part 6 Code of Practice (Looked After and Accommodated*

Children) (Welsh Government, Version 2, April 2018) (*Part 6 Code of Practice*), the Children (Secure Accommodation) (Wales) (Amendment) Regulations 2016 (SI 2016/312) (W 102) and the Children (Secure Accommodation) (Wales) (Amendment) Regulations 2018 (SI 2018/391) (W 68). Secure accommodation should be based on the needs of the child, never because of inadequacies of staffing or resources in residential accommodation, nor because a child is being a nuisance. It may never be used as a punishment, see *Court Orders and Pre-Proceedings for Local Authorities* (DfE, April 2014), Chapter 4, paragraph 40.

The provisions for secure accommodation of children applicable to their age group are set out at para 8.7.5.

Secure accommodation orders need to be compatible with the ECHR. The ECHR allows minors to be detained by lawful order for the purpose of educational provision. The courts must ensure that any secure accommodation order makes educational provision. Failure to do so would be a breach of the ECHR, see *Re K (Secure Accommodation Order: Right to Liberty)* [2001] 1 FLR 526.

Useful practice guidelines are available from the Secure Accommodation Network at www.secureaccommodation.org.uk.

8.1   Restricting liberty with a secure accommodation order

The effect of a secure accommodation order is to restrict a child's liberty. Local authorities should pay careful regard to the guidance in their use of restriction of liberty. There is a distinction between placing a child in an environment (secure unit), from which he cannot run away and in which he is safeguarded, and the temporary restriction of a child's liberty, for example, locking him in a room, something which is not allowed in mainstream residential care units. It is, however, permissible in certain circumstances to use approved forms of physical restraint as part of a structured behavioural management strategy in order to protect a child or young person from hurting himself or others, but not to prevent a child from leaving a room or (if the child is of sufficient age) a building unless there is an immediate risk of serious harm.

8.1.1   Safeguards

The making of secure accommodation orders is subject to strict regulation. Some of the key safeguards are as follows:

(a)   *Court Orders and Pre-Proceedings for Local Authorities* (DfE, April 2014), Chapter 4, paragraph 41 provides that restricting the liberty of the child does not mean that the restriction should only be considered as a 'last resort'. Restricting the liberty of a child could offer a positive option. A decision to apply for an order under section 25 of the CA 1989 should be made on the basis that this represents the best option to meet the particular needs of the child. The placement of a child in a secure children's home should, wherever practicable, arise as part of the local authority's overall plan for the child's welfare.

(b)   *Court Orders and Pre-Proceedings for Local Authorities* (DfE, April 2014), Chapter 4, paragraph 47 provides that it is the role of the court to safeguard the child's welfare from inappropriate or unnecessary use of secure accommodation, by satisfying itself that those making the application have demonstrated that the statutory criteria have been met. The guidance provides that proceedings under section 25 of the CA 1989 are specified proceedings for the purposes of section 41(6), and therefore that the court is required to appoint a children's guardian for the child unless it is of the opinion that it is unnecessary to do so in order to safeguard the child's interests. The child should also be given the opportunity to be legally represented in the proceedings.

(c)   *Guide to the Children's Homes Regulations, including the Quality Standards* (DfE, April 2015), Annex B, paragraph 1.6 provides that restricting the liberty of a child is a serious step which should only be taken where it is necessary and where other alternatives have been considered. This does not mean that all other alternatives must have been tried. But in order to apply to the court for an order to restrict a child's liberty under section 25 of the CA 1989, it is vital that the local authority has made a careful assessment that this is the most appropriate option to meet the child's particular needs. The placement of a child in a secure children's home should, wherever practicable, arise as part of the local authority's overall plan for the child's welfare. Also, paragraph 1.7 of this guidance provides that secure placements should only continue for as long as they remain appropriate to meet the needs of the child. The plan for the child should be kept under careful monitoring and review from the outset of the secure placement to ensure that there will be continuity of care and education and where necessary any specialist intervention or support once the child is no longer detained.

(d)   Regular inspection and review by, in particular, the Secretary of State (to approve secure unit), and the Department for Education (educational facilities).

(e)   Time limits on the duration of secure accommodation orders.

(f)   Care plans required by court on review of the orders.

(g)   The appointment of a children's guardian, unless considered not necessary, and the right to an independent visitor.

(h)   The 'three wise men (or women)'. The local authority keeping a child in a secure unit must appoint at least three people, one of whom must not be a local authority employee, to review the placement within one month, and thereafter at 3-monthly intervals. The task of these three people is to ensure that the criteria justifying secure accommodation still applies, that the placement is necessary and that no other description of accommodation is appropriate. See further on reviews at para 8.7.1.

The local authority must keep good case records, with details listed in regulation 17 of the Secure Accommodation Regulations 1991, and the *Guide to the Children's Homes Regulations, including the Quality Standards* (DfE, April 2015), paragraph 1.46.

With secure orders, the complication in the law is that the routes to the order and the rules applicable vary according to the court to which the child has been remanded. The grounds for the application in each of these circumstances are set out in para 8.3, and procedures are set out in para 8.4.

8.1.2   Criminal cases (secure orders)

Juveniles may be detained by the police under circumstances specified in section 38 of the Police and Criminal Evidence Act 1984 (PACE). Under section 38(6), the juvenile shall be moved to local authority accommodation unless the custody officer certifies that either it is impracticable to do so or, in the case of a juvenile over 12 years old, no secure accommodation is available and other local authority accommodation would not be adequate to protect the public from serious harm from him. The remanding of juveniles to local authority accommodation in this way by the police is covered by the provisions of section 25 of the CA 1989. There are also safeguards for young people who have been arrested, which protect their interests in detention and during questioning.

The *Guide to the Children's Homes Regulations, including the Quality Standards* (DfE, April 2015), Annex B, paragraph 1.35 provides that the effect of regulation 6 of the Secure Accommodation Regulations 1991 is that section 25 of the CA 1989 applies with modifications to children detained under section 38(6) of PACE. For these children, the criteria in section 25(1) of the CA 1989 are modified so that the children may not be placed, and if placed, may not be kept in secure accommodation unless it appears that any accommodation other than that provided for the purpose of restricting liberty is inappropriate because the child is likely to abscond from such other accommodation; or the child is likely to injure himself or other people if he is kept in any such other accommodation.

Where a child has been remanded by a criminal court to local authority accommodation, under section 23 of the Children and Young Persons Act 1969, then the child may be the subject of an application for secure accommodation under section 25 of the CA 1989. Section 23 of the Children and Young Persons Act 1969 would apply to children who are: (a) charged with or convicted of an offence which would carry a sentence of 14 years or more for a person over 21 years old; (b) charged with or convicted of an offence of violence, or who have a previous conviction for violence; or (c) detained under section 38(6) of PACE. It should be noted that for the purposes of the Legal Aid, Sentencing and Offenders Act 2012, section 23 of the Children and Young Persons Act 1969 is omitted. Under section 130 of the Criminal Justice Act 1988, if juvenile offenders are remanded to local authority accommodation, and placed in secure units, their time so spent will be deducted from their eventual custodial sentence.

8.1.3   Use of secure accommodation in civil cases

Every local authority is under a duty to take reasonable steps designed to avoid the need for children within its area to be placed in secure accommodation, within the meaning given in section 25 of the CA 1989, and in section 119 of the SSW(W)A 2014 (Schedule 2, paragraph 7(c) to the CA 1989). Local authorities also have a duty to 'encourage children within their area not to commit criminal offences' (Schedule 2, paragraph 7(b)). The local authority looking after the child is under a duty to safeguard and promote the child's welfare (section 22(2)). Note, in particular, section 22G requires local authorities to take such steps, as far as are reasonably practicable, to ensure that there is sufficient accommodation in their area which meets the needs of looked after children.

8.2   How long can a child be kept in secure accommodation?

8.2.1   Where no court order made

Without the authority of the court, a child may only have his liberty restricted for up to 72 hours, either consecutively or in aggregate within any period of 28 consecutive days (regulation 10(1) of the Secure Accommodation Regulations 1991).

However, regulation 10(2) of the Secure Accommodation Regulations 1991 gives an exception where, if the court authorises secure accommodation for less than 28 days, on the day when the court order expires, the 28-day period mentioned in regulation 10(1) starts running afresh from that day, ignoring any time spent in secure accommodation before the court order.

Also, the limit to 72 hours is given some limited flexibility by virtue of regulation 10(3), so as to meet the difficulties which may be faced by local authorities in arranging for secure applications to be heard at short notice, in circumstances where the 72-hour period expires late on a Saturday, a Sunday or a public holiday. Regulation 10(3) therefore gives special provisions for days either side of public holidays by granting a limited extension of the 72-hour time limit.

Note that where a child has been placed in local authority accommodation under section 20(1) of the CA 1989, a person with parental responsibility can remove the child at any time (section 20(8)), unless the exceptions in section 20(9) apply. This includes removal from secure accommodation. Note the Welsh equivalent provisions relating to accommodation under sections 75–76 of the SSW(W)A 2014.

8.2.2   Secure order (child on remand in a criminal case)

Where the child has been remanded by a criminal court, the duration is for the period of the remand, with a maximum order of 28 days (regulation 13 of the Secure Accommodation Regulations 1991).

8.2.3   Civil cases and children not on criminal remand – secure accommodation orders

If the child is not on remand, then the maximum period under section 25 of the CA 1989 or section 119 of the SSW(W)A 2014 is:

• up to 3 months on the first application (regulation 11 of the Secure Accommodation Regulations 1991); and

• up to 6 months on subsequent applications (regulation 12).

The period of detention runs from the date the order was made, not the date the child was actually placed in the unit, see *Re B (Minor) (Secure Accommodation)* [1994] 2 FLR 707.

Any period in the secure unit before a secure accommodation order is made should be deducted from this, see *C (Minor) v Humberside County Council & Another* [1995] 1 FCR 110, in which the justices making a care order had no power to order that a child kept in secure accommodation for one month should then be kept in the secure unit for a further 3 months.

In the case of *In Re W (Minor) (Secure Accommodation Order)* [1993] 1 FLR 692, it was held that the court should consider the shortest appropriate period, rather than order the maximum period available as a matter of course.

Also, in *R v Oxfordshire County Council (Secure Accommodation)* [1992] Fam 150, it was decided that once an order is made, it should only be for so long as is necessary and unavoidable.

If the criteria for detention in secure accommodation cease to apply, the child must be released, see *LM v Essex County Council* [1999] 1 FLR 988. Therefore, the local authority could not lawfully continue to keep a child in secure accommodation within the maximum period specified in the order at a time when it did not consider the criteria under section 25 of the CA 1989 continued to be met. The remedy for the child was an application to the High Court for a writ of *habeas corpus*.

8.2.4   Adjournments

If there is an adjournment of an application for secure accommodation, then, under section 25(5) of the CA 1989, the court may permit the child to be kept in secure accommodation under an interim order during the adjournment.

In the case of *Birmingham City Council v M* [2008] EWHC 1085 (Fam), it was held that the court could not adjourn a secure accommodation application solely in order to keep the children's guardian and solicitor engaged in the case and supporting the child. Furthermore, if the adjournment was not justified (e.g. to obtain further information or for reasons of procedural fairness), then the court should hold the substantive hearing. This followed on from the previous decision in *Re B (A Minor) (Secure Accommodation)* [1994] 2 FLR 707.

8.3   Grounds for application

8.3.1   Children detained in criminal cases

Where a child has been detained under section 38(6) of PACE, then the child may be the subject of an application for secure accommodation under section 25 of the CA 1989.

The effect of section 38(6) of PACE is that where a custody officer authorises an arrested juvenile to be kept in police detention, subject to the exceptions below, the custody officer shall direct that the arrested juvenile is moved to local authority accommodation. The exceptions are: (a) that, by reason of such circumstances as are specified in the certificate, it is impracticable for him to do so; or (b) in the case of an arrested juvenile who has attained the age of 12 years, that no secure accommodation is available and that keeping him in other local authority accommodation would not be adequate to protect the public from serious harm from him. The effect of section 38(6A) of PACE is that the term 'protecting the public from serious harm from him' shall be construed as a reference to protecting members of the public from death or serious personal injury, whether physical or psychological, occasioned by further such offences committed by him.

8.3.2   Children in civil cases

Children who are looked after by a local authority and accommodated in care homes, independent hospitals, nursing homes and mental nursing homes, or accommodated by health authorities, National Health Service trusts or local authorities in the exercise of education functions, are subject to the provisions of section 25 of the CA 1989. See regulation 7 of the Secure Accommodation Regulations 1991. Section 25 of the CA 1989 provides that if subject to the provisions of the section, a child who is being looked after by a local authority in England or Wales may not be placed, and, if placed, may not be kept, in accommodation in England or Scotland, provided for the purpose of restricting liberty, unless it appears:

(a)   that:

   (i)   he has a history of absconding and is likely to abscond from any other description of accommodation; and

   (ii) if he absconds, he is likely to suffer significant harm; or

(b)   that if he is kept in any other description of accommodation he is likely to injure himself or other persons.

At this juncture, it is important to note some of the changes that have been brought in surrounding secure accommodation orders obtained in England and Wales, to place children in Scotland. In the cases of *Re X (A Child) and Y (A Child)* [2016] EWHC 2271 (Fam), the then President of the Family Division, Sir James Munby, posed the question as to whether a judge in England can make a secure accommodation order under section 25 of the CA 1989 if the child is to be placed in a unit in Scotland. If not, can the same outcome be achieved by use of the inherent jurisdiction of the High Court, and in either case, will the order made by the English judge be recognised and enforced in Scotland? These issues arose because of the shortage of places in secure accommodation units in England, so that local authorities in England look to making use of available places in secure accommodation units in Scotland. His Lordship decided that a judge in England cannot make a secure accommodation order under section 25 if the child is to be placed in a unit in Scotland (and the same applies, if an order is made under section 119 of the SSW(W)A 2014), and that although, in principle, a judge, in exercise of the inherent jurisdiction, can make an order directing the placement of a child in secure accommodation in Scotland, the order would not be recognised in Scotland. Subsequently, section 10 of the Children and Social Work Act 2017 has now made provision for the fact that Schedule 1 to this Act allows for local authorities in England and Wales to place children in secure accommodation in Scotland, and clarifies the provision for placement by local authorities in Scotland of children in secure accommodation in England and Wales.

8.3.3   Deprivation of liberty and secure accommodation

As the case of *London Borough of Southwark v F* [2017] EWHC 2189 (Fam) illustrates, the local authority needs to consider a deprivation of liberty (DoL) application in situations where, despite a secure accommodation order being granted, a unit is not available for the child. This case related to a 14-year-old, who was subject to a full care order. The local authority had lodged an application for a secure accommodation order, but because it had been unable to identify a suitable secure placement, it lodged an application for a DoL order, alongside the application for a secure accommodation order. The plan at that stage was for the child to be placed in a residential unit, with 2:1 supervision, until a secure unit could be identified for him. The objective underpinning this was to secure the child in a residential placement, and to reinforce it with appropriate additional safeguarding measures. Given the limited secure accommodation units available, His Lordship provided (at [14]–[15]) that there was an impasse in respect of which the court was unable to achieve a resolution. The judgment was delivered in open court because it was a matter that fell within 'the public interest', and in this respect, the court followed the approach of the then President of the Family Division in the case of *Re X (A Child) (No 3)* [2017] EWHC 2036 (Fam), in which the President had set out similar comments. The later cases of *Re A–F (Children)* [2018] EWHC 138 (Fam) and *Re A–F (Children) (No 2)* [2018] EWHC 2129 (Fam) are particularly helpful in looking at the interface between secure accommodation, DoL and Article 5 of the ECHR. These and other subsequent cases are considered further at para 8.9.

8.3.4   Welfare of the child and secure accommodation

In the case of *Re M (A Minor) (Secure Accommodation Order)* [1995] 2 FCR 373, the welfare of the child was held by the court to be relevant, but not paramount in proceedings under section 25 of the CA 1989, and therefore application of the welfare checklist, although useful, was not obligatory.

A child may be placed in a secure unit under section 25(1) of the CA 1989 to prevent her injuring another child, which may be inconsistent with putting the welfare of the secured child first. The court's duty mirrors that of the local authority under section 20(1)(b). The court must ascertain whether the section 25 conditions are satisfied, and if so, make the order if this accords with the duty of the local authority to safeguard and promote the welfare of the child. The children's guardian will assist the court in deciding these questions, see *Re M (Secure Accommodation Order)* [1995] Fam 108.

If the child is voluntarily accommodated by the local authority, i.e. not subject to a care order, a person with parental responsibility may remove the child from the secure accommodation at any time (sections 20(8) and (9) and 25(9) of the CA 1989). In the decision of *Re M (A Child) (Secure Accommodation)* [2018] EWCA Civ 2707, Peter Jackson LJ stated (at [4]) that 'absconding' for the purposes of the criteria set out, means something more than trivial disobedient absence, and that it may connote an element of escape from an imposed regime. The court needs to give it the 'ordinary' meaning and recognise behaviour that can be properly described as absconding in all the circumstances of the individual case.

8.4   Practice and procedure

In some situations, secure accommodation orders can be made in respect of 17-year-olds who do not consent. This was the situation in the case of *Re W (A Child)* [2016] EWCA Civ 804, in which the child appealed, as she argued that since she was 17 years of age, the court lacked jurisdiction to make her the subject of the secure accommodation order without her consent. The Court of Appeal took the view that when the child was judged at being at risk, then the local authority was under an obligation to accommodate her. The court found that section 20(3) of the CA 1989 does not require the child to consent to being accommodated. Once she is accommodated, under section 20(3), this then provides the gateway to an application under section 25. However, parental consent was required in this situation, as any person with parental responsibility can remove a child from accommodation provided by the local authority unless the child was over 16, and he or she objected to being removed. The equivalent provision in Wales is section 76(2) and (3) of the SSW(W)A 2014.

8.4.1   Application

Where a child is being looked after by a local authority (even if the child is accommodated by another body) that local authority should be the applicant for the order. In other circumstances, pursuant to rule 12.3 of the FPR 2010, other potential applicants include those who are providing accommodation for the child, i.e.:

- local authority;

- health authority;

- Secretary of State;

- National Health Service trust established under section 25 of the National Health Service Act 2006, or section 18(1) of the National Health Service (Wales) Act 2006; or

- National Health Service Foundation Trust.

Once made, an application may only be withdrawn with leave of the court.

8.4.2   Forms

The application should be made on Form C1 together with supplemental Form C20, in accordance with FPR 2010 PD 5A. Note that it is important to stipulate on Form C20 as to whether the application is being made under section 25 of the CA 1989 and/or section 119 of the SSW(W)A 2014.

If the application is made to the High Court in wardship, it should be by summons and the ward should be named as a party. It is suggested that it should be made by seeking to invoke the court's inherent jurisdiction by using Form C66, see FPR 2010 PD 5A.

8.4.3   Venue

In relation to secure accommodation applications, consider the *President's Guidance: Jurisdiction of the Family Court: Allocation of Cases within the Family Court to High Court Judge Level and Transfer of Cases from the Family Court to the High Court* (24 May 2021). Paragraph 18 of the guidance provides that, except as specified in the Schedule to the guidance, every family matter must be commenced in the Family Court, and not in the High Court. A secure accommodation application does not come within the Schedule to this guidance, and hence, must be made to the Family Court. The allocation of the secure accommodation application within the Family Court will be regulated by the Family Court (Composition and Distribution of Business) Rules 2014 (as amended in 2021).

8.4.4   Respondents

Respondents should be served with a copy of the application in Form C1 with Form C20, and Form C6 notice of the proceedings with the date and place of hearing (rule 12.8 of the FPR 2010 and PD 12C, paragraph 1.1(1)).

Given that these applications are, by their very nature, emergency proceedings, service should be one day before the hearing (FPR 2010 PD 12C, paragraph 2.1).

Pursuant to rule 12.3 of the FPR 2010, certain people are automatically respondents to the application:

(a)   those believed to have parental responsibility for the child;

(b)   those who had parental responsibility prior to the care order, if one is in force;

(c)   the child.

Others may be joined as respondents, and automatic respondents may be removed by direction of the court. See rules 12.3(3) and 16.2 of the FPR 2010.

8.4.5   Notice

Applications for secure accommodation are made on one day's notice (FPR 2010 PD 12C, paragraph 2.1).

The following people are entitled to notice of the proceedings, with the date, time and place of the hearing:

(a)   a local authority providing accommodation for the child;

(b)   any person with whom the child was living at the time proceedings were commenced;

(c)   a person providing a refuge for the child under section 51 of the CA 1989 (FPR 2010 PD 12C, paragraph 3.1).

Regulation 14 of the Secure Accommodation Regulations 1991 provides a list of people who should be informed of the application as soon as practicable if the child is placed in a secure unit in a community home, and the application is to keep the child there:

(a)   the child's parents;

(b)   any person with parental responsibility for the child;

(c)   the child's independent visitor;

(d)   any other person the local authority considers should be told.

8.4.6   Service

Rule 6.23 of the FPR 2010 provides that service may be effected by personal service, in accordance with rule 6.25, by first class post, through the DX or other service providing delivery on the next business day, leaving it at a place specified; by fax or email in accordance with FPR 2010 PD 6A or through any other means of electronic communication in accordance with PD 6A. Rule 6.26 provides that a party to the proceedings must give an address at which that party may be served with the documents relating to those proceedings, and that a party's address for service must be the business address of a solicitor acting for the party to be served; or where there is no solicitor acting for the party to be served, an address at which the party resides or carries on business.

Service on a child may be through her solicitor or the children's guardian, or, with leave of the court, service on the child herself, see rule 6.31 of the FPR 2010. The time for service may be abridged by the court, or waived altogether, see rule 4.1(3)(a).

8.5   Role of the children's guardian

Secure accommodation applications under section 25 of the CA 1989 come within Part III and hence, a reading of section 41(6) does not bring them strictly within the definition of 'specified proceedings'. Section 41(6) defines 'specified proceedings' as any proceedings:

(a) on an application for a care order or supervision order;

(b) in which the court has given a direction under section 37(1) and has made, or is considering whether to make, an interim care order;

(c) on an application for the discharge of a care order or the variation or discharge of a supervision order;

(d) on an application under section 39(4);

(e) in which the court is considering whether to make a child arrangements order with respect to the living arrangements of a child who is the subject of a care order;

(f) with respect to contact between a child who is the subject of a care order and any other person;

(g) under Part V;

(h) on an appeal against (i) the making of, or refusal to make, a care order, supervision order or any order under section 34; (ii) the making of, or refusal to make, a child arrangements order with respect to the living arrangements of a child who is the subject of a care order; or (iii) the variation or discharge, or refusal of an application to vary or discharge, an order of a kind mentioned in sub-paragraph (i) or (ii);

(iv) the refusal of an application under section 39(4); or (v) the making of, or refusal to make an order under Part V; or

(hh) on an application for the making or revocation of a placement order, within the meaning of section 21 of the Adoption and Children Act 2002);

(i)   which are specified for the time being, for the purposes of this section, by rules of court.

However, given the general provision under rule 16.2 of the **FPR** 2010, the court may make a child a party to proceedings if it considers it is in the best interests of the child to do so. Given that the child is ordinarily a respondent to these proceedings, the effect of rule 16.4(1) is that the court will appoint a children's guardian for a child in such cases. By having a guardian for the child, this will be a protective measure, intended to ensure that children in secure units have had their wishes and feelings made known to the court, and that the court has been advised of the most appropriate way forward in the best interests of the child. It is also important to note that in practice, there may be a secure accommodation order application running alongside a care application which is a 'specified proceeding' and where in many cases, a guardian will have been appointed. The guardian in the care case will in practice be the guardian in the secure accommodation application.

8.6   Contact

Children in secure units have the right to reasonable contact with members of their family, as children in care (see Chapter 7, para 7.6.5 and Chapter 12, para 12.5). It will often be the case that a local authority will lodge care proceedings alongside a secure accommodation application. If the child is in care, then a contact order under section 34 of the CA 1989 may be made if necessary.

8.7   Rights of the child

The rights of the child are as follows:

*   three persons to review placement (regulation 15 of the Secure Accommodation Regulations 1991);

*   duty on local authority to keep detailed case records (regulation 17);

*   education whilst accommodated;

*   entitlement to appropriate therapy where necessary;

*   regular inspection of the secure unit by the Social Services Inspectorate from the Department of Health, who must approve the unit;

- inspection by the Department for Education, because children there are receiving education whilst accommodated;

- regional placement committees, who check the resources and conditions of the unit;

- time limits on the duration of secure accommodation orders;

- care plans on review of the orders;

- independent visitor;

- consultation, and to have wishes and feelings ascertained (section 22(4) of the CA 1989);

- consultation with parents and those with parental responsibility (section 22(4)); and

- 'free' public funding to be represented on section 25 application.

In relation to the detailed case records referred to above, the *Guide to the Children's Homes Regulations, including the Quality Standards* (DfE, April 2015), Annex B, paragraph 1.46 provides that in addition to the records required through regulations 37, 38 and 39 of the Children's Homes (England) Regulations 2015 (SI 2015/541), regulation 17 of the Secure Accommodation Regulations 1991 requires each person, organisation or local authority responsible for the management of the secure children's home to keep records giving details of:

- the name, date of birth and sex of the child;

- details of the care order or other statutory provision under which the child is in the home and details of any local authority involved with the placement;

- the date and time of the placement, the reason for the placement and the name of the offer authorising the placement and where the child was living before the placement;

- persons informed under regulations 9, 14 or 16(3);

- court orders made under section 25 of the CA 1989;

- secure accommodation reviews undertaken under regulation 15;

- the date and time of any occasion when the child is locked in his own room in the children's home other than during his usual bedtime hours, the name of the person authorising this action, the reason for it and the date and time on which the child ceases to be locked in that room; and

- the date and time of his discharge and his address following the discharge from the secure children's home.

8.7.1   Reviews

Reviews are governed by regulations 15 and 16 of the Secure Accommodation Regulations 1991, and the *Guide to the Children's Homes Regulations, including the Quality Standards* (DfE, April 2015), Annex B, paragraphs 1.37–1.45 and in Wales, regulations 10 and 11 of the Children (Secure Accommodation) (Wales) Regulations 2015 and the *Part 6 Code of Practice*. In the High Court decision of *A Borough Council v E & Others (No 2) (Refusal of Secure Accommodation Order)* [2021] EWHC 2699 (Fam), it was argued on behalf of the child that it was an unprecedented step for a local authority to ignore the outcome of its own Secure Accommodation Review Panel.

In relation to secure criteria reviews, regulation 15 of the Secure Accommodation Regulations 1991 provides that the first review must be held within one month of the start of the placement, and thereafter reviews must take place at intervals not exceeding 3 months. In Wales, the *Part 6 Code of Practice*, paragraph 742 provides that each local authority which decides to place a child in secure accommodation must appoint at least three people to review the decision within 15 working days of the start of the placement. At least one of these should be neither a member, nor an officer of the local authority. Further reviews must take place at intervals not exceeding 3 months while the placement continues. Regulation 16 in England and regulation 11 in Wales require the persons appointed to be satisfied as to whether or not the criteria for keeping the child in secure accommodation continue to apply and as to whether any other type of accommodation would be appropriate for the child. The child's wishes and feelings, as far as is practicable, need to be taken into account, as well as in particular those of the child's parent, any other person who has parental responsibility for the child, and of anyone else who has had the care of the child. The views of the child's independent visitor, where one has been appointed, also need to be considered, as well as those of the local authority managing the secure accommodation in which the child is placed, if not managed by the local authority looking after the child.

The *Guide to the Children's Homes Regulations, including the Quality Standards* (DfE, April 2015), Annex B, paragraph 1.41 provides that the purpose of the review meetings is only to review the issue of whether or not the conditions for detaining the child in secure accommodation still apply. The secure accommodation review is not a substitute for and does not replace the statutory review of the child's overall care plan, which must be chaired by the child's IRO. Also, paragraph 1.44 provides that if the review panel recommends that the criteria for restricting the child's liberty no longer apply, or that the placement is no longer necessary or another type of placement would be appropriate, then the local authority must urgently convene a statutory review of the child's care plan, chaired by its

IRO. The review should consider how the child's needs will be met in a non-secure setting and plan how this move will be managed so that it takes place in a way that is least disruptive to the child concerned.

8.7.2 Attendance at court

Children and young people subject to applications have the right to be present in court. Rule 12.14(3) of the FPR 2010 gives the court power to exclude a child who wants to attend court if it is in the child's interest to do so and he or she is represented, although rule 12.14(4) requires the court to give the guardian, the child's solicitor and child, if of sufficient understanding, the opportunity to make representations about the child's attendance. In *Re K (A Child)* [2011] EWHC 1082 (Fam), the court held that there is no presumption that a child should not attend. The only reason to prevent the attendance of a child who wishes to attend is if attendance may cause her psychological damage.

8.7.3 Public funding

Public funding is available to a child subject to an application under section 25 of the CA 1989 who wishes to be legally represented. Public funding therefore for secure accommodation cases is 'free', i.e. non-means and non-merits tested when representing the child.

Applications for public funding for parents in secure accommodation cases may be refused on the basis that their legal representation is not necessary as representations will be made by both the local authority and the advocate on behalf of the child. Therefore, it is not common for public funding to be made available for parents in secure accommodation applications.

8.7.4 Right to legal advice

Section 25(6) of the CA 1989 provides that the court hearing the application cannot make the secure order unless the child is legally represented, except where he has been informed of his right to legal advice and representation, and had the opportunity, but failed or refused to apply. If a child is not notified of the application for the secure order, the matter may not be heard, as set out in *Re AS* [1999] 1 FLR 103, in which the court decided that natural justice required notification to the child of the application. However, in the later case of *Re C (Secure Accommodation Order: Representation)* [2001] 1 FLR 857, the Family Division decided that the decision to hear the secure application was not outside a reasonable exercise of the court's discretion.

8.7.5   Age of child

A child under the age of 13 may not be kept in secure accommodation without the authority of the Secretary of State (regulation 4 of the Secure Accommodation Regulations 1991 and Annex B, paragraph 1.13 of the *Guide to the Children's Homes Regulations, including the Quality Standards* (DfE, April 2015)). In Wales, prior approval of Welsh Government is required regarding children aged under 13, under regulation 13 of the Children (Secure Accommodation) (Wales) Regulations 2015.

If the child is over 16 years of age, and is also accommodated under section 20(5) of the CA 1989, or section 76 in Wales, then an application for secure accommodation cannot be commenced in respect of the child. However, if an application had been commenced prior to the child's 16th birthday, then a secure order can be made, which can then continue beyond the birthday for that child, see *Re G (Secure Accommodation)* [2000] 2 FLR 259. Wards of court may only be placed in secure accommodation with a direction from the wardship judge.

8.8   Appeals and the Human Rights Act 1998

Appeals in family proceedings are governed by Part 30 of the FPR 2010, as well as PD 30A, which provides a codified procedure for appeals. It does not cover appeals to the Court of Appeal or the Supreme Court, both of which are covered by Part 52 of the Civil Procedure Rules 1998 (SI 1998/3132).

In relation to secure accommodation orders, FPR 2010 PD 30A, paragraph 2.1 is relevant here, in that this provides that permission is not required to appeal against the decision of a bench of two or three lay magistrates, or a lay justice. The appeal here would lie to a judge of circuit judge level sitting in the Family Court, or a judge of High Court Judge level sitting in the Family Court where a Designated Family Judge or a judge of High Court Judge level considers that the appeal would raise an important point of principle or practice. In relation to appeals against the decision of a judge sitting in the Family Court, permission is generally required, subject to various exceptions. These are set out in rule 30.3(2), which provides that permission to appeal is not required where the appeal is against: (a) a committal order; (b) a secure accommodation order under section 25 of the CA 1989; or (c) a refusal to grant *habeas corpus* for release in relation to a minor. Therefore, permission to appeal would not be required where the appeal is against a secure accommodation order (rule 30.3(2)(b)).

In relation to appeals from a circuit judge or recorder, the appeal would lie to the High Court Judge (sitting in the High Court), except where paragraph 5 of the table in FPR 2010 PD 30A, paragraph 2.1 applies.

The Human Rights Act 1998 and Article 5 of the ECHR are relevant to decisions of local authorities and the courts in secure accommodation issues. Article 5 confirms the right to liberty and security of a person and Article 8 protects the right to family life. Article 5 refers to the detention of minors for 'educational supervision' or for the purpose of 'bringing them before the competent legal authority'.

Acts of public authorities and the courts which do not comply with the Human Rights Act 1998 or the ECHR may be challenged by complaint, judicial review or appeal.

8.9   Deprivation of liberty orders

As mentioned at para 8.3.3, a local authority needs to consider an application for a DoL order in appropriate cases. Such applications have risen in number and complexity over the years. The question will therefore be raised as to whether the proposed restrictions to the child constitute a DoL for the purposes of Article 5 of the ECHR, such that the High Court is being invited to exercise its jurisdiction. If so, the court will be invited to authorise those steps as being in the child's best interests.

As discussed at para 3.6, in relation to orders under the inherent jurisdiction of the High Court in relation to children, and wardship, the public funding is means and merits tested for all parties. This will cover, in particular, applications for DoL orders.

8.9.1   What constitutes a deprivation of liberty?

To understand this area, it is necessary to consider, first, the case of *Storck v Germany* [2006] 43 EHRR 6. In this decision by the European Court of Human Rights, it was established that there are three broad elements comprising a DoL for the purposes of Article 5(1) of the ECHR. These are: (a) an objective element of confinement to a certain limited place, for a not negligible period of time; (b) a subjective element of absence of consent to that confinement; and (c) the confinement imputable to the state. Only where all three components are present will the circumstances amount to DoL and therefore engage Article 5 of the ECHR.

Following on from the position set out in the *Storck* case, it is also necessary to consider the so-called 'acid test'. This has been referred to in many significant court decisions, such as in *Cheshire West and Chester Council v P* [2014] UKSC 19, [2014] AC 896 and more recently in *Re A-F (Children)* [2018] EWHC 138 (Fam). This latter case, handed down by the then President of the Family Division, considered the interface between care proceedings brought in the Family Court, and the requirements of Article 5 of the ECHR. His Lordship emphasised that there were two aspects of the 'acid test' for determining a DoL, these being 'complete supervision and control' and not being 'free to leave'. His Lordship provided that there may be situations where a person is under constant supervision and control, but they are still free to leave, should they express the desire so to do. Conversely, it is possible for a person to not be free to leave, but not under such continuous supervision and control as to lead to the view that they are deprived of their liberty. Therefore, His Lordship stressed that there was a clear distinction between a 'deprivation of liberty' within the meaning of Article 5, and a 'restriction on liberty of movement'. There were many aspects of the normal exercise of parental responsibility that interfered with a child's freedom of movement, but which did not involve a DoL, engaging Article 5, even if they involved a restriction on liberty of movement.

In practice, how can a local authority (and, subsequently, the court) determine whether the restrictions that are proposed for the child are those that can be implemented within the exercise of parental responsibility, rather than requiring authorisation through a High Court order? The case of *Re RD (Deprivation or Restriction of Liberty)* [2018] EWFC 47 considered this question. Here, the child was placed in a residential placement, and she had restrictions placed on her liberty. On the facts, even though there were many restrictions upon her liberty, the court was satisfied that the regime at the placement did not constitute a deprivation of her liberty for the purposes of Article 5 of the ECHR, and therefore an order was not necessary. More recently, in *LA v CP and DT and P* [2023] EWHC 133 (Fam), MacDonald J was faced with an application by the local authority for the court to make an order under its inherent jurisdiction that authorised restrictions which it said amounted to a deprivation of the child's liberty for the purposes of Article 5(1) of the ECHR. The key issue in this case was that the local authority sought to include authorisation to restrict the use by the child of her mobile telephone. The court was aware that in previous judgments, it had been the practice to include provisions removing or restricting the use of a child's mobile phone in orders authorising restrictions, such as in the decision of *Salford City Council v NV, AM, M (By her Children's Guardian)* [2019] EWHC 1510 (Fam). In the current case, the child was subject of a final care order and His Lordship took the view that within this context, pursuant to section 33(3)(b) of the CA 1989, the local authority was able to determine the extent to which her parents may meet their parental responsibility for her. In such circumstances, if her parents were to take an opposing view regarding the restriction or removal of her mobile phone, tablet and laptop and access to social media to that which the local authority considered necessary to safeguard and promote her welfare, then the local authority was able to exercise parental responsibility in their place, unless the steps it wished to take were of such magnitude that they should not be taken without sanction by the court. In the circumstances, the court could see no principled objection to the local authority seeking to remove or restrict the use of the child's mobile phone, tablet and laptop and use of social media under the powers conferred on it by section 33(3)(b) of the CA 1989, provided it was necessary to do so in order to safeguard and promote her welfare. At [60], His Lordship did, however, accept that there may well be circumstances that contemplated the use of physical restraint or other force to remove a mobile phone or other device from a 16-year-old adolescent, even in order to prevent significant harm. In such circumstances, this was a grave step and one which would require sanction by the court, rather than simply the exercise by the local authority of its power under section 33(3)(b), not least because such actions would likely constitute an assault.

Consider the recent decision in *Peterborough City Council v Mother* [2024] EWHC 493 (Fam). Here, the local authority sought a DoL order in respect of a child, aged 12, who was severely disabled. In refusing the application, Lieven J was of the view that the test to determine whether there was a DoL, was as to whether the individual was under constant supervision and control and not free to leave. It was axiomatic that the child was not free to leave because of some action (or inaction) of the state. However, on the facts of the current case, the child was incapable of 'leaving' because of a combination of her physical and mental disabilities, not by reason of any restraints placed upon her. The child was undoubtedly under close supervision and control, but that was not in order to prevent her leaving. The close supervision was to meet her care needs. It was not for the purpose of preventing her leaving, because she was wholly incapable of leaving, not only because of physical inability, but also because she was unable to form any desire or intent to leave. Therefore, the court decided that it would be difficult to see how one can be deprived of something that one is incapable of doing.

In this context, it is important to note the other recent judgment of Lieven J, who has handed down the decision in *Re J (Local Authority consent to Deprivation of Liberty)* [2024] EWHC 1690 (Fam). Here, Her Ladyship refused to grant a DoL order in respect of a 14-year-old boy. Her Ladyship decided that the decision to deprive the child of his liberty was not a decision of such magnitude as to fall outside the local authority powers, but rather an exercise of its statutory duties to him under s 33(3)(b) of the CA 1989. Her Ladyship was of the view that given the local authority had a care order, it could exercise its responsibility under s 33(3)(b) of the CA 1989, so as to provide the consent to the restrictions. The authors would suggest that this position is quite a departure from the previous judgments relating to children under 16, such as the position set out in *Re A-F (Children)* [2018] EWHC 138 (Fam) referred to above. This recent judgment by Lieven J will therefore have a significant impact concerning DoL applications for children in the future.

Given the cases discussed above, the authors would suggest that it is imperative that practitioners take legal advice at an early stage and to consider multi-agency meetings and decision making, so as consider whether the intended restrictions to the child's liberty are such that an application for authorisation of DoL is required, and if so, to lodge an application as soon as possible. Failure to do so could result in not only significant harm to the child, but also significant failings in duties towards the child and family. This was the position in the case of *In NHS Trust v ST (Refusal of Deprivation of Liberty Order)* [2022] EWHC 719 (Fam). Here, the court found that the local authority had been aware for approximately a month that the child was in a placement that was manifestly ill-equipped to meet her needs, and in which it was depriving her of her liberty for the purposes of Article 5 of the ECHR. Also, the NHS Trust acknowledged that the child had been deprived of her liberty in extremely challenging situations for over a month before the matter was brought before the court, and that neither the local authority nor the NHS Trust had taken any steps to seek to bring the matter before the court in a timely manner to seek authorisation for the consequent breach of the child's Article 5 rights.

8.9.2   Applications for a deprivation of liberty order and the National DoL List

In the decision of *Re A-F (Children)* [2018] EWHC 138 (Fam) referred to at para 8.9.1, the children were subject to final care orders. The court emphasised that where a child is subject to a care order (whether interim or final), neither the local authority nor a parent can exercise their parental responsibility in such a way as to provide a valid consent for the purposes of the *Storck* component. In this judgment (particularly within [45]–[55]), the President set out the processes and procedures for pursuing DoL orders in some detail. Of particular importance, His Lordship stated that a 'confinement' will be lawful if, as a matter of substance, it is both necessary and proportionate. There is no need for the court to make an order specifically authorising each element of the circumstances constituting the 'confinement'. Instead, it is sufficient if the order authorises the child's DoL at the particular placement, as described generally in some document. Furthermore, if a substantive order (interim or final) is to be made authorising a DoL, there must be an oral hearing in the Family Division (this can be before a section 9 judge). In terms of party status, the child must be a party to the proceedings and have a guardian and, if possible, the children's guardian who is acting or had acted for the child in the care proceedings. The President also emphasised that the evidence in support of the application should address, in particular, the nature of the regime in which it is proposed to place the child, identifying and describing, in particular, those features which it is said do or may involve 'confinement' as well as to why it is said that the proposed placement and regime are necessary and proportionate in meeting the child's welfare needs. The views of the child, the child's parents and the IRO, the most recent care plan, the minutes of the most recent looked after children review or other statutory review and any recent reports in relation to the child's physical and/or mental health should be provided. The President set out that the review of the authorisation is crucial to the continued lawfulness of any 'confinement'. There should be, in particular, regular reviews by the local authority, a review by a judge at least once every 12 months, and the matter must be brought back before the judge without waiting for the next 12-monthly review if there has been any significant change.

In this context, the current President of the Family Division had introduced the National DoLs Court on 4 July 2022, so that this court would deal with applications seeking authorisation to deprive children of their liberty. The court would be based at the Royal Courts of Justice. Recently, the President has provided that the National DoLs Court is no longer to operate under that title and, instead, following the publication of the protocol by the President, dated September 2023, headed *Revised National Listing Protocol for Applications that seek Deprivation of Liberty Orders Relating to Children under the Inherent Jurisdiction*, in future, all initial applications are to be dealt with as part of the National DoL List. This will continue to be overseen as part of the work of the Family Division. Therefore, as from 2 October 2023, all Form C66 applications seeking orders to deprive any child of their liberty (DoL orders) should continue to be issued centrally in the Royal Courts of Justice.

8.9.3 Use of the inherent jurisdiction and position surrounding the child's consent

When making an application for a DoL order, the local authority is inviting the court to invoke its inherent jurisdiction, and in making the order, the court needs to consider the issue of the child's consent. These were some of the issues that were specifically considered by the Supreme Court in *Re T (A Child)* [2021] UKSC 35. One key question was whether it was a permissible exercise of the High Court's inherent jurisdiction to make an order authorising a local authority to deprive a child of his or her liberty rather than use the secure accommodation legislation. At [119], Lady Black said that Parliament had made it very clear that it was not intended that the inherent jurisdiction should be entirely unavailable to local authorities, and that it was appreciated that there could be cases in which it would be necessary to have recourse to this because there was reason to believe that the child would otherwise be likely to suffer significant harm. This was evident from section 100(3)–(5) of the CA 1989. Like the express prohibitions in section 100(1) and (2), the more general conditions imposed by section 100(3)–(5) were shaped to confine the local authority to orders otherwise available to it, but building in a safety net where those other orders would not achieve the required result in a risky situation. The Supreme Court set out that if the local authority cannot apply for an order under section 25 of the CA 1989, because there was no section 25-compliant secure accommodation available, the inherent jurisdiction can, and will have to, be used to fill that gap, without clashing impermissibly with the statutory scheme.

The other key question that was considered by the Supreme Court was that if the High Court could have recourse to its inherent jurisdiction to make an order of this type, then what was the relevance of the child's consent to the proposed living arrangements? The child argued that consent was highly relevant to the evaluation of whether it was in the child's best interests to make the orders sought, and that, on the facts of this case, it was contrary to her best interests to make the order, given her consent to the regime arranged for her. However, at [162], Lady Black stated that when the court considers the local authority's application, any consent on the part of the child will form part of the circumstances that it evaluates in deciding upon its order. The child needs to be (and is) protected by the institution of the proceedings and the consequent involvement of the court. His or her personal autonomy will be respected by being fully involved in those proceedings, and being able to express views about the care that is being proposed, as ensured by the procedures stipulated by statute (for section 25) and by case law (for the inherent jurisdiction). In any case where the local authority is authorised to deprive the child of his or her liberty but, when it comes to putting the restrictive arrangements into practice, the child is in fact consenting to them in circumstances where that consent is valid and sufficient, there would be no DoL. In that situation, the local authority would simply be providing the child with accommodation.

8.9.4 Court of Protection and deprivation of liberty applications

Where there is an application before the court for a DoL order, and the child is approaching 16, there needs to be consideration as to whether the child's welfare needs to continue to be met through the family jurisdiction or transferred to the Court of Protection. The Court of Protection has jurisdiction in relation to children who have attained the age of 16 years, and who lack capacity within the meaning of the Mental Capacity Act 2005. The position was considered in *Re A-F (Children) (No 2)* [2018] EWHC 2129 (Fam). The court explained that in considering possible transfer to the Court of Protection, a number of factors needed to be considered, such as whether the children required the continuing protection of looked after reviews and the support of the IRO. If there were existing care proceedings, then one had to also consider the fact that the parental responsibility lay with the local authority children's social care department, which would be much more familiar with practice and procedure in the Family Court and the Family Division, than with the practice and procedure in the Court of Protection. The children's guardian would also be able to continue exercising that role, so long as the case remained within the Family Court and the Family Division; and the court said it was doubtful whether the children's guardian would be able to act as litigation friend in the Court of Protection.

In this context, it is also important to note the decision *In the Matter of D (A Child)* [2019] UKSC 42. Here, the Supreme Court decided that it was not within the scope of parental responsibility for a parent with parental responsibility to consent to the living arrangements for a 16- or 17-year-old, which would otherwise amount to a DoL, in circumstances where the child lacked mental capacity. A DoL order would need to be sought to sanction the arrangements in such circumstances. Furthermore, consider paragraph 7 of the protocol by the President of the Family Division, dated September 2023, headed *Revised National Listing Protocol for Applications that seek Deprivation of Liberty Orders Relating to Children under the Inherent Jurisdiction.* Here, the President has provided that if the child or young person is aged 16 or 17 and there is reason to believe they may lack capacity and would be likely to be transferred to the Court of Protection at the age of 18, then the court should transfer the case to the Court of Protection in accordance with the guidelines.

8.9.5 Shortage of placements and ongoing difficulties

As already discussed, applications for DoL have increased significantly over the last few years. This has largely been down to the very limited availability of secure accommodation units, and also the fact that some of the units are unable to meet the specifically identified needs of the child concerned. Therefore, a 'bespoke' regime may be sought in such circumstances, in the form of a DoL placement, which would require court authorisation. The difficulty in securing such placements has been identified in a number of significant decisions by the senior judiciary. For example, Cobb J, in *Re S (Child in Care: Unregistered Placement)* [2020] EWHC 1012 (Fam), emphasised that the absence of satisfactory secure provision was a chronic problem which, in recent years, had become ever more acute to the significant detriment of a large number of young people in society. In *Re Z (A Child) (DOLS: Lack of Secure Placement)* [2020] EWHC 1827 (Fam), the local authority had approached over 30 institutions, including in Scotland, via a central agency, and despite daily phone calls and updates, no secure placement was available. There were about 40 children awaiting secure placements at that time. Subsequently, in *Lancashire County Council v G (No 4) (Continuing Unavailability of Regulated Placement)* [2021] EWHC 244 (Fam), MacDonald J, at [4], said that the reality was that the court was again, reduced to little more than a rubber stamp in circumstances where the continuing lack of options before the court essentially obviated the courts' ability to apply the welfare test. As matters stood, in the same way as there were no secure accommodation places to accommodate the child, and despite the local authority having continued its diligent search, there were no regulated non-secure placements in the jurisdiction available and able to take the child. At [32], His Lordship said that, once again, the court must authorise the continued deprivation of the child in an unregulated placement that was not fully equipped to meet her complex needs by reason of the fact that the court had no other option. The court said that the placement was in the child's best interests only because it was the sole option available to the court to prevent the child from causing herself serious and possibly fatal harm.

Given the increasing difficulties with insufficient facilities for meeting children's needs, the President of the Family Division, Sir Andrew McFarlane, set out his judgment in *Re X (Secure Accommodation: Lack of Provision)* [2023] EWHC 129 (Fam). Here, at [1], His Lordship said that the primary purpose of this judgment was for the court, once again, to draw public attention to the very substantial deficit that existed nationally in the provision of facilities for the secure accommodation of children. There were an increasing number of children and young people under the age of 18 years, whose welfare and behaviour required that they be looked after within a secure regime which restricted their liberty. These specialist units were limited in number and, at present, the number of secure beds was far out-stripped by the number of vulnerable young people who need to be placed in them. Courts were regularly told that, on any given day, the number of those needing a secure placement exceeded the number of available places by 60 or 70. It was not the role of the courts to provide additional accommodation; all the court could do was to call out the problem and to shout as loud as it can in the hope that those in Parliament, government and the wider media would take the issue up. At [5]–[6], the President stated that within the current proceedings it was accepted that no criticism could attach to the local authority, or the individual social workers, who had striven to find a suitable secure placement. The point to be made most firmly was that the situation faced by the local authority was one that was faced by every other local authority in England and Wales on a regular basis.

8.9.6 Deprivation of liberty orders and enforceability in Scotland

It will be the case that sometimes local authorities in England and Wales have to consider the placement of children in Scotland. In para 8.3.2, we set out the position surrounding the legality of secure accommodation orders made in England and Wales for children who may be placed in a secure unit in Scotland. What is the position regarding a DoL order in such circumstances? This has been considered and provided for within the Cross-border Placements (Effect of Deprivation of Liberty Orders) (Scotland) Regulations 2022 (SI 2022/225). These Regulations make provision for a DoL order granted by a High Court in England, Wales or, as the case may be, Northern Ireland to have effect in Scotland as if it were a compulsory supervision order in certain circumstances and for certain purposes. This means that a local authority in England, Wales and the Northern Irish health and social care trusts do not need to petition the Court of Session to have DoL orders granted via the inherent jurisdiction of the High Court to be recognised in Scotland. These regulations therefore allow cross-border placements to take place. However, there is a need to meet certain conditions. The local authority in the country that is placing the child retains responsibility for implementing the order, and it needs to meet these conditions. The local authority needs to complete a notice and an undertaking, so as to confirm that it will meet the conditions set. It needs to ensure the order is sent to Scottish Ministers, the local authority and health board for the area where the child is to be placed, as well as to the placement provider, and amongst others, the Children and Young People's Commissioner for Scotland and the inspectorate, Social Care and Social Work Improvement Scotland. Further guidance is set out in the *Cross-Border Placements (Effect of Deprivation of Liberty Orders) (Scotland) Regulations 2022 – Practice Guidance, Notice and Undertaking Template* (Scottish Government, June 2022).

8.9.7 Unregistered placements and supported placements

As emphasised in para 8.9.5, there is a mounting shortage of secure accommodation and DoL placements for children across England and Wales.

The situation has become even more difficult with the passing of further regulations in England, which has led to tighter restrictions on children's placements. In particular, the effect of the Care Planning, Placement and

Case Review (England) (Amendment) Regulations 2021 (SI 2021/161) is that, from 9 September 2021, it is a criminal offence to place any child under 16 in an unregistered or unregulated placement. More specifically, the reference to 'unregulated setting' has been replaced with the term used in section 22C(6)(d) of the CA 1989, namely 'other arrangements'. The effect of these 2021 amendment regulations is to introduce the additional regulation 27A, which prohibits the placement of a child under 16 in any such 'other arrangement', save for a limited number of situations. Where has this left applications for DoL orders in such 'other arrangements'? In *Tameside Metropolitan Borough Council v AM & Others* [2021] EWHC 2472 (Fam), the court decided that, in appropriate cases, it remained open to the High Court to authorise, under its inherent jurisdiction, the DoL of a child under the age of 16 in such placements, but it would be limited, and by authorising this, the court was not providing immunity from prosecution. In authorising the placement, the court would need to be satisfied that there was the rigorous application of (what was then) the President's Guidance of November 2019 entitled *Placements in unregistered children's homes in England or unregistered care home services in Wales* and the addendum thereto dated December 2020. Recently, this guidance has been replaced by the *Revised Practice Guidance on the Court's approach to unregistered placements* issued by the President of the Family Division, dated September 2023. One key aspect of this revised guidance is that the President has emphasised that it is not for the court to become a regulatory body or the overseer of the regulatory process. The court's role in DoL applications is to exercise its inherent jurisdiction to ensure that any DoL is not itself unlawful, whether as an unlawful detention under the common law, or a breach of Article 5 of the ECHR. That is the extent of the court's powers, and the court's role should not go beyond those powers. Therefore, paragraphs 8 and 9 of this guidance stipulate that the courts, when considering a DoL application, should enquire into whether the proposed placement is registered or unregistered. If it is unregistered it should enquire as to why the local authority considers an unregistered placement is in the best interests of the child. Furthermore, the court may order the local authority to inform Ofsted/Care Inspectorate Wales within 7 days if it is placing a child in an unregistered placement.

Lastly, various provisions set out in the Supported Accommodation (England) Regulations 2023 (SI 2023/416) have been implemented. These Regulations extend to England and Wales but apply in relation to England only. The regulations apply to the accommodation of 16- and 17-year-old looked after children in accordance with section 22C(6)(d) of the CA 1989 and care leavers in accordance with section 23B(8)(b) of the CA 1989. In particular, they provide for registration with Ofsted of the person responsible for carrying on or managing supported accommodation.

9 Education Supervision Orders

The Education Act 1996, combined with the provisions of section 36 of, and Schedule 3 to, the CA 1989, authorises the prosecution of parents who fail to ensure that their child receives a proper full-time education. A local authority has an obligation under sections 444A and 444ZA of the Education Act 1996 to take legal action so as to enforce school attendance. This is done through its Education Welfare Service. The legislation is the same across England and Wales, although the Welsh Government issues separate guidance on school attendance in Wales.

Parents have the right to educate their children other than in school, provided that the child receives a 'proper education' as described below. The local education authority may agree, under the Education Act 1996, to help parents to arrange education otherwise than at school. The Department for Education guidance, *Working together to improve school attendance (Guidance for maintained schools, academies, independent schools, and local authorities)* (May 2022 and updated September 2023), paragraph 9, provides that the law entitles every child of compulsory school age to an efficient, full-time education suitable to their age, aptitude, and any special educational needs they may have. It is the legal responsibility of every parent to make sure their child receives that education either by attendance at a school or by education otherwise than at a school. Furthermore, paragraph 10 goes on to provide that where parents decide to have their child registered at school, they have an additional legal duty to ensure their child attends that school regularly. This means their child must attend every day that the school is open, except in a small number of allowable circumstances, such as being too ill to attend or being given permission for an absence in advance from the school.

Section 36(4) of the CA 1989 states that 'a child is being properly educated only if he is receiving efficient full-time education suitable to his age, ability and aptitude, and any special educational needs he may have'. Under section 437(1) of the Education Act 1996, a local education authority which is concerned about a child's education may serve notice on parents to show that the child is being properly educated. If the parents fail to comply or to provide the required proof, then the local authority may serve on parents a 'school attendance order', requiring the parents to register the child at a named school (section 437(3) of the Education Act

1996). Failure to comply with this order constitutes an offence, and on prosecution, the court may direct the local authority to apply for an education supervision order.

9.1   Effects of an education supervision order

Paragraphs 107 and 108 of the above Department for Education guidance, *Working together to improve school attendance (Guidance for maintained schools, academies, independent schools, and local authorities)* provides that where a voluntary early help plan or formal parenting contract has not been successful, an education supervision order, made under section 36 of the CA 1989, can be a useful alternative to provide formal legal intervention without criminal prosecution. In deciding whether to progress to an education supervision order, the school and local authority should have exhausted voluntary support and be clear that making the order would be beneficial for the pupil and parent(s). Where safeguarding concerns exist, the lead practitioner should also discuss with the school's designated safeguarding lead and the local authority children's social care department to agree that an education supervision order would be a more suitable option than a section 17 (children in need) or section 47 (child protection) plan. In all cases, local authorities must fully consider using an education supervision order before moving forward to prosecution. The education supervision order gives the local authority a formal role in advising, helping and directing the pupil and parent(s) to ensure the pupil receives an efficient, full-time, suitable education.

The education supervision order places the child under the supervision of a local authority. It differs from supervision orders made under section 31. School refusal is no longer by itself a ground for care, but it may be evidence of neglect, lack of parental control, underlying emotional problems, or that the education system may be failing to meet the needs of the child. School refusal may, therefore, form part of the section 31 grounds (see Chapter 7, para 7.2, and *Re O (A Minor) (Care Order: Education Procedure)* [1992] 2 FLR 7).

Schedule 3, paragraph 12(1) to the CA 1989 sets out the supervisor's duty to 'advise, assist and befriend and give directions to the supervised child and to his parents, in such as way as will ... secure that he is properly educated'.

Schedule 3, paragraph 12(3) to the CA 1989 provides that the supervisor should take into account the wishes and feelings of the child and parents, including, in particular, their wishes as to the place at which the child should be educated. Directions made should be reasonable and such that the parents and child are able to comply with them. Persistent failure to comply with directions given under the education supervision order may lead to prosecution (Schedule 3, paragraph 18(1) to the CA 1989). Local authorities can prosecute in the magistrates' courts for persistent non-compliance with the education supervision order and parents (upon conviction) will be liable to a fine of up to £1,000. There are various defences to a prosecution for failure to comply with an education supervision order, which include showing that all reasonable steps were taken to comply; that the directions were unreasonable; that there was compliance with directions or requirements in the education supervision order; and that it was not reasonably practicable to comply with both the direction and with the requirement or directions mentioned (Schedule 3, paragraph 18(2) to the CA 1989).

Directions might require the child to attend meetings with the supervisor or with teachers at the school to discuss progress, or to cover medical assessment or examination, or assessment by a clinical psychologist. They should be confirmed in writing, and the parents informed.

The effect of Schedule 3, paragraph 13 to the CA 1989 is that parents lose their right to have the child educated at home or to move the child to another school while an education supervision order is in force, and they have no right of appeal against admissions decisions.

9.2 Duration

The education supervision order will subsist for one year, or until the child is no longer of compulsory school age, whichever is the earlier (Schedule 3, paragraph 15(1) and (6) to the CA 1989). It may be discharged earlier, on the application of the child, the parents or the local authority (Schedule 3, paragraph 17(1)).

It may be extended for up to 3 years if application is made within 3 months before the expiry date, and it can be extended more than once (Schedule 3, paragraph 15 to the CA 1989). It will cease on the making of a care order (Schedule 3, paragraph 15(6)(b)).

9.3 Grounds for application

Under section 36(3) of the CA 1989, an education supervision order may only be made if the court is 'satisfied that the child concerned is of compulsory school age and is not being properly educated'; section 36(4) states that 'a child is being properly educated only if he is receiving efficient full-time education suitable to his age, ability and aptitude and any special educational needs he may have'.

Where a child is subject to a school attendance order under section 437 of the Education Act 1996 which is in force, but with which the child is not complying, or is a registered pupil of a school which he is not attending regularly within the meaning of section 444, there is a presumption that the child is not being properly educated (section 36(5) of the CA 1989).

Note that an education supervision order may not be sought in respect of a child who is already subject to a care order (section 36(6) of the CA 1989).

Before making an application for an education supervision order, the local authority is required under section 36(8) of the CA 1989 to consult the appropriate local authority, if different.

The children's services department may seek the assistance of other local authority departments in the provision of services for the child. This fits in with the general duty to comply with requests from other local authority departments pursuant to section 27(1)–(3) of the CA 1989.

9.4   Practice and procedure

9.4.1   Application

The applicant for the education supervision order is the local authority, and the application should be made on Form C110A, together with supplemental Form C17, as the application is under Part IV of the CA 1989. Applications are 'family proceedings' under section 8(3) and (4) of the CA 1989, and therefore the menu of orders is available to the court (see Table 13.1). The principles in section 1 apply, see Chapter 2. An application may not be made in respect of a child subject to a care order (section 36(6)).

9.4.2   Venue

Cases should be commenced in the Family Court and may only be transferred to the High Court in the limited situations set out in the *Jurisdiction of the Family Court: Allocation of Cases within the Family Court to High Court Judge Level and Transfer of Cases from the Family Court to the High Court* (24 May 2021). This is considered in more detail in Chapter 14.

9.4.3   Notice

FPR 2010 PD 12C, paragraph 2.1 provides that 7 days' notice of the hearing or directions appointment must be given, including the date and venue of the application.

A local authority providing accommodation for the child, or the person with whom a child is living, or the manager of a refuge providing accommodation for the child under section 51 of the CA 1989, may be served with notice of the application, on Form C6A, pursuant to FPR 2010 PD 12C, paragraph 3.1.

9.4.4 Respondents

Every person with parental responsibility for the child is a respondent, as is the child. Respondents should be served with notice of the application, together with a copy of the application Form C110A and supplement in Form C17.

9.4.5 Service

The normal rules of service apply, as well as the methods of service, see rule 6.23 of the FPR 2010 and PD 6A. The time for service may be abridged by the court or waived altogether (see rule 4.1(3)(a)).

The applicant needs to confirm service, at or before the hearing, so as to confirm when, by whom and which document(s) were served.

9.5 Rights of the child

The rights of the child are:

(a)   the child's welfare is paramount;

(b)   to be consulted on schooling issues;

(c)   to have wishes and feelings taken into consideration;

(d)   to be a respondent in the application;

(e)   to receive directions that are reasonable;

(f)   to advice, assistance and befriending from the supervisor.

9.6 Variation, discharge and appeals

Discharge can be on the application of the child, the parents or the local authority designated in the order (Schedule 3, paragraph 17(1) to the CA 1989). On the discharge application, the court may order the local authority to investigate the child's circumstances under section 37 and Schedule 3, paragraph 17(2).

The order may be extended for up to 3 years on application by the authority within 3 months before the expiry date, and the order can be extended more than once (Schedule 3, paragraph 15 to the CA 1989).

9.6.1   Appeals

Rule 30.1 of the FPR 2010 sets out that the provisions in Part 30 apply to appeals to: (a) the High Court; and (b) the Family Court. All parties to an appeal must comply with FPR 2010 PD 30A. Rule 30.3(1B) and (2) of the FPR 2010 specifically set out when permission to appeal is or is not required against a decision or order of the Family Court. See Chapter 17 for more detail on appeals.

Interestingly, the ECHR envisages the use of secure accommodation to detain a minor for 'educational supervision' (Article 5).

However, read in conjunction with Article 8 (right to family life) of the ECHR, it is unlikely that in the United Kingdom this would encourage courts to take a step in that direction.

10 Police Powers under the Children Act 1989

The police have powers under section 46 of the CA 1989 referred to as 'police protection', which do not need a court order. The ground for action is that police have reasonable cause to believe the child would otherwise suffer significant harm (section 46(1)).

The Department for Education guidance, *Court orders and pre-proceedings: For local authorities* (April 2014), Chapter 4, paragraph 30 provides that the police powers should only be used in exceptional circumstances, where there is insufficient time to apply for an emergency protection order, or for reasons relating to the immediate safety of the child.

Also, paragraph 37 of this guidance provides that neither the officer, the designated officer, nor the local authority acquire parental responsibility for a child who is in police protection following the exercise of powers under section 46 of the CA 1989. The designated officer must nevertheless do what is reasonable in all the circumstances to promote the child's welfare, bearing in mind that the child cannot be kept in police protection for more than 72 hours (section 46(6) and (9) of the CA 1989).

10.1 Police powers and responsibilities

The powers of the police are:

- to remove a child to a safe place and keep him there (section 46(1)(a) of the CA 1989);

- to prevent a child's removal from a safe place (section 46(1)(b));

- no power to enter premises without a warrant unless section 17 of PACE is satisfied (section 17 includes, amongst other situations, saving life and limb, prevention of serious damage to property, or arrests);

- to safeguard and promote the child's welfare (section 46(9)(b)).

Each area must have a 'designated police officer' responsible for carrying out the duties imposed by the CA 1989, who can apply for emergency protection if necessary (section 46(3)(e) and (7)).

The police must, under section 46(3) of the CA 1989, inform the local authority of their action, the reasons for it, and the child's whereabouts; inform the child (if he is capable of understanding), and discover his wishes and feelings; and, under section 46(4), take reasonable steps to inform parents, those with parental responsibility, and those with whom the child was living, of the action, the reasons for it and future plans.

10.2   Contact with child

Pursuant to section 46(10) of the CA 1989, in relation to contact, the designated officer must also allow the following persons to have such contact with the child as, in the officer's opinion, is both reasonable and in the child's best interests:

*   the child's parents;

*   anyone else who has parental responsibility for the child;

*   anyone with whom the child was living immediately before he was taken into police protection;

*   any person named in a child arrangements order as a person with whom the child is to spend time or otherwise have contact;

*   anyone who has in his favour an order relating to contact with the child under section 34 of the CA 1989;

*   anyone acting on behalf of any of the above.

Note that, in appropriate circumstances, an application should be made for an emergency protection order, as opposed to the police exercising powers of police protection.

11 Instructions and Case Preparation in Family Proceedings

Family proceedings should be non-adversarial. Advocates may be instructed to represent children, parents, other parties or local authorities. Effective advocacy depends more on thorough preparation of the case, coupled with good negotiation skills with all parties throughout the proceedings, than on the final presentation in court.

The first task is to elicit from all sources available as much information as possible about the circumstances of the case, the client and the child. All evidence relevant to the welfare of the child should be available to the court.

11.1 Action plan on receipt of instructions from an adult or local authority

- Arrange to interview the client or instructing social worker as soon as possible.

- Where appropriate, check the public funding situation and complete the necessary forms.

- Obtain copies of all applications and documents which have been filed with the court.

- Find out whether there are other relevant proceedings current or pending. If there are, obtain details.

- Find out whether there have been previous proceedings in relation to the child(ren) or the family. If so, ask for copies of all previous/existing court orders and copies of documents filed with the court. Consent and appropriate directions by the court may be necessary to authorise and facilitate disclosure of documents from another court or from other proceedings.

- Ascertain who the other parties are. Check whether they have instructed legal representatives, and obtain details.

- Identify any other people who should be made parties to the proceedings or notified of the proceedings in accordance with the rules, and take appropriate action.

- Let the court and all other parties (or their advocates if they are represented) and the children's guardian know you are instructed in the matter, and write, inviting communication and offering co-operation. (See Chapter 15 if being instructed by the children's guardian on behalf of the child.)

- Interview potential witnesses.

- Follow FPR 2010 PD 12A and other relevant FPR 2010 Practice Directions.

11.2   Interviewing clients

Cases involving family breakup or issues of child protection are stressful for all the parties concerned. It is essential to establish a relationship of trust with clients, giving them space in the initial interview to express their feelings, whilst at the same time keeping the interview focused on taking background history and instructions. Set aside sufficient time to allow clients to fully express all they have to say and offer appropriate refreshments – this can provide a welcome break. A checklist may assist to keep the interview focused on the information required. Below are sample checklists of some basic issues to cover when interviewing parents, social workers and medical witnesses, to which can be added specific issues relevant to each case.

11.2.1   Checklist for information from parents

- Full name and address.

- Home telephone number. (Any restrictions on its use?)

- Work telephone number. (Any restrictions on its use?)

- Mobile telephone number. (Any restrictions on its use?)

- Email address. (Any restrictions on its use?)

- Names of all the children of the family and their dates of birth.

- Who are the parents of each child of the family?

- Who has parental responsibility for the child?

- Where does each child of the family live, if they do not live with the client?

- What are the present contact arrangements with the children living elsewhere?

- Partner and family members living in client's household. This will be of particular relevance so as to ensure there are appropriate assessments undertaken of 'connected persons', see in particular the assessment process as set out in regulations 24–25 of the 2010 Regulations, and the Welsh equivalent in regulations 25–28 of the 2015 Regulations.

- Does this client, any member of the family or the child(ren) have any special needs, cultural issues, language difficulties, disabilities or difficulties, of which the court, children's guardian and other parties need to be aware? In particular, if there are issues surrounding the client parent having a learning disability, there should be a referral to the adult disability team. In this context, see the *President's Guidance: Family Proceedings: Parents with a Learning Disability* (10 April 2018), issued by the then President of the Family Division, Sir James Munby. The President had stated that the primary purpose in issuing this guidance was to bring to the attention of practitioners and judges, the very important *Good Practice Guidance on Working with Parents with a Learning Disability 2016* (DoH/DfES, updated September 2016) issued by the Working Together with Parents Network and the Norah Fry Centre for Disability Studies, School for Policy Studies, University of Bristol. This and more recent guidance are referred to specifically at para 11.2.4.

- Consider the need for any participation directions, as per Part 3A of the FPR 2010 and PD 3AA. This came into effect on 27 November 2017, and has the effect under rule 3A.4 that the court must consider whether a party's participation in the proceedings (other than by way of giving evidence) is likely to be diminished by reason of vulnerability and, if so, whether it is necessary to make one or more participation directions. Before making such participation directions, the court must consider any views expressed by the party about participating in the proceedings. More recently, in *Re X and Y (Domestic Abuse: Participation Directions: Obligations to Consider)* [2024] EWFC 121 (B), Williams J (at [11]) stated that whilst the court is under an obligation to provide a fair hearing which takes account of matters which diminish a party's ability to participate and to give evidence, where a party is legally represented the obligation to consider how a party will participate fairly lies firstly, both temporally and procedurally, on the legal team. That is both good practice and in accordance with professional duties (as is use of the Advocates Toolkit) but also is the route Part 3A of the FPR 2010 provides. This recent judgment emphasises that the court is entitled to assume that a represented party's lawyers are satisfied they can participate fairly if the issue is not raised.

- Also consider whether there may be an issue as to the parent client lacking litigation capacity. If so, there may need for a referral to be made to a psychologist or psychiatrist, so as to assess litigation capacity. This may lead to a possible invitation for the Official Solicitor to become involved, see in particular Part 15 of the FPR 2010, relating to protected parties and also the Practice Note of January 2017 issued by the Official Solicitor, *The Official Solicitor to the Senior Courts: Appointment in Family Proceedings and Proceedings under the Inherent Jurisdiction in Relation to Adults* (updated in May 2023 to update the contact details for the Official Solicitor). The Practice Note specifically covers the guidance on appointing the Official Solicitor as litigation friend of a child in family proceedings or a protected party, and for dealing with requests from the court for the Official Solicitor to act as, or appoint counsel to act as, an advocate to the court. Also issued in 2021 was the updated *Official Solicitor's Referral Form*, which specifically provides that the litigation friend checklist must also be completed and sent with the referral. Additionally, there is the Family Justice Council guidance, *Capacity to Litigate in Proceedings involving Children* (April 2018), containing important material to assist courts in addressing capacity issues relating to parties to family law proceedings. It includes, in particular, a checklist for the appointment of a litigation friend, including the Official Solicitor, a draft certificate of capacity, notes for assessors, a draft letter to an independent expert and/or treating clinician in public law proceedings, together with the Official Solicitor's certificate of capacity, a draft letter to a friend or family member of an unrepresented person whose capacity is in question to seek information, and a list of suggested information relevant to the finances of the protected party to support an application for public funding. Also included in the guidance are draft orders when inviting the Official Solicitor to act as litigation friend, and for the provision of directions for disclosure against third parties.

- Also consider whether there may be an issue as to jurisdiction, and in particular, whether there is a need to contact another country if the child, parent or other relative has a connection with another country. As mentioned in para 7.4.2, for children matters prior to the exit from the EU, the Brussels II Regulation (Council Regulation (EC) 2201/2003 of 27 November 2003 concerning jurisdiction and the recognition and enforcement of judgments in matrimonial matters and the matters of parental responsibility (BIIR)) is still relevant. Therefore, recognition and enforcement provisions of BIIR still apply to proceedings instituted before the end of the transition period as governed by Part 3 of the EU-UK Withdrawal Agreement. Given that the BIIR has been revoked, for cases starting after the end of the transition period, the courts need to apply the Hague Convention on Jurisdiction, Applicable Law, Recognition, Enforcement and Cooperation in Respect of Parental Responsibility and Measures for the Protection of Children 1996 (1996 Hague Convention). There is specific guidance by the Ministry of

Justice, 'Family law disputes involving the EU: guidance for legal professionals', dated 31 December 2020. In particular, Article 8 of the 1996 Hague Convention provides for the transfer of jurisdiction to another contracting state where a court with jurisdiction considers a court in another contracting state is better placed to hear the case. This therefore is what was provided for previously in Article 15 of BIIR. In *Re N (Children)* [2016] UKSC 15, Lady Hale emphasised that the assessment of whether a transfer would be in the best interests of the child should be based on the principle of mutual trust and on the assumption that the courts of all states are, in principle, competent to deal with a case. As an example, in *AM and GM v KL and VL* [2023] EWFC 15, the court had to consider the question as to whether the court had jurisdiction in respect of the subject children, each of whom all parties accepted were habitually resident in this jurisdiction, and if so, whether the court should exercise that jurisdiction. There may also be a need to obtain relevant information for use in Family Court proceedings by using the *Protocol: Communicating with UK visas and immigration (UKVI) – In family proceedings* (17 May 2018). This protocol enables the Family Court to communicate with UK Visas and Immigration, the relevant division of the Home Office, to obtain immigration and visa information for use in Family Court proceedings. In this context, also note the *Guidance from the President of the Family Division: Liaison between the courts and British Embassies and High Commissions*, dated March 2022. The President stated that courts exercising family jurisdiction in England and Wales regularly deal with cases where children have been wrongfully removed to a foreign country or have been retained there wrongfully, most commonly by a parent or relative. In such situations, the guidance sets out the situations where consular assistance may be sought, via the Foreign, Commonwealth and Development Office in London, from the relevant British Embassies, High Commissions or Consulates abroad.

- Obtain general information about this client, including background, education, attainments, current or past employment, interests and significant life events.

- Does this client or any partner, family member, carer or cohabitee have any convictions or cautions for offences which may affect an assessment of their capacity to care for the child(ren)? For example, conviction for an offence listed in Schedule 1 to the Children and Young Persons Act 1933, drink- or drug-related offences, etc?

- Convictions should be disclosed to the court, see *Re R (Minors) (Custody)* [1986] 1 FLR 6.

- Does the client or any family member have any particular skills or attributes relevant to their parenting ability?

- Have there been any previous court orders or applications made to a court in respect of this child, or any other child of the family or any family member?

- Other people or bodies involved with the family who may be able to assist in providing information:

  - schools attended by the child(ren);

  - playgroups;

  - voluntary organisations/religious organisations;

  - therapists;

  - GP/hospital;

  - health visitor;

  - community, religious or other agencies or organisations involved with the family.

- How does the client see the present situation? Obtain:

  - details of the circumstances that led up to this application;

  - a description of the current situation and presenting problems;

  - details of the client's wishes, feelings and concerns;

  - the client's instructions as to what he or she wishes to happen in this case (subject to the legal advice the client may receive now or later).

- Does the client have any comments to make or explanations to offer about causation of any injuries or harm alleged, or the child's emotional problems?

- What contact has the client had to date with social services or other professionals about this child?

- Has the client requested or received any help, advice or resources from social services?

- What would the client like to see happen in the future concerning the child(ren)?

- What would the child(ren) like to happen?

- What does the client think that others will say about the situation? (Often a very revealing question.)

- Can the client think of others who may be able to offer relevant information about the child or family?

11.2.2 Checklist for *Public Law Outline* requirements on information from local authorities and social workers

The PLO checklist (as set out in FPR 2010 PD 12A) is such that it ensures that social workers and local authorities have provided all the information and documentation that is required of them. The pre-proceedings checklist (set out in Chapter 7, at para 7.7.4) is to be followed.

If the SWET document approach is not being followed, then the annex documents to be attached to the application form (Form C110A) are the following:

- social work chronology;
- social work statement and genogram;
- current assessments relating to the child and/or the family and friends of the child to which the social work statement refers and on which the local authority relies;
- care plan;
- index of checklist documents.

The chronology prepared for court and social work statements are factual accounts of recent events leading to the application.

Checklist documents are those that are already existing on the local authority files, and are considered in Chapter 7, at para 7.7.4.

Note that the letter before proceedings sets out in clear terms what is considered to be the problem. The Department for Education guidance, *Court orders and pre-proceedings: For local authorities* (April 2014), in paragraphs 30–31 set out that unless the local authority considers that the level of risk requires an immediate application to court, it should send a letter before proceedings to parents and/or others with parental responsibility. The letter is the formal written notification that proceedings are likely. The guidance specifically provides that the letter should set out a summary, in simple language, of the local authority's concerns, what support has already been provided, what parents need to do, what support will be provided for them to avoid proceedings, including timescales, and information on how to obtain legal advice and advocacy. The letter needs to emphasise how important it is for the parent to seek legal representation.

The letter will enable the parents and/or persons with parental responsibility, to obtain legal assistance and advice, so as to address the concerns. A standard template letter is set out in the guidance.

When writing the care plan and any written agreements (contract of expectations), there is a need to bear in mind the welfare checklists under the CA 1989 and the Adoption and Children Act 2002, if relevant, as well as the 2010 Regulations, or the Welsh equivalent, namely the 2015 Regulations.

In the re-launch of the PLO on 16 January 2023, the President of the Family Division stated that the PLO pre-proceedings process, with the engagement of parents and a thorough assessment exercise, is essential.

11.2.3   Checklist for basic initial information from medical witnesses

There is guidance in Part 25 of the FPR 2010 and PDs 25A, 25B and 25C as to the content of the letter of instruction to an expert and also the required content of an expert's report. See Chapter 18 for discussion of the instruction of experts, expert evidence and medical reports. In addition to this, the checklist below indicates the basic information which might be included in the report of a medical witness:

- Medical witness's full name.

- Health centre/surgery/hospital address/post held.

- Relevant qualifications and experience.

- Nature, extent, venue and duration of examination(s) of the child:
    - date, duration and venue of first examination;
    - reason for referral;
    - observations of child on examination;
    - appearance, demeanour, attitude to examination and others present;
    - note any statements made by the child or by others that are relevant;
    - any abnormalities in physical or mental state;
    - marks, abrasions, wounds, skeletal survey, pain, tenderness;
    - unusual features or appearance of any part of the body.

- Body map showing location of areas of injury, bruising.

- Colour photographs (of great help to a court if the child/family is willing to allow this, but beware, if sexual abuse is alleged, photography may remind child of the abuse or be further abusive).

- Description of the general health of the child.

- Full description of the child's injuries/abnormalities, with an explanation of the medical terms used.

- Is it possible to give a time of the occurrence of any injuries noted?

- When the injuries occurred, would they have caused pain to the child? Would he or she have cried out, screamed in pain? Does it still hurt? How soon afterwards would it stop hurting? Should a caring adult have noticed/treated the child's discomfort/pain?

- Were there attempts to treat the injuries/or to cover them up?

- Is there any evidence of brittle bones or other congenital factor likely to contribute to these injuries or explain them?

- If anyone was questioned about the injuries, note who was questioned, who was present, their reactions and demeanour in response to questioning, specific questions used and responses given.

- Note any comments or explanations offered of how the injuries/abnormalities occurred.

- Does any explanation given by adults agree/conflict with the medical or psychiatric diagnosis?

- Describe diagnosis, treatment given or recommended following examination and prognosis.

- Note date(s), venue and duration of subsequent examinations.

- Record any other relevant or significant health issues within the family (including parents, siblings, other relatives), particularly any issues affecting the parents' or carers' ability to look after the child, or affecting the general health and welfare of the child or close family members.

- Health history of the child, in chronological order, including:

  - physical development;

  - height/weight/centile charts;

  - developmental assessments according to age;

  - visual/hearing/neurological/speech/language assessments;

  - evidence of emotional problems/abnormalities (Have they been diagnosed as a congenital disorder, or is there possibly some other cause?);

  - evidence of physical problems/abnormalities (Do they constitute an illness or 'disability' within the meaning of the CA 1989? Have they been diagnosed as a congenital disorder, or is there possibly some other cause?);

- treatment(s) given to the child and the effect of treatment;

- advice offered to the family/child about medical care and whether the advice was taken up and acted upon.

• Up-to-date information about the child's development.

• Other information concerning the child's welfare that is relevant for the helping agencies and the court.

Medical witnesses should bear in mind the welfare checklist whilst writing their report. It is a useful reference concerning the best interests of the child shared by the court, the children's guardian and the professionals in the case.

Also, they need to ensure that any opinions expressed are objective, relevant, and supported by observations.

The names and addresses of doctors and other health professionals who have been involved with the child/family, or to whom the child has been referred for specialist treatment or examination should be included. They may be able to give additional relevant information.

A list of 'dates to avoid' should be included, i.e. times when unavailable for court, conferences and meetings.

11.2.4   Working with parents with a learning disability and participation directions

As mentioned at para 11.2.1, it is important to note the guidance provided surrounding working with parents with a learning disability. In particular, consider the case of *A Local Authority v G (Parent with Learning Disability)* [2017] EWFC B94, in which the court stated (at [35]) that where a parent has a learning disability, the court must make sure that the parent is not being disadvantaged simply because of his or her disability. The essential question is whether the parenting that can be offered is good enough if support is provided. The court referred to *Re D (No 3)* [2016] EWFC 1, in which the then President of the Family Division, Sir James Munby, had endorsed and recommended what was said by Gillen J in *Re Guardian and A (Care Order: Freeing Order: Parents with a Learning Disability)* [2016] NI Fam 8. The court stated (at [8]) that the publication, *Good Practice Guidance on Working with Parents with a Learning Disability 2016* (DoH/DfES, updated September 2016), issued by the Working Together with Parents Network and the Norah Fry Centre for Disability Studies, School for Policy Studies, University of Bristol, was written to emphasise the need for effective joint working between adult and children's services.

These matters have been addressed further and, in particular, in *Nottinghamshire County Council v XX & Others* [2022] EWFC 10. Here, Knowles J commented (at [105]–[109]) that the publication *Learning about the Good Practice Guidance on Working with Parents with a Learning Disability* (first published in 2007 and amended in 2016 and 2021) should be more widely disseminated to both children and family social workers and adult social care workers. It must be an essential part of continuation training for such social workers and their managers. Furthermore, there must be timely referrals to adult social care for a parent with learning difficulties in his or her own right, and parents with learning difficulties involved with children's social care where a child is on a child protection plan should have their own advocate as a priority. Additionally, the support available to a parent with learning disabilities in his or her own right should be distilled into a simple document identifying what is available, how often it is available, the timescales for its availability, and who is responsible for its delivery.

This was a substantive issue that was raised in the decision of *Re S (Vulnerable Party: Fairness of Proceedings)* [2022] EWCA Civ 8. The care proceedings were listed for a fact-finding hearing, and the appellant, who was the intervenor in the proceedings, argued that the court had made findings against her, but her cognitive issues were not considered nor adjustments made to ensure her fair participation. She therefore argued that the findings that were made were unsafe. The Court of Appeal emphasised that to comply with the obligation under rule 3A.9 of the FPR 2010, the judge conducting the CMH at the start of care proceedings should as a matter of course investigate whether there are, or may be, issues engaging Part 3A of the FPR 2010, and that the parties' advocates should as far as practicable be in a position to respond. Legal representatives should be particularly vigilant to detect possible vulnerabilities in their clients when they are unable to meet them in person. On the facts, the intervenor's difficulties were not immediately evident to her lawyer, who only became concerned about her client's level of understanding towards the end of the hearing.

Therefore, in practice, we would suggest that there may be a need, in appropriate cases, for a cognitive assessment to be undertaken to assess any cognitive disability and advice should be sought as to how to assist the person in the future, not just in terms of communication at court, but also in liaising with other professionals and engaging in assessments. If there is a need for assessing a person with disabilities, practitioners will be familiar with the PAMS (Parental Assessment Manual) and more recently, the 'ParentAssess' specialist form of assessment tools used in such circumstances where parents have learning disabilities or additional needs. Note that cognitive assessments should not be seen as being directed routinely, as emphasised recently in *West Northamptonshire Council v The Mother*

(Psychological Assessments) [2024] EWHC 395 (Fam), whereby Lieven J set out some guidance on when such applications should be made, and the approach that the Family Court should take. In particular, at [25]–[27], Her Ladyship set out that it had been argued that a psychological assessment would be useful in determining what support the mother would need to help care for the child in the future. However, Her Ladyship set out that this was not the purpose of the application under Part 25 of the FPR 2010. Further, and in any event, that type of analysis was one that all social workers should necessarily be very familiar with and there was nothing in this case which justified going beyond normal good social work practice. The test is one of necessity and did not mean that a report would be 'nice to have' or might help in determining what psychological support the parent might need in the future. This was not necessary to resolve the proceedings and therefore, the application was refused.

In terms of participation directions, and specifically those relating to communication and support in the conduct of proceedings, guidance may be sought, from perhaps a psychologist or other professional, as to whether the party may benefit from an intermediary/and or lay advocate. What is meant by these terms? In rule 3A.1 of the FPR 2010, an 'intermediary' is defined as a person whose function is to: (a) communicate questions put to a witness or party; (b) communicate to any person asking such questions the answers given by the witness or party in reply to them; and (c) explain such questions or answers so far as is necessary to enable them to be understood by the witness or party or by the person asking such questions. In *Re C (Lay Advocates) (No 2)* [2020] EWHC 1762 (Fam), Keehan J at [10] and [11] stated that the term 'lay advocate', for the purposes of this judgment, meant a person who is qualified and/or has experience of assisting and supporting a party in proceedings who has an intellectual impairment or learning difficulties which compromises their ability to process and comprehend information given to them. The function of the lay advocate is to ensure that the party does understand the information provided and is able to respond to the same and, thereby, is enabled to participate effectively in the proceedings. This assistance and support will be required both in court during the proceedings and out of court for the purposes of taking instructions and preparing the party's case for the court proceedings. In this case, the proposal was for HMCTS to fund an individual with experience of dealing with persons with learning difficulties to be made available to the mother and father both during court proceedings to help explain what was going on, and at all meetings with the solicitor to help explain advice given and pass instructions. The individual would also meet with the mother and father to reinforce what they had been told by their solicitors and what they had heard at court. His Lordship said that in respect of proceedings in court, it appeared that the individual's role was, in fact, largely the same as someone who would usually be described as an 'intermediary', although the role was broader than acting as such for the purposes of cross-examination (for which an intermediary is most commonly used). Outside court, in meetings with the solicitor, it appeared the individual's role was to ensure advice was understood and instructions given.

As for the arrangements and costs in instructing an intermediary at court, there is the guidance and booking form provided by HMCTS, called *Request an HMCTS approved intermediary assessment* of February 2023. The process is that if there is a need for an intermediary (which may sometimes come in the form of a recommendation following a cognitive assessment), then there needs to be an intermediary assessment carried out to see what services and assistance the person would require. You would be expected by HMCTS to use this form to request an assessment of the client's needs and, thereafter, to book an intermediary to support the client for a court hearing or at a conference. In terms of funding, the services provided by approved intermediaries are mostly funded by HMCTS, with no charges or payments required by legal representatives. The exception is for pre-hearing conferences in the Family Court, for which the costs can be met by the Legal Aid Agency (LAA), if appropriate.

In terms of meeting the costs of a 'lay advocate', guidance is set out in *Re C (Lay Advocates) (No 2)* [2020] EWHC 1762 (Fam) (discussed above), where Keehan J provided that: (a) HMCTS will fund the provision of a lay advocate, in appropriate circumstances, for a party at court hearings; and (b) the LAA will fund the provision of a lay advocate, if satisfied that it is a justifiable and reasonable disbursement, to support and assist a party in communicating with his or her solicitor and/or counsel out of court. Subsequently, the *Guidance on Remuneration of Expert Witnesses*, dated September 2020 (Version 6), was updated to reflect the position with payment for the costs of intermediaries and lay advocates by the LAA. This guidance has since been reinforced in Version 7 of this guidance, of September 2022.

11.3 Preparation of the case

Good advocacy is not just an ability to speak persuasively in court. It is mostly good preparation. A good grasp of the facts of the case, the issues and the relevant law will generate confidence when putting forward an argument or making a point. Research on an issue will assist an advocate to ask questions that are useful to the court. Effective child and family law advocates are non-adversarial in approach, willing to negotiate and, when in court, they are courteous, clear, concise and accurate, having read all the case documentation thoroughly before the hearing.

A sound knowledge of the relevant law and the rules of evidence and procedure is essential, and it is also vitally important to keep up to date with changes.

When researching legal material on the internet, reliable sources should be used. Legislation is kept up to date at www.legislation.gov.uk and court judgments are published on The National Archives website, 'Find case law' and on the BAILII website.

11.4 Burden of proof and standard of proof in child law cases

Generally, the person alleging a fact must prove it. In child protection, the burden of proof is with the local authority. The standard of proof the local authority must reach is on a balance of probability, that is 'it is more likely than not' that there is actual or a potential risk of significant harm to the child. Neither the seriousness of any allegations nor the seriousness of the consequences should make any difference to the standard of proof to be applied in determining the facts, see *Re B (Children) (Care Orders: Standard of Proof)* [2008] UKHL 35, [2008] 2 FLR 141. This ruling was subsequently applied in *Re S-B (Children)* [2009] UKSC 17. The Supreme Court also decided that there are particular benefits in some cases in identifying the perpetrator. For example, by doing so, identification will allow the parties to work with the parent, and other members of the family, on the basis of the judge's findings. Also, the children would, in later life, know the truth about who injured them.

In the later case of *Re A (A Child)* [2015] EWFC 11, the then President of the Family Division, Sir James Munby, emphasised various fundamental points. In particular, it was for the local authority to prove, on a balance of probabilities, the facts upon which it relied. The findings of fact must be based on evidence, not suspicion or speculation. The case of *Re BR (Proof of Facts)* [2015] EWFC 41 also emphasised the need for facts to be based upon evidence and not suspicion.

11.5 Special evidence rules in child law cases

Child law cases should be non-adversarial. The focus of the case is the welfare of the child. The rules of evidence in child protection differ from other areas of law. The CA 1989 encourages admission of actions affecting the child without these becoming the basis for prosecution. In wardship proceedings the strict rules of evidence do not apply, see Butler-Sloss LJ in *Re H (Minor), Re K (Minors) (Child Abuse: Evidence)* [1989] 2 FLR 313 at

332–33. The general rules of evidence in non-child law cases render certain evidence inadmissible, i.e. that relating to character, hearsay and opinion. In child law cases this evidence is admissible, see Table 11.1.

11.5.1 Character

In child law cases, consideration of the character of those who care for the child is vitally important, and evidence of convictions and medical and psychiatric history is admissible.

11.5.2 Best evidence and hearsay

The hearsay rule provides that witnesses may only give an account of what they themselves actually experienced as evidence of the truth of the alleged event. If a witness tells the court what someone else said, the words quoted cannot be admitted as proof that the thing reported actually happened. If A tells the court that, 'On 14 July 2023, B said, "C hit me"', under the hearsay rule, this statement proves only that on that day B was alive and able to speak; that B spoke to A and that A heard his words; but it is not sufficient to prove that C did, in fact, hit B. B personally would have to come and give evidence of the event.

In children law cases, however, the court requires all relevant evidence, and in certain circumstances it admits hearsay. The wishes and feelings of children are important, and quotations from others about the child or of what the child said can be vital.

The combined effect of section 96(3) of the CA 1989, and the Children (Admissibility of Hearsay Evidence) Order 1993 (SI 1993/621) is that, in civil proceedings, evidence given in connection with the upbringing, maintenance or welfare of a child shall be admissible notwithstanding any rule of law relating to hearsay. Family proceedings are defined in sections 8(3) and 105 of the CA 1989. Section 4 of the Civil Evidence Act 1995 contains helpful criteria in the assessment of hearsay evidence. The court often requires the originals of all notes produced, including those made contemporaneously, not just the neatly typed copies made subsequently. Notes should be written up at the time or as soon as possible after the event recorded. If notes are made days after an event, their reliability may be questioned. See, in particular, the case of *Re P (Children)* [2010] EWCA Civ 672, where the Court of Appeal decided that a generalised finding can be made against the respondent in a care case. The evidence in this case took the form of the foster carer's diary, which contained statements made by the child as to allegations of sexual abuse directed towards the respondent. The court was satisfied that the diary entries were an accurate record of statements made by the child.

Table 11.1   Admissible evidence in care proceedings

ORAL EVIDENCE MAY BE GIVEN BY:		ANY WITNESS MAY PRODUCE ALL OR ANY OF THESE:	
The child	Provided that the court is satisfied on enquiry that the child understands the duty to tell the truth. Also consider *Re W* [2000] EWCA Civ 57	*Photographs*	Provided they are produced by the taker, who has unretouched the negatives and can produce the originals
Any witness of fact	Hearsay rule not applicable in family proceedings. Witness may not give opinions	*Tape recordings*	Provided they are shown to be original and not tampered with
An expert witness	May give fact and opinion, can refer to charts, notes, tables and reference works	*X-rays*	As for photographs
		Other objects	For example, clothing, weapons, are admissible provided they are relevant
		Video recordings	If they are of an incident, they are admissible as for photographs. Admissibility and content of interviews may be questioned
Notes may be used provided that		They were made contemporaneously with events or sufficiently soon thereafter for the memory of the person making the note to be clear	
Documentary evidence Proof of convictions/acquittals. Also, see rule 23.6 of the FPR 2010 about the use of plans and photographs as evidence. There are special rules for computer records. Documents copied by the children's guardian may be adduced in evidence (section 42 of the CA 1989)			
Self-producing documents			
Memorandum of conviction		Admissible under section 7(2) of the Rehabilitation of Offenders Act 1974, Schedule 13, paragraph 35 to the CA 1989 and section 73 of PACE	
Medical certificate		Admissible under section 26 of the Children and Young Persons Act 1963	

11.5.3 Opinion

Witnesses may give factual or expert evidence. Witnesses of fact may not give their opinion and are expected to restrict themselves to a full and accurate account of what happened. The court draws inferences from the facts. Experts may draw inferences, and offer opinions based on the facts, research and their own learning and experience. They should behave in a professional manner and be impartial, see Chapter 18.

11.5.4 Statements made by children's guardians

Under section 41(11)(a)–(b) of the CA 1989, the court may take account of any statement contained in the report of a children's guardian, and of any evidence given in respect of matters referred to in the guardian's report. The court has the power to regulate its own proceedings, and will assess the weight to give to such evidence. The children's guardian has access to (and may cite) local authority records, see section 42; and should draw to the attention of the court for directions any local authority papers which are relevant, but which the local authority does not intend to disclose, see *Re C (Expert Evidence: Disclosure: Practice)* [1995] 1 FLR 204.

See, in particular, FPR 2010 PD 16A. Paragraph 6.10 provides that where the children's guardian inspects records of the kinds referred to in: (a) section 42 of the CA 1989 (right to have access to local authority records); or (b) section 103 of the Adoption and Children Act 2002 (right to have access to adoption agency records), the children's guardian must bring all records and documents which may, in the opinion of the children's guardian, assist in the proper determination of the proceedings to the attention of: (a) the court; and (b) unless the court directs otherwise, the other parties to the proceedings.

11.5.5 No professional privilege for medical or psychiatric reports

Medical records must be disclosed on production of a witness summons. There is a need for full and frank disclosure of material in all matters relating to children because the welfare of the child is of paramount importance. This includes medical reports unfavourable to a client's interests, see *Essex County Council v R (A Minor)* [1993] 2 FLR 826, and *Oxfordshire County Council v M* [1994] 1 FLR 175, in which the Court of Appeal upheld this principle. Communications between lawyer and client remain privileged.

In relation to the issuing of a witness summons, rule 24.2 of the FPR 2010 provides for a witness summons to be issued by the court, requiring a witness to attend court to give evidence, or to produce documents to the court. The prescribed form is set out in FPR 2010 PDs 24A and 5A. If a person seeks to have a summons issued less than 7 days before the date of the hearing, permission of the court is required.

Also note Article 13 of the Family Procedure (Modification of Enactments) Order 2011 (SI 2011/1045), which amends the Magistrates' Courts Act 1980 so as to enable a magistrate, in family proceedings, to issue a witness summons.

11.5.6   Case management hearings – ordering the evidence

Delay must be avoided (section 1(2) of the CA 1989). Case management hearings enable the court to control the preparation of evidence and listing hearings.

In care cases, the various forms referred to in FPR 2010 PDs 12A and 5A should be used. Also, note the *Advisory Notice by Mr Justice Peel, Judge in Charge of the Standard Orders* (May 2023), which contains the updates to the *Practice Guidance: Standard Children and Other Orders* (June 2018), issued by the then President of the Family Division, Sir James Munby. These contain many standard orders for use in children proceedings, including, for example, case management orders, disclosure orders, personal protection orders and various private children law orders. All of these standard orders are available on the Courts and Tribunals Judiciary website, at www.judiciary.uk/guidance-and-resources/advisory-notice-by-mr-justice-peel-judge-in-charge-of-the-standard-orders/.

Permission of the court is required to withhold documents from a party, see the case of *A Local Authority v M & M (by their Guardian) & Others* [2009] EWHC 3172 (Fam), where Hedley J considered withholding some of the documents from the respondent father, and even providing for some documents to be redacted, but on the facts, took the more Draconian step of discharging him as a party.

Where one party seeks to prevent another from seeing a document, an application should be made on notice, see *Re M (Disclosure)* [1998] 2 FLR 1028. The directions may also stipulate the venue of any assessments to be carried out, who should accompany the child and to whom the results should be given.

In the later case of *Re X and Y (Children)* [2018] EWHC 451 (Fam), the father had been found guilty of several sexual abuse offences against his children, and was sentenced to 22 years in prison. The pre-sentence report set out that father was considered a risk of physical, sexual and emotional harm to children, and he was made subject to a sexual offences prevention order. The circumstances of the case were exceptional. The father was discharged as a party to the placement order proceedings and to the contact proceedings. This was a just and proportionate decision within the context of the Convention rights in play. Also (at [55]), the court granted the local authority declarations through the court's inherent jurisdiction, that it be absolved from various statutory obligations set out in the CA 1989 to consult, refer to and/or inform the father about aspects of the children's progress, development and/or well-being. In this context, see also the later decision in *LA v XYZ (Restriction of Father's Role in Proceedings)* [2019] EWHC 2166 (Fam).

The court's permission is required for disclosure of documents to experts unless the instruction of the expert has been directed by the court, in which case documents can be released (Part 25 of the FPR 2010 and PDs 25A and 12G).

Permission of the court is required for the disclosure of documents to a non-party, although see rules 12.70–12.75 of the FPR 2010 and PD 12G, which allow communication of information in some limited cases.

Permission of the court is required for medical or psychiatric examinations or assessments of children, pursuant to section 38(6) and (7) of the CA 1989.

See also *Re X (Disclosure for the Purposes of Criminal Proceedings)* [2008] EWHC 242 (Fam), [2008] Fam Law 725 and *Re M (Case Disclosure to Police)* [2008] Fam Law 618, Baron J. Also, in the case of *A Local Authority v DG & Others* [2014] EWHC 63 (Fam), Keehan J referred specifically to the *2013 Protocol and Good Practice Model: Disclosure of information in cases of alleged child abuse and linked criminal and care directions hearings* (October 2013) (*2013 Protocol and Good Practice Model*), which was issued by the President of the Family Division, the Senior Presiding Judge, the Director of Public Prosecutions and other bodies. This model provided guidance on the procedures to be followed when there are linked care proceedings and criminal proceedings especially in relation to applications for disclosure between the two sets of proceedings. Subsequently, in the decision of *In the matter of H (Children)* [2018] EWFC 61, the then President of the Family Division, Sir James Munby (sitting as a judge of the High Court), emphasised that various protocols had been set up over the years about sharing of information. In particular, His Lordship referred to the *2013 Protocol and Good Practice Model*. His Lordship stated that these protocols were not working as well as one would wish for them to and, therefore, there needed to be an improved understanding across the jurisdictions of how the others work, as well as introducing mechanisms to facilitate collaborative, joined-up or even joint decision-making. Subsequently, in *Lancashire County Council v A, B and Z (A Child Fact-Finding Hearing Police Disclosure)* [2018] EWHC 1819 (Fam), Knowles J (at [46]–[55]) set out some practical solutions to the problems evident in the operation of both the national and local protocols insofar as police disclosure into the family justice system is concerned. Her Ladyship stated that this guidance should be followed pending the publication of any guidance from the President of the Family Division. The *Disclosure of Information between Family and Criminal Agencies and Jurisdictions: 2024 Protocol* is now in place. This has become effective as from 1 March 2024 and it replaces the *2013 Protocol and Good Practice Model*. This new Protocol relates to all private and public family law proceedings, including contemplated public law proceedings, and all material held by the police. The Protocol is in three parts, namely: Part A (disclosure from the police to family proceedings), Part B (disclosure sought by an investigator) and Part C (linked directions hearings). As many practitioners will be aware, under the *2013 Protocol and Good Practice Model*, it was common to complete the Annex H police disclosure order, which would typically invite the police to provide disclosure within 28 days. The new Protocol requires the completion of the form at Annex 1, and the local authority is required to review any police information and material already in its possession as standard practice before making any requests to the police for information. Paragraphs 1.3–1.4 of the Protocol provide that at the outset of contemplated public law proceedings, where the local authority representative believes that there will be police material relevant to the central issues in the case, he or she must notify the police of the existence of contemplated proceedings/ongoing proceedings and seek relevant material by submitting the form at Annex 1 to the police. The police will respond by providing disclosure, as a general rule, within 20 business days, unless an alternative timescale is negotiated and approved by the court. Paragraph 1.6 of the Protocol provides that in private law proceedings, representatives must complete the form at Annex 1 when instructed to do so by the court, and that all Annex 1 applications must be submitted to police with a copy of the Annex 5. Without this, applications for disclosure will be rejected. The police will respond by providing disclosure as soon as reasonably possible.

Expert witnesses are widely used, and advocates build up good working relationships with them. See Chapter 18 for instruction of experts, judicial guidance, how to find the right expert and resource issues. Before the CMH (where there may be an application made for the instruction of an expert), the advocate should ascertain whether experts are available, how long assessments will take, cost, public funding position, and any assistance the experts may require. The expert should confirm availability, enabling the court to fix a suitable hearing date for issues resolution. See, in particular, Part 25 of the FPR 2010 and PDs 25A–25D, which set out the provisions surrounding instruction of experts in cases. See also the Legal Aid Agency, *Guidance on the Remuneration of Expert Witnesses in Family Cases*

(September 2022, Version 7), available at https://assets.publishing. service.gov.uk/media/6332c60ee90e0711d00beda9/Guidance_on_ the_Remuneration_of_Expert_Witnessesv7.pdf (and watch for any subsequent amendments). This guidance sets out, amongst other things, the rates of payment for expert services.

11.6 Court procedure at the hearing

Procedure is addressed separately in the chapters dealing with each order. However, hearings follow a reasonably consistent pattern common to most applications under the CA 1989.

11.6.1 Notes of evidence

Rule 23.9 of the FPR 2010 provides that in proceedings in a Family Court, before a lay justice or lay justices, the court shall keep a note of the substance of the oral evidence given at a directions appointment or at a hearing of any proceedings.

11.6.2 Order of evidence

Part 22 of the FPR 2010 sets out specific issues and requirements relevant to evidence.

In particular, rule 22.1 of the FPR 2010 provides for the court to control the evidence by giving directions as to:

- the issues on which it would seek evidence to be provided;
- the nature of the evidence which it requires, in order to decide the issues; and
- the way it was going to be placed before the court.

It is therefore very important for legal representatives to have a clear idea of which witnesses they would wish to attend court and why. For example, is the witness required for purposes of giving evidence on threshold, contact or disposal? It should always be ensured that consideration is given to whether the evidence of the witness can be agreed, in order to avoid the witness being called, in accordance with the overriding objective under Part 1 of the FPR 2010. Therefore, at the IRH (the purpose of which is to narrow down the salient issues in the case, and even finalising the case), legal representatives should be prepared and clear about which witnesses are to be called and what they will go on to prove. In this context, it is important to note the use of rule 25.10, relating to the use of written questions to court directed experts. Rule 25.10 provides that unless the court directs otherwise, or a practice direction provides otherwise, the written questions must be proportionate, may be put once only, must be put within 10 days beginning with the date on which the expert's report was served, and must be for the purpose only of clarification of the report. By using this provision, it may result in narrowing down the issue(s) in dispute, and potentially avoiding the need for the expert to attend court for the purposes of cross-examination. Rule 22.4 sets out the format of a witness statement, and in particular that it needs to comply with PD 22A. It must also contain a statement of truth (PD 17A).

Rule 22.1 of the FPR 2010 allows the court to exclude evidence that would otherwise be admissible and can limit the cross-examination (rule 22.4).

Unless the courts create a variation of procedure, the order of evidence in a care matter tends to be as follows:

(a)   applicant;

(b)   any party with parental responsibility for the child;

(c)   other respondents (including a child who is separately represented);

(d)   the children's guardian;

(e)   the child, if he is not a party and there is no children's guardian. (This is a situation mainly relevant to private law cases, since in most cases under Part IV of the CA 1989 there is a children's guardian appointed and a child of sufficient age to instruct a lawyer separately will be a party.)

11.6.3   Extent of evidence

There are some limitations on the courts regulating their own proceedings. They may hear some evidence, even if the matter is agreed. It is not normally sufficient to file statements and to rely on these to support a case, calling no oral evidence at all, although this may occur in some circumstances.

In *Re F (Minor) (Care Order: Procedure)* [1994] 1 FLR 240, a magistrates' court which had heard evidence from the local authority but refused to hear the evidence of the father was held to be wrong. The justices should have heard the evidence from both sides. In *S v Merton London Borough Council* [1994] 1 FCR 186, an FPC, as it was then, was criticised for making its decision on submissions only, and it was held that some evidence at least is required. See Munby J (as he was then) on bundles in *Re X and Y (Court Bundles)* [2008] EWHC 2058 (Fam).

Consider rule 22.2 of the FPR 2010, which provides that, generally, any fact which needs to be proved by the evidence of witnesses is to be proved: (a) at the final hearing, by their oral evidence; and (b) at any other hearing, by their evidence in writing. There is an exception to this rule, however, where it is stated that the general rule does not apply to applications under Part 12 for secure accommodation orders, interim care orders, interim supervision orders, or where an enactment provides otherwise. One particular example referred to is in the case of an application for an emergency protection order, whereby section 45(7) of the CA 1989 provides that the evidence may be take into account when the court is hearing an application.

11.6.4   Case management hearing/issues resolution hearing: key checklist matters for advocate to consider

- List of witnesses.
- Dates to avoid (prior engagements of):
    - parties;
    - witnesses of fact;
    - expert witnesses;
    - advocate.
- Information and assistance for court proceedings:
    - reference material;
    - exhibits;
    - intermediary/lay advocate;
    - support advocate;
    - interpreter;
    - visual aids in court;
    - live/video links; tape recorder/player;
    - security;
    - wheelchair access;
    - hearing loop.
- Information for expert witnesses:
    - documents in case;
    - exhibits to be sent to expert or in expert's possession;
    - chronology;
    - arrangements for conference/meeting of experts.

- Permission of the court or consents necessary:
  - disclosure of documents, information, exhibits;
  - medical or psychiatric examinations and their venue, who will accompany child, to whom results are to be given;
  - bloods, swabs, hair strand, fingernail, scram (secure continuous remote alcohol monitor) bracelet;
  - other special testing;
  - excuse party/child attendance at court;
  - accommodation of child;
  - withholding information from party (inherent jurisdiction declaration).
- Statements and reports to be filed with the court:
  - parties; witnesses; experts; chronology; reports; other;
  - documents from files, statements or reports;
  - consent of the court required for late filing and reliance upon.
- Service:
  - applicant and parties; those entitled to notice of the proceedings; those entitled to be respondents; children's guardian; others.

11.7   Courtroom skills

11.7.1   Court manners

Proceedings are non-adversarial, and in an inevitably emotional situation, a calm advocate can assist everyone greatly in family proceedings. Forms of address are set out in Table 11.2.

As a result of the Covid-19 pandemic, and the consequential lockdowns, there was a need to ensure that court hearings were still being conducted to meet demand. Many hearings became remote and even after the series of lockdowns and after the recovery period, various types of hearings across England and Wales are still being conducted remotely, when appropriate to do so. In the Practice Guidance, *COVID 19: National Guidance for the Family Court*, dated 19 March 2020, the President had set out the procedure for Family Court hearings to take place remotely, either via email, telephone, video or Skype. Where the requirements of fairness and justice required a court-based hearing, and it was safe to conduct one, then a court-based hearing should take place. There were also the various updated versions of the *Remote Access Family Court Guidance*, constantly updated by Mr Justice MacDonald. At the time of writing, dependent on where one practises, there may still be many types of hearings that are run remotely.

Table 11.2   Judiciary and legal representatives – forms of address

Level	*Forms of address*
Magistrates/lay justices	Your Worship, Sir or Madam (usually pronounced Ma'am)
Legal adviser	Sir or Madam (pronounced Ma'am)
Deputy/District Judge	Judge
Recorder	Your Honour
Circuit Judge	Your Honour
High Court and Court of Appeal Judges	My Lord or My Lady (usually pronounced by the Bar as M' Lord or M' Lady)
Barristers	'My (learned) friend, counsel for X or Mr, Mrs or Ms ...' etc
Solicitors, chartered legal executives, and other legal representatives (referring to each other)	'My friend, legal representative for X or Mr, Mrs or Ms ...' etc

Whether in-person or remote, children cases are almost always listed just by the court case reference number or otherwise anonymised. It is therefore essential to be familiar with the case number. When conducting remote hearings, ensure that you and your client have good access to the internet, are in a private setting and have an efficient means of taking instructions. Clients need to be aware that hearings held remotely are just as formal as those held in person.

If conducting an in-person hearing, we would advise that you should greet other parties and advocates on arrival at court, letting the court usher know of your arrival. Ushers will enter the names of everyone present on their court list, noting who are the parties, advocates and witnesses.

In court, stand while the judge or magistrates enter the room, and wait for them to be seated before sitting down yourself. Figure 11.1 illustrates a typical courtroom layout and seating when appearing before lay justices. The court may conduct their proceedings seated. Check with the legal adviser to the court or the usher. The general rule is that advocates or witnesses should stand whilst speaking or when giving evidence, until invited to sit.

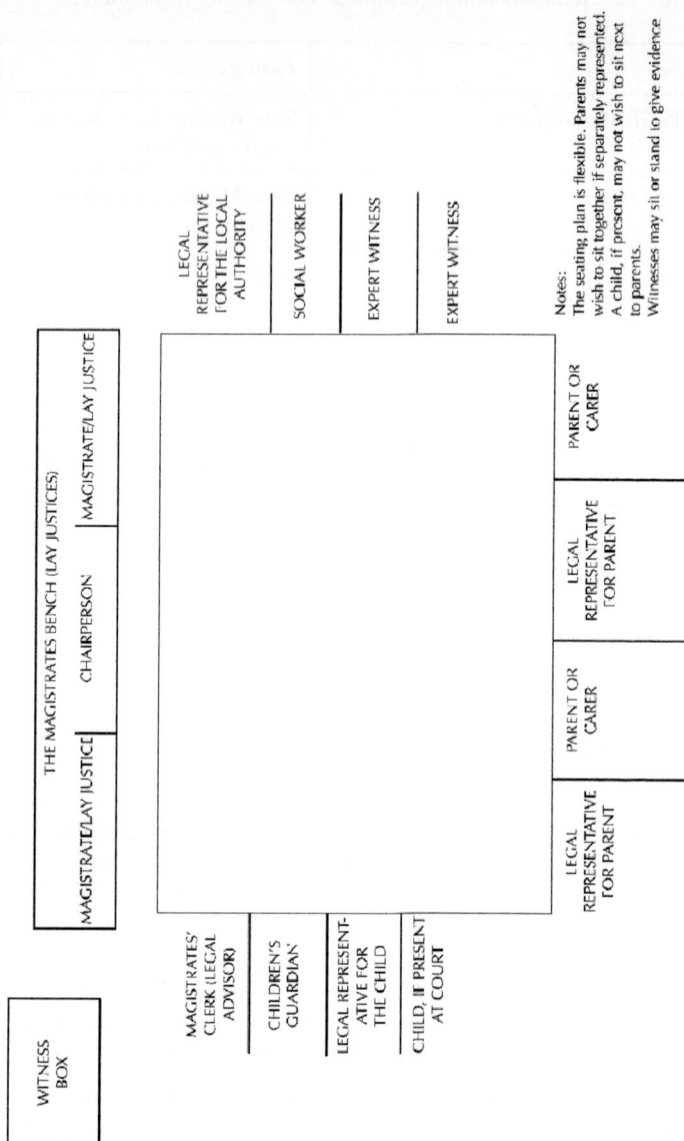

THE MAGISTRATES BENCH (LAY JUSTICES)

MAGISTRATE/LAY JUSTICE | CHAIRPERSON | MAGISTRATE/LAY JUSTICE

WITNESS BOX

MAGISTRATES' CLERK (LEGAL ADVISOR)

CHILDREN'S GUARDIAN

LEGAL REPRESENTATIVE FOR THE CHILD

CHILD, IF PRESENT AT COURT

LEGAL REPRESENTATIVE FOR THE LOCAL AUTHORITY

SOCIAL WORKER

EXPERT WITNESS

EXPERT WITNESS

LEGAL REPRESENTATIVE FOR PARENT

PARENT OR CARER

LEGAL REPRESENTATIVE FOR PARENT

PARENT OR CARER

Notes:
The seating plan is flexible. Parents may not wish to sit together if separately represented. A child, if present, may not wish to sit next to parents.
Witnesses may sit or stand to give evidence

Figure 11.1   Layout of typical case before lay justices (magistrates)

The applicant's advocate usually introduces other advocates and the parties to the court, or sometimes the judge or magistrate may invite people to introduce themselves. To be prepared, check the names of parties, other advocates and witnesses before going into court.

The task of an advocate is to present the facts and the law to the court and to put forward to the court his or her client's point of view in a reasoned and courteous manner. In children and family cases, questioning should be to elicit clarity and detail, and not be belligerent or adversarial. Advocates will therefore be asking questions of witnesses to clarify statements filed with the court or to elicit new information. A good tip for advocates is not to ask questions to which the answer is unknown (unless, of course, such a question is absolutely necessary), otherwise, be prepared for surprises in the answer.

Do not interrupt another advocate or witness when they are addressing the court. Allow them to finish what they are saying, then request the court's permission to correct any factual or legal errors. Do not interrupt an advocate who is asking questions, wait, let the advocate finish and then speak.

Advise witnesses that, when giving evidence, they should turn slightly to face the bench/judge and maintain eye contact with the judge or the magistrates, while addressing all answers to them (rather than looking back towards the advocate asking the questions). This is not only good court practice, but it also very effectively prevents advocates from interrupting the witness's evidence, as to do so would then seem discourteous to the judge or magistrates. If an over-enthusiastic or aggressive advocate interrupts before a witness has said all that he wanted to, advise the witness to turn to the judge or bench and say, politely, that before he answers the new question, he would first like to finish the point that he wanted to make in response to the original question.

Making audible comments or critical 'asides' in court to other advocates, parties or others is not acceptable, and is unprofessional.

Outside the courtroom, maintain quiet, professional courtesy to everyone. Remember that the parties are likely to be under stress and be aware of their feelings. Loud conversations between advocates discussing the case, comments about others, jokes, holiday memories and personal family/pet anecdotes are not professionally appropriate.

If a client wishes to say something to his or her advocate in the courtroom as the evidence unfolds, the client should do so quietly, and if it is necessary to have a longer conversation, an adjournment may be sought to take instructions.

If using hard copies of documents, bring to court sufficient spare copies of documents and draft orders for the court and all the parties and witnesses who may need to have one. The original goes to the judge or bench. If there are magistrates, each should have a copy if possible. If you are typing up the case management order on your laptop, tablet or other electronic device, it is important to ensure that you can email it into the court, and to the other parties, so that everyone can consider carefully the contents of the proposed order before it is approved by the court. The order will need to be uploaded on the family law portal through the MyHMCTS portal.

The examination of witnesses follows the order of evidence. Each witness is called to the witness box, sworn in by the usher or legal adviser (or requested to affirm) and then examined in chief. Questions which suggest an answer are 'leading questions' and are generally forbidden in examination in chief; one must not 'lead the witness'. For example, ask 'What time of day was it when … ?' not 'Was it three o'clock when … ?'.

In relation to litigants in person, note the guidance in *Litigants in person: guidelines for lawyers* (Bar Council, CILEX and the Law Society, 2015). It provides practical advice to lawyers and litigants in person, particularly, when lawyers face litigants in person in the civil courts and tribunals. The guidelines discuss the relationship between the client's interest and the interests of the administration of justice, and the extent to which a lawyer can properly provide assistance to a litigant in person. The guidelines also discuss the role of McKenzie Friends. Also see the *Advice for Litigants in Person* guidance on the Courts and Tribunals Judiciary website issued in June 2022. This provides particular guidance for litigants in person on telephone and video hearings.

The other parties may then cross-examine the witness, for example to test the evidence or to check facts, and the party calling the witness may re-examine to clarify points already made. One may not usually raise new evidence in re-examination unless with the permission of the court. The court should then be offered the opportunity to ask any questions of the witness that it wishes. If the witness is not likely to be required further, permission of the court is required to discharge the witness before he or she leaves the court. Some witnesses, particularly experts, may be asked to remain either in court, on the premises or 'on call' in case they are needed again.

Traditionally, the applicant opens the case and outlines his or her case to the court. The other parties then have the opportunity to make a speech to the court, but they will usually do so at the end of the case. The children's guardian or the child's advocate will often be the last to speak.

If there are submissions on law during the case, the order of address follows the order of evidence.

When the case is completed, the court should stand for the magistrates or judge to leave the room.

These notes are necessarily brief, but there are many good books and courses on advocacy. By far the best way of learning courtroom skills is to sit in on cases (with the permission of the court and the parties) alongside experienced advocates, some of whom will be on the Law Society Children Law Accredited Scheme, so as to learn by observation – not necessarily to copy their style. You will, over time and with practice, develop your own individual strengths and skills as an advocate, and become efficient, confident and a cogent professional.

11.8   Transparency

11.8.1   Media attendance and reporting hearings

Accredited representatives of the media (journalists) and duly authorised lawyers (legal bloggers) are entitled to attend most types of Family Court hearings about children, although held in private. This is set out in rule 27.11 of the FPR 2010 and PD 27B. However, these reporters are not normally permitted to publish information relating to the proceedings without first obtaining leave of the court, in accordance with section 12 of the Administration of Justice Act 1960.

These statutory reporting restrictions have meant that reporters rarely attend. However, following the Transparency Review conducted by the President of the Family Division which reported in October 2021, a Reporting Pilot began in three courts (Cardiff, Carlisle and Leeds) where reporters who attended could publish information about cases, subject to a transparency order that ensures anonymity and non-identification of children. On 15 May 2023, the pilot was extended to private children law in those three courts. In January 2024, this pilot was extended to 16 more courts with regard to public law hearings before judges. At the time of writing, it is anticipated that this pilot will be incrementally rolled out to more courts across England and Wales in the next few years, including hearings before magistrates. It is therefore important to be aware that there may be reporters at a hearing and that children's privacy rights should be considered, in the context of the aspiration for more openness in family justice. The Transparency Project, a legal educational charity that legal bloggers can write for, has guides for pilot courts and others available on its website, such as, 'What to do if a reporter attends your hearing'.

11.8.2   Objections to attendance

Parties who want to raise objections to reporters' attendance at hearings need to satisfy the court that exclusion is necessary, in the interests of any child concerned in, or connected with, the proceedings; for the safety or protection of a party, a witness in the proceedings or a person connected with such a party or witness; or for the orderly conduct of the proceedings; or justice will otherwise be impeded or prejudiced (rule 27.11(3) of the FPR 2010). Where a request for leave to publish is made, or there is consideration of relaxing or further restricting the standard transparency order in a Reporting Pilot court, the court will balance the rights of privacy of individuals in the case with the media's rights of freedom of expression, under Articles 8 and 10 of the ECHR.

It should also be noted that parents should not share information about their cases under the Administration of Justice Act 1960 unless they are consulting lawyers or other people who are helping them, under a list of exemptions in rules 12.73 and 12.75 of the FPR 2010. There is some relaxation of this rule in Reporting Pilot courts if parents are speaking to reporters. In all cases brought under section 97(2) of the CA 1989, individual children are prohibited from being publicly identified while they are subject to proceedings. However, anonymising a child does not allow the sharing of information under section 12 of the Administration of Justice Act 1960 if the exemptions or permissions are not in place.

Judgments in the higher courts (and sometimes at circuit judge and district judge level) may be published on The National Archives website 'Find case law' and on the BAILII website, but children will normally be anonymised. Practitioners acting for children should therefore always bear in mind the possibilities of publication and its impact, whether in the media or through judgments. On 19 June 2024, the President issued new judicial guidance on anonymisation and publication, which can be found on the Courts and Tribunals Judiciary website.

12 Children's Rights

The law affecting the rights of children includes the CA 1989, the UN Convention on the Rights of the Child (UNCRC) (ratified by the United Kingdom in 1991) and the Human Rights Act 1998 (in force in the United Kingdom from 2 October 2000), which incorporates the ECHR and its Protocols into UK law. Other legislation affords specific rights to children and families, for example in mental health, and is cited below where relevant.

Under section 22(4) of the Human Rights Act 1998, all proceedings brought by a public authority are subject to the ECHR, even where the alleged breach of these rights occurred before the coming into force of the Human Rights Act 1998.

12.1 To accept or refuse medical treatment

No adult or child competent to make their own medical decisions may be given medical treatment without their consent. Treatment without consent (save in emergencies) may incur liability for damages for assault or constitute an offence in criminal law. Detention in hospital or any other place without consent could constitute an unlawful DoL in breach of Article 5 of the ECHR. The law on DoL is discussed in Chapter 8.

It is important to make a clear distinction between two situations in which consent may be required. The first is where doctors seek to carry out diagnostic assessments which may be necessary before deciding on the best method of treatment, and/or medical, psychiatric or psychological treatments necessary to maintain the child's health and welfare. The second category is where medical, psychiatric or psychological assessments are sought for purely forensic purposes and directed by the court.

Depending on the child's age and other considerations, in special circumstances the courts may overrule a child's refusal of necessary treatment, but the courts will be far less willing to overrule a child's refusal of an assessment for forensic purposes.

The issue, therefore, is at what age can a child give valid consent?

12.1.1   Children aged over 16 (but under 18)

Under section 8 of the Family Law Reform Act 1969, at the age of 16, a young person gains the right to give informed consent to surgical, medical or dental treatment. Examinations or assessments must impliedly be included. The consent of the young person is as valid as that of an adult. Under the Mental Capacity Act 2005, like adults, 16- and 17-year-olds are presumed to have decision-making capacity, unless it is established that they are unable to make decisions for themselves in relation to the matter because of an impairment of, or a disturbance in the functioning of, the mind or brain.

If a young person consents to recommended medical or dental treatment, therefore (even if his or her parents disagreed for some reason), the medical or dental practitioner would be protected from a claim for damages for trespass to the person.

However, if the young person refuses the recommended treatment – although those with parental responsibility for the young person may give a valid consent which will have the effect of protecting the medical or dental practitioner from claims for damages for trespass to the person – it should be noted that as the age of the young person increases towards 18, his or her refusal and the reasons for it are important considerations for parents and the court.

In the event of a dispute about consent for medical treatment, the issue should be taken before the High Court, either under its inherent jurisdiction or under section 8 of the CA 1989 for a specific issue order. For example, in a case where over-16s were refusing blood transfusions on religious grounds, their lack of consent was overruled by the High Court exercising its inherent jurisdiction, a decision upheld by the Court of Appeal in *E v Northern Care Alliance NHS Foundation Trust* [2021] EWCA Civ 1888, [2022] 1 FLR 1255.

In circumstances requiring sterilisation, termination of a pregnancy or surgical interventions to save or prolong the child's life, if the child is a ward of court, the High Court's consent is required.

If parents refuse to allow medical treatment and the child needs it, the High Court can provide the requisite authority under its inherent jurisdiction.

Changes made to section 131 of the Mental Health Act 1983 by section 43 of the Mental Health Act 2007 mean that when a young person of 16 or 17 has capacity (as defined in the Mental Capacity Act 2005) and does not consent to admission for treatment for mental disorder (because he or she is overwhelmed, does not want to consent or refuses to consent), he or she cannot then be admitted informally on the basis of the consent of a person with parental responsibility (see *Mental Health Act 1983: Code of Practice* (DoH, 2015), Chapter 19).

12.1.2   Children aged under 16

The legal situation for consent by children aged under 16 but who are judged to be '*Gillick* competent' is similar to that for young people aged over 16, described in para 12.1.1. For those who are not considered to be '*Gillick* competent', decisions concerning medical treatment are made for them by those with parental responsibility and, where necessary, the courts will intervene or assist in the ways described above.

In *Gillick v West Norfolk and Wisbech Area Health Authority* [1986] AC 112, the House of Lords formulated the concept now known colloquially as '*Gillick* competence' in which the ability of a child under 16 to make her own medical decisions is evaluated according to chronological age considered in conjunction with the child's mental and emotional maturity, intelligence and comprehension.

Lord Scarman made it clear in the *Gillick* case that:

> It will be a question of fact whether a child seeking advice has sufficient understanding of what is involved to give a consent valid in law. Until the child achieves the capacity to consent, the parental right to make the decision continues save only in exceptional circumstances. Emergency, parental neglect, abandonment of the child, or inability to find the parent are examples of exceptional situations.

'*Gillick* competence' has been reviewed in a number of subsequent cases. A notable case was *R (Axon) v Secretary of State for Health* [2006] EWHC 37 (Admin), in which a mother challenged through judicial review the Department of Health guidance for confidentiality on the issue of the provision of abortion for her daughter aged 15, without the mother's knowledge. The court held that the *Gillick* decision remained authoritative as to the lawfulness of the provision by health care professionals of confidential advice and treatment to young people under 16, without parental knowledge or consent. The *Gillick* guidelines must, however, be strictly observed.

In *Re S (Minor) (Refusal of Treatment)* [1995] 1 FCR 604, it was held that a girl of almost 16 suffering from thalassaemia major should continue with her treatment, despite her refusal to do so on religious grounds. The discontinuance of treatment would have resulted in her death within a few weeks. The court acknowledged that at 18 she could refuse and effectively end her life, but expressed the hope that in the intervening period she might change her mind or that gene therapy would relieve her condition.

See also *Re L (Medical Treatment: Gillick Competency)* [1998] 2 FLR 810 and *Re M (Child: Refusal of Medical Treatment)* [1999] 2 FCR 577, where a heart transplant was authorised for a 15-year-old girl.

Understanding the potential consequences of refusing treatment or assessment increases with the child's age, maturity, intelligence and level of understanding, influenced by the detail of the information provided. The *Reference Guide to Consent for Examination or Treatment* (DoH, 2nd edn, 2009), pages 32–38 should be consulted.

Where a child under the age of 16 lacks capacity to consent (i.e. is not '*Gillick* competent'), consent may be given on the child's behalf by any one person with parental responsibility if the matter is within the scope of parental responsibility (formerly termed the 'zone of parental control' as defined by the Mental Health Act 1983) or by the court. The scope of parental responsibility is explained in the *Mental Health Act 1983: Code of Practice* (DoH, 2015), Chapter 19. Those giving consent on behalf of child patients must have the capacity to consent to the intervention in question, be acting voluntarily and be appropriately informed. The best interests of the child must be a significant consideration when exercising the power to consent. Even where a child lacks capacity to consent on his or her own behalf, it is good practice to involve the child as much as possible in the decision-making process.

Where necessary, the courts have power to overrule the refusal by a person with parental responsibility for any necessary mental or medical assessment and/or treatment of a child. Certain important decisions, such as sterilisation for contraceptive purposes, should be referred to the courts for guidance, even if those with parental responsibility have given consent for the operation.

For medical and psychiatric treatment in the context of supervision orders, see para 12.2.1.

12.1.3   Children who lack capacity to make a decision

Where a child is unable to make a legally valid decision for himself because he is not *Gillick* competent or lacks capacity under the Mental Capacity Act 2005, the High Court in its inherent jurisdiction may consent on the child's behalf. The High Court may order reasonable force to be used to ensure compliance with necessary treatment, see *A Metropolitan Borough Council v DB* [1997] 1 FLR 767.

Where a child under 18 lacks capacity to consent to being detained for social care reasons, the Supreme Court has held that consent of the child's parents is not sufficient to avoid this being a DoL (*Re D (A Child)* [2019] UKSC 42, [2020] 1 FLR 549). A local authority with parental responsibility for a child could not deprive the child of his liberty without court authority. If the restrictions on the child's liberty fell within normal parental control for a child of that age, they would not require a DoL authorisation, but if restrictions went beyond normal parental control, the court's authorisation was required. The law on DoL is discussed in Chapter 8.

12.1.4 Where no available person has parental responsibility

In situations where an immediate decision or action is needed and no one with parental responsibility is available, section 3(5) of the CA 1989 provides:

> a person who:
>
> > (a) does not have parental responsibility for a particular child; but
> >
> > (b) has care of the child,
>
> may ... do what is reasonable in all the circumstances of the case for the purpose of safeguarding or promoting the child's welfare.

This section is intended for use by neighbours, relatives or others, such as foster carers, looking after children who may need to take the child urgently to the GP or dentist, but should not be used to give consent for major medical decisions.

12.2 To accept or refuse medical or psychiatric assessment

Child protection often necessitates medical or psychiatric examination or assessment. The *Report of the Inquiry into Child Abuse in Cleveland* (HMSO, 1987) demonstrated that repeated medical examinations can themselves be abusive. The court has wide power to set limits by directions, for example, the place and time of an examination, person(s) to be present, person(s) to conduct the examination and person(s) or authorities to whom the results shall be given.

12.2.1 Circumstances in which the court may direct medical or psychiatric examination or assessment which the child has a right to refuse

In the following circumstances, a child of sufficient understanding has the right to refuse to consent to medical or psychiatric examination:

(a) interim care order (section 38(6) of the CA 1989);

(b) interim supervision order (section 38(6));

(c) emergency protection order (section 44(6)(b) and (7));

(d) child assessment order (section 43(8)).

In supervision orders, the child may be directed to undergo a medical, but not a psychiatric, examination, but (where the child has sufficient understanding to exercise his right of consent) the court may make this direction only if the child consents (Schedule 3, paragraph 4 to the CA 1989). The court may order psychiatric or medical treatment of a child under a supervision order in specified circumstances and consent is required of a child who has sufficient understanding to exercise his or her right of consent (Schedule 3, paragraph 5).

Doctors must check whether the child is capable of giving an informed decision, and that he consents, before proceeding with an examination. Even if the court has directed an examination with the child's consent, if, when the child is with the doctor he then refuses, the doctor should not proceed, but should refer the matter back to the court. If the court agrees that this is an informed decision, then usually the court will respect the refusal. In one case where the refusal to attend a psychiatric assessment ordered under section 38(6) of the CA 1989 placed a 15-year-old in serious danger, the High Court invoked the inherent jurisdiction to overrule the refusal in the child's best interests (*South Glamorgan County Council v W and B* [1993] 1 FLR 574).

12.3   To make his or her own application to the court

Under section 10(8) of the CA 1989, children of sufficient age and understanding may make their own applications for section 8 orders, with leave of the court.

Following *Re SC (Minor) (Leave to Seek Residence Order)* [1994] 1 FLR 96, where the child is the applicant, his welfare is paramount because the provisions of section 10(9) of the CA 1989 do not apply. (Section 10(9) sets out the criteria for the court's consideration in granting leave for all other applicants, and it has been held that the child's welfare is not paramount in those applications.) Also, everyone with parental responsibility for the child should have notice of the application, see Chapter 13, para 13.2.2.

Children may seek other orders under the CA 1989, with leave, including discharge of:

- care;

- supervision;

- emergency protection;

- section 8 orders;
- parental responsibility orders;
- parental responsibility agreements.

The decision as to whether a child is of sufficient age and understanding to apply is a matter initially for the solicitor instructed by the child, but ultimately for the court to decide, see *Re CT (Minor) (Wardship: Representation)* [1993] 2 FLR 278. The court can appoint a children's guardian for the child under rule 16.4 of the FPR 2010 or a litigation friend, usually the Official Solicitor, under rules 16.5–16.16 and PD 16.

12.4 To request confidentiality and, in the event of disagreement with the children's guardian, to instruct a solicitor separately

Where a child is subject to care or supervision applications, the child has a solicitor appointed for him or her by the children's guardian or the court. The child's solicitor takes instructions from the children's guardian and from the child. A child of sufficient age and understanding may request client confidentiality with his or her solicitor on specific issues or generally.

A child of sufficient age and understanding may disagree with the recommendations of the children's guardian, remaining a party with his own solicitor. The guardian will notify the court and continue unrepresented or appoint another solicitor. The procedure is governed by rule 16.29(2)–(3) of the FPR 2010. The ethics, duties and responsibilities of the solicitor for the child are discussed in Chapter 15.

A court's assessment of whether the child has the ability to instruct a solicitor will be case-specific and based on a broad consideration of all relevant factors and any opinions from solicitors and experts. It should not be driven by welfare factors or by a theoretical comparison between protection and autonomy, but by a practical assessment of the child's understanding. There are no legal presumptions for or against separate representation (*Re C (Child: Ability to Instruct a Solicitor)* [2023] EWCA Civ 889).

12.5 Rights of a child in care

Rights of children who are looked after by the local authority are covered in Chapter 7.

12.6   UN Convention on the Rights of the Child

The UNCRC has been ratified by the UK government but is not incorporated into UK law. This means that it is persuasive on the courts rather than binding in the same way as is the ECHR. In Wales, government ministers and local authorities are obliged to pay due regard to the UNCRC when making decisions that affect children (Rights of Children and Young Persons (Wales) Measure 2011; SSW(W)A 2014). Article 12 of the UNCRC states that children who are capable of forming their own views have a right to express these in matters affecting them and to have due weight placed on their views in accordance with their age and maturity, in particular, to be heard in any judicial or administrative proceedings affecting them. This Article is increasingly cited in the courts as reflecting awareness of taking young people's own views into account, for example, *Mabon v Mabon* [2005] EWCA Civ 634.

13 Other Orders available to the Court in Family Proceedings

The CA 1989 empowers the court to make certain orders of its own volition in 'family proceedings', defined in section 8(3) and as including Parts I, II and III; the Matrimonial Causes Act 1973; the Family Law Act 1996; the Adoption and Children Act 2002; and others. There is a menu of orders available in family proceedings (see Table 13.1) from which the court may choose, subject to the principles of section 1 of the CA 1989. Note that the court should make no order unless it is necessary for the welfare of the child, see Chapter 2. The court cannot, however, intervene in family proceedings to impose orders for care, supervision, secure accommodation, emergency protection or child assessment, in the absence of an application by a local authority.

13.1 Orders in family proceedings

Family assistance orders require no application, but the parties must agree to their making. Special guardianship orders may be made of the court's own volition, but require the consent of the person in whose favour the order is made, see Chapter 3.

13.2 Section 8 orders

Section 8(1) of the CA 1989 created the original section 8 orders: contact, prohibited steps, residence and specific issue, all available in all family proceedings. In April 2014, orders for contact or residence were replaced by child arrangements orders. Child arrangements orders regulate arrangements relating to where, when, and with whom a child is to live, spend time or otherwise have contact. The court may regulate, on an application or of its own volition, the child's residence and contact with others; prohibit specified steps without leave of the court; and deal with any specific issues arising in the child's upbringing.

Table 13.1   Menu of orders available in family proceedings

Family proceedings (section 8(4) of the CA 1989)	Orders available without application	Orders available only by application
Any proceedings under the inherent jurisdiction of the High Court in relation to children	Child arrangements orders, specific issue or prohibited steps – if no care order in force (section 8 of the CA 1989)	Application by father, second female parent or step-parent for parental responsibility (section 4 of the CA 1989)
Parts I, II and IV of the CA 1989	Guardianship (section 5 of the CA 1989)	Termination of parental responsibility (section 4 of the CA 1989)
Matrimonial Causes Act 1973		Financial provision (section 15 of the CA 1989)
Schedule 5 to the Civil Partnership Act 2004	Family assistance orders (section 16 of the CA 1989)	Care or supervision (section 31 of the CA 1989)
Adoption and Children Act 2002	Direction to the local authority to investigate (section 37 of the CA 1989)	Education supervision (section 36 of the CA 1989)
Domestic Proceedings and Magistrates' Court Act 1978		Child assessment (section 43 of the CA 1989)
Schedule 6 to the Civil Partnership Act 2004	Welfare report (section 7 of the CA 1989)	Emergency protection (section 44 of the CA 1989)
Part III of the Matrimonial and Family Proceedings Act 1984	Special guardianship (section 14A of the CA 1989)	
Family Law Act 1996		

Sections 11 and 12 of the Crime and Disorder Act 1998	Direction to the local authority to investigate (section 37 of the CA 1989) Non-molestation order (section 42 of the Family Law Act 1996) Exclusion requirement (section 38A or section 44A of the CA 1989)	Recovery order (section 50 of the CA 1989) Child arrangements order regarding with whom the child will live, where there is a care order in force (section 8 of the CA 1989) Adoption and placement orders (Adoption and Children Act 2002) Occupation order (sections 33–38 of the Family Law Act 1996) Child safety order (sections 11 and 12 of the Crime and Disorder Act 1998)

Some applicants are entitled to apply, and others must first seek the leave of the court. The following are entitled under section 10 of the CA 1989 to apply for any section 8 order:

(a)   any parent or guardian, or special guardian of a child, section 10(4)(a) (this will include the unmarried father of a child whether or not he has parental responsibility); and section 10(4)(aa), any person who by virtue of section 4A has parental responsibility for the child;

(b)   any person in whose favour a child arrangements order, specifying living with, or an older residence order, is in force with respect to the child, section 10(4)(b).

The following are entitled to apply for child arrangements orders (but not a prohibited steps order or a specific issue order):

(a)   any party to a marriage or civil partnership (whether or not subsisting) in relation to whom the child is a child of the family, section 10(5)(a) (this provision enables a step-parent to seek an order);

(b)   any person with whom the child has lived for a period of at least 3 years, section 10(5)(b) (section 10(10) provides that the 3-year period need not be continuous but must have begun not more than 5 years before, or ended more than 3 months before, the making of the application);

(c)   any person who:

(i)   in any case where a child arrangements order in force with respect to the child regulates arrangements relating to with whom the child is to live or when the child is to live with any person, has the consent of each of the persons named in the order as a person with whom the child is to live;

(ii)   in any case where the child is in the care of a local authority, has the consent of that authority; or

(iii) in any other case, has the consent of each of those (if any) who have parental responsibility for the child.

(d)   any person who has parental responsibility for the child by virtue of provision made under section 12(2A).

Under sections 10(5A) and 10(5B) of the CA 1989, added by the CYPA 2008, respectively, a relative of a child is entitled to apply for a child arrangements order regulating with whom the child will live if the child has lived with the relative for a period of at least one year immediately preceding the application.

13.2.1 Leave to apply

Any other person needs leave to apply for an order under section 8 of the CA 1989, including the child. The court must be satisfied that a child applicant has sufficient understanding to make the proposed application (section 10(8)). FPR 2010 PD 16A sets out matters which the court will take into consideration when deciding if it is in the child's best interests to be made a party under rule 16.2. An application for a child arrangements order, specifying living with, in respect of a child who is subject to a care order, if successful, would have the effect of discharging the care order.

Note that in *Re A (Care: Discharge Application by a Child)* [1995] 2 FCR 686, Thorpe J held that a child's application to discharge care was not one which required leave of the court. See also *Re W (A Child) (Care Proceedings: Child's Representation)* [2016] EWCA Civ 1051, [2017] 2 FLR 199 regarding a child's own application.

13.2.2 Considerations on application for leave

Where the person applying for leave is not the child, section 10(9) of the CA 1989 applies. This requires that on applications for leave the court should have regard to various considerations which do not include the paramountcy principle. On the issue of leave, the welfare of the child is not of paramount importance, because an application for leave is not a trial of the substantive issue. The factors listed in the section are not exhaustive, see *Re B (A Child) (Paternal Grandmother: Joinder as Party)* [2012] EWCA Civ 737, [2012] 2 FLR 1358.

Section 10(9) of the CA 1989 sets out the factors to which the court should have particular regard:

(a)   the nature of the proposed application;

(b)   the applicant's connection with the child;

(c)   any risk that there might be of that proposed application disrupting the child's life to such an extent that he would be harmed by it; and

(d)   where the child is being looked after by a local authority:

   (i)   the authority's plans for the child's future; and

   (ii)   the wishes and feelings of the child's parents.

13.2.3 Duration

Other than a child arrangements order that specifies whom a child will live with, orders under section 8 of the CA 1989 subsist until the child reaches 16, unless they are brought to an end earlier by the court or made of limited duration (section 91(11)). They may, in exceptional circumstances, be extended until the child reaches 18 (section 9(6)). Orders regarding residence (a child arrangements order, specifying living with) subsist until the child is 18, unless ended by the court. There is no such provision under the CA 1989 as an 'interim section 8 order' but, instead, only a full order of limited duration, see *S v S (Custody Jurisdiction)* [1995] 1 FLR 155 and also *Re M (Official Solicitor's Role)* [1998] 2 FLR 815.

13.2.4   When the court may not make an order under section 8 of the Children Act 1989

Section 9(1) of the CA 1989 establishes restrictions on making section 8 orders.

No court shall make any order under section 8 of the CA 1989 (other than an order as to whom the child will live with) with respect to a child who is in the care of the local authority.

A child arrangements order regulating residence will result in the automatic discharge of the care order and a care order automatically discharges a section 8 order (section 91(2)).

Section 9(2) of the CA 1989 states, 'No application may be made by a local authority for a child arrangements order and no court shall make such an order in favour of a local authority'.

Section 9(3) of the CA 1989 imposes restrictions on the application to the court for leave to apply for section 8 orders by some foster carers. All foster carers need leave of the court to apply for a section 8 order unless they are entitled to apply. If they have fostered the child within the preceding 6 months, they will need the consent of the local authority before seeking leave to apply unless they are related to the child or the child has lived with them for at least one year preceding the application.

Section 9(5)(a) of the CA 1989 forbids a court to make a specific issue or prohibited steps order 'with a view to achieving a result which could be achieved by making a child arrangements order'. Specific issue and prohibited steps orders are regarded as quite formidable powers, to be used sparingly and only where appropriate.

Section 9(5)(b) of the CA 1989 forbids a court to exercise its power to make a specific issue or prohibited steps order 'in any way which is denied to the High Court (by section 100(2)) in the exercise of its inherent jurisdiction with respect to children'.

The essential purpose of section 100(2) of the CA 1989 is to ensure that local authorities seeking some measure of control over a child do so by way of proceedings under Part IV or Part V and not by invoking wardship. Section 9(5)(b) applies the same principle to section 8 proceedings.

Section 9(6) of the CA 1989 prohibits the making of any section 8 order which is to have effect for a period which will end after the child has reached the age of 16, unless the circumstances are exceptional. Note that subsection (6) does not apply to a child arrangements order to which subsection (6B) applies (i.e. a child arrangements order if the arrangements regulated by the order relate only to either or both of: (a) with whom the child concerned is to live; and (b) when the child is to live with any person).

13.2.5 Welfare reports in applications under section 8 of the Children Act 1989

Under section 7 of the CA 1989, the court may, when considering any question under the Act, ask for a report on the welfare of the child. The court may direct that a report be prepared by a Cafcass or Cafcass Cymru officer or by a local authority. This refers to the court's power to direct Cafcass to provide a report to assist its decision making in a section 8 application. In practice, Cafcass officers may now work with parents towards dispute resolution without a report being written, see FPR 2010 PD 12B. A section 7 direction should be made to a local authority only where the family is already known to the authority.

13.3 Contact (spending time with, or otherwise having contact with)

In private law proceedings, an order made under section 8 of the CA 1989 regulating contact means an order requiring the person with whom a child lives or is to live, to allow the child to visit the person named in the order, or for that person and the child otherwise to have contact with each other.

This order governs contact by direct and indirect means, including visits, staying over, telephone calls, tapes, videos, letters, cards and presents.

Contact orders generally will expire when the child reaches 16, unless there are exceptional circumstances (section 9(6) of the CA 1989).

Contact orders lapse if the parents live continuously together for more than 6 months (section 11(6) of the CA 1989).

13.3.1   Contact disputes

Children in private law disputes often find themselves caught up in bitter arguments between their parents about the arrangements for contact. This has the potential to cause children significant harm over time, and is often very difficult to manage. Orders for contact are not always successful and do not deal with the underlying conflict, which often results in allegations and counter-allegations, and in the entrenchment of the positions of both parents. Allegations of domestic abuse are a feature of at least half the cases that go to court. The procedures in FPR 2010 PD 12J should be followed.

Where allegations or concerns about domestic abuse exist, the court should first conduct a fact-finding hearing to determine whether the allegations are true, but only where they would (if found to be true) have an impact on the decisions to be made about the child's welfare (*Re H-N (Children) (Domestic Abuse: Finding of Fact Hearings)* [2021] EWCA Civ 448, [2021] 2 FLR 1116 and *K v K (Fact-finding Hearing in Private Family Proceedings)* [2022] EWCA Civ 468, [2022] 2 FLR 1064).

The Child Arrangements Programme was introduced as an attempt to intervene early and effectively to resolve disputes. The Programme is now set out in FPR 2010 PD 12B. Under the Programme, if alternative dispute resolution has failed, the court will list the application for a dispute resolution appointment to follow the preparation of reports under section 7 of the CA 1989 or other expert report. At the dispute resolution appointment, the court will identify and narrow the key issues to be determined and give final case management directions.

At the time of writing, a Pathfinder Pilot is operating in courts in parts of Dorset, parts of Wales and in Birmingham. This process aims to divert cases from court where there are no safety issues and to focus at an earlier stage on those cases where there are concerns about domestic abuse or child abuse (see FPR 2010 PD 36Z). It is intended to extend the Pathfinder Pilot to more courts in the near future.

The court has the option to use activity orders (see para 13.3.2) to try to break deadlocked cases; however, ultimately, it is only a change in the behaviour and attitude of parents that will result in a reduction of the conflict in such situations.

In some circumstances the court will order supervised contact in private law proceedings. Contact centres can provide a useful facility for the supervision of contact, but not all cases are suitable for such an arrangement.

This then leaves one-to-one supervision as the other alternative option. If there are no friends or family considered to be sufficiently neutral to provide this then a professional contact supervisor will be required. This results in one of the parties having to finance this arrangement as there are no other means available to facilitate the funding of such arrangements, and it will be rare.

Cafcass has developed practice guidance called the *Child Impact Assessment Framework*, which applies to high conflict, domestic abuse and alienation. Chapter 16 covers this in more detail and the Cafcass website should be checked for the latest position.

13.3.2   Activity orders

Sections 11A–P were added to the CA 1989 by the Children and Adoption Act 2006 and are intended to facilitate and enforce contact orders where there is hostility between parties. They set out provisions for contact activity directions (sections 11A–B and 11E–F); contact activity conditions (sections 11C–F); monitoring contact (sections 11G–H); enforcement (sections 11I–N); and compensating for financial loss (sections 11O–P). These were renamed 'activity directions' and 'activity conditions' as a result of the CFA 2014. Activities relate to referrals to services and programmes which are designed to promote safe contact, such as counselling or anger management. These facilitation and enforcement provisions are not used very often, with the courts instead tending to rely on FPR 2010 PD 12B.

13.4   Prohibited steps

A prohibited steps order means an order that no step which could be taken by a parent in meeting his parental responsibility for a child, and which is of a kind specified in the order, shall be taken by any person without the consent of the court. This order enables the court to spell out those matters which are to be referred back to it for a decision. An example is an application to stop a child being known by a different surname, as in *Dawson v Wearmouth* [1999] 1 FLR 1167.

13.5   Residence (living with)

A child arrangements order settling the arrangements to be made as to the person with whom the child is to live has replaced the former description of a residence order. A 'shared residence order' refers to a former residence order under section 11(4) of the CA 1989 made in favour of two people who do not live together, where the child spends a substantial amount of time in each household. However, section 11(4) is now repealed, because a child arrangements order is flexible and can cover shared residence.

The court may make conditions and directions if necessary to facilitate the implementation of any order made under section 8 of the CA 1989. Where a child arrangements order is supported by the local authority as an alternative to a child being looked after, the carer is entitled to apply for a financial allowance under Schedule 1, paragraph 15 to the CA 1989.

13.5.1　Residence and parental responsibility

Child arrangements orders do not remove parental responsibility from anyone else who has it. Parental responsibility can be given to the person in whose favour a 'living with' order is made, remaining while the order is in force (section 12(2) of the CA 1989, and see Chapter 3). These orders generally expire when the child reaches 18, see para 13.2.3.

Section 12(1) of the CA 1989 specifically requires the court to make an order under section 4 giving parental responsibility to a father in favour of whom it makes a child arrangements order for residence if he would not otherwise have it. The court may not bring that parental responsibility order to an end while the section 8 order remains in force (section 12(4)). There is an additional effect of the combined operation of section 12(2) and (4) for an unmarried father, which is that discharge of a residence order, or its expiry by effluxion of time, will not automatically result in the discharge of his parental responsibility for his child. He continues by implication to have parental responsibility for his child until the child reaches 18, unless it is specifically discharged by court order under section 4(4).

The CA 1989 does not allow parental responsibility given under this section to cover agreement to adoption, nor does it permit the appointment of a guardian for the child (section 12(3) of the CA 1989).

Section 13(1)(b) of the CA 1989 generally prohibits the removal of a child from the United Kingdom without the written consent of every person who has parental responsibility for the child or the leave of the court, whilst section 13(2) makes an exception permitting a person in whose favour a child arrangements order for residence is made to take the child abroad for a period of less than one month.

A parent who fears that a child may be removed abroad permanently on the pretext of a short holiday may apply for a prohibited steps order excluding the effect of section 13(2) of the CA 1989. Where the question of the removal of the child from the jurisdiction is anticipated, the court may, on the making of the living with order, give leave either generally, or for specified purposes (section 13(3)).

Where a child is subject to a child arrangements order, specifying living with, or to a care order, no person may change that child's surname without the written consent of every person with parental responsibility for that child, or leave of the court: section 13(1)(a) of the CA 1989; see *Re A (A Child: Joint Residence/Parental Responsibility)* [2008] EWCA Civ 867.

13.6 Specific issue

A specific issue order means an order giving directions for the purpose of determining a specific issue which has arisen, or which may arise, in connection with any aspect of parental responsibility for a child. Examples include medical vaccination or investigations, as in *Re C (A Child) (HIV Test)* [1999] 2 FLR 1004, and more recently in *Re Permission to Arrange Covid-19 Vaccination* [2022] EWFC 112.

This order enables either parent to submit a particular dispute to the court for resolution in accordance with the child's best interests. The order was not envisaged as a way of giving one parent the right to determine issues in advance, nor was it intended to be a substitute for a residence or contact order.

Applications for specific issue or prohibited steps orders cannot be made in respect of children subject to care orders (section 9(1) of the CA 1989).

13.7 Supplementary provisions

Section 11(1) of the CA 1989 instructs the court to 'draw up a timetable with a view to determining the question without delay' and 'to give such directions as it considers appropriate for the purpose of ensuring, so far as is reasonably practicable, that the timetable is adhered to'.

Section 11(2) of the CA 1989 permits rules of court to 'specify periods within which specified steps must be taken in relation to proceedings in which such questions arise' and 'to make other provision ... for the purpose of ensuring, so far as is reasonably practicable, that such questions are determined without delay'.

Section 11(3) of the CA 1989 states that where a court has power to make a section 8 order, it may do so at any time in the course of the proceedings in question, even though it is not in a position to dispose finally of those proceedings.

Where there is an order for residence or 'living with' in force, as a result of which the child lives, or is to live, with one of two parents who each have parental responsibility for him, the order shall cease to have effect if the parents live together for a continuous period of more than 6 months (section 11(5) of the CA 1989).

Section 11(6) of the CA 1989 has the effect that a child arrangements order, specifying spending time with, or otherwise having contact with his other parent, shall cease to have effect if the parents live together for a continuous period of more than 6 months.

Orders made under section 8 of the CA 1989 may contain directions, impose conditions, be made for a specified period or contain provisions for a specified period; and make such incidental, supplemental or consequential provisions as the court thinks fit (section 11(7)).

13.8   Practice and procedure in applications under section 8 of the Children Act 1989

Procedure is governed by Part 12 of the FPR 2010.

13.8.1   Mediation Information and Assessment Meetings and non-court dispute resolution

One of the key provisions brought about by the FPR 2010, in April 2011, was the requirement for attendance at a Mediation Information and Assessment Meeting (MIAM). That is, as prerequisite to making an application for a private children law order, the proposed applicant is required to attend a MIAM unless they are exempt from doing so. As of April 2024, there have been changes to the MIAM expectations, brought about by the Family Procedure (Amendment No 2) Rules 2023 (SI 2023/1324). That is, FPR 2010 PD 3A, paragraph 7 is amended, so that if an applicant claims a MIAM exemption, the court will issue proceedings, but will inquire into the exemption claimed. In private law proceedings, the court must make this enquiry at the stage at which the case is allocated to a level of judge (often referred to as the 'gatekeeping stage'). If the court is of the view that a MIAM exemption has not been validly claimed, or is no longer applicable, the court may direct the applicant or the parties to attend a MIAM, and may adjourn proceedings for that purpose.

Furthermore, FPR 2020 PD 3A, paragraph 10B now provides that the court will want to know the parties' views on using non-court dispute resolution as a way of resolving matters. Consequently, each party is now required to file with the court and serve on all other parties, standard Form FM5, setting out their views on using non-court dispute resolution: (a) at least 7 days before the first hearing in the proceedings which is held on notice to all parties; or (b) within such other period before that hearing as the court may direct; and (c) if required by the court, each party must file with the court and serve on all other parties an updated version of that standard form: (i) at least 7 days before a subsequent hearing; or (ii) within such other period before a subsequent hearing as the court may direct.

13.8.2   Applications

Freestanding applications should be on Form C100 and, where applicable, Form C1A, or on Form C2 if the application is made in existing 'family proceedings'. Form C1A should be added if there are any risks to parties or children identified in Form C100 (FPR 2010 PD 12B, paragraphs 8.1–8.10).

If the application is for leave only, then, unless it is made without notice (see Chapter 18), the applicant for leave must complete Form C2 giving reasons for the application and requesting leave in writing, and to file and serve the request together with the draft of the application on Form C1 to each respondent (rules 18.2–18.8 of the FPR 2010).

As discussed at para 3.6, for the purposes of public funding in relation to private children law cases, the effect of LASPO, as from 1 April 2013, has brought significant changes, principally concerning the 'merits' test. Therefore, in terms of eligibility for public funding to cover private children law applications, there is a requirement to satisfy both the 'means' and 'merits' tests. In terms of the merits test, one has to show the 'gateway evidence' of 'domestic violence' or 'child abuse', as defined in the regulations. The Civil Legal Aid (Procedure) (Amendment) (No 2) Regulations 2017 (SI 2017/1237), as from 8 January 2018, had the effect of removing the time limitation as to how far back the evidence of 'domestic violence' or 'child abuse' can be relied upon.

13.8.3   Venue

Applications are made to the Family Court, where they are allocated to a level of judge in accordance with the *President's Guidance on Allocation and Gatekeeping for Proceedings under Part II of the Children Act 1989 (Private Law)* (22 April 2014) (as amended in 2020), issued in accordance with rule 21 of the Family Court (Composition and Distribution of Business) Rules 2014 (as amended in 2021).

13.8.4   Notice of application for orders under section 8 of the Children Act 1989

Under FPR 2010 PD 12C, notice shall be served on:

(a)   any local authority providing accommodation for the child;

(b)   persons caring for the child when the proceedings commence;

(c)   any person providing refuge in which child is staying;

(d)   any person whom the applicant believes is named in the court order, which is still in effect, relating to the child;

(e)   any party whom the applicant believes is a party to pending proceedings relating to the child;

(f)   every person with whom the applicant believes the child has lived for 3 years prior to the application.

Notice of the proceedings is on Form C6A, giving the date, time and venue of the hearing. It should be served at least 14 days before the hearing (FPR 2010 PD 12C, paragraph 2.1).

13.8.5   Respondents

Under rule 12.3 of the FPR 2010, the following are automatically respondents to an application under section 8 of the CA 1989:

(a)   everyone with parental responsibility for the child;

(b)   if a care order is in force, everyone with parental responsibility when the order was made;

(c)   parties to proceedings leading to an order for which variation or discharge is now sought.

Respondents should be served with a copy of the application with the date of hearing endorsed on it, together with notice of the proceedings on Form C6A. It should be served at least 14 days before the hearing (FPR 2010 PD 12C).

Under rule 12.3 of the FPR 2010, anyone may apply on Form C2 to be joined as a respondent or may be made a respondent by court order without application. The same applies if respondents wish to be removed. If the person requesting party status has parental responsibility for the child, the court must grant that person's request.

13.8.6   Service

The rules about serving a document are contained in rules 6.23–6.39 of the FPR 2010 and PD 6A. Service can be carried out by delivery to the solicitor acting for the person to be served, personally, by document exchange, facsimile transmission, email or first class post; or by delivery to the person himself, either personally or by first class post to his last known residence (see para 8.4.6).

The court has the power under the rules to abridge, waive or vary the manner of service (rule 6.35 of the FPR 2010).

Under FPR 2010 PD 12B, paragraph 8.12, on receipt of Form C7 and any Form C1A filed by the respondent(s), the court shall send a copy of each form to Cafcass or Cafcass Cymru, in electronic format where possible, and shall send copies to the applicant. Also, paragraph 13.7 specifically provides that the letter/safeguarding report done by Cafcass or Cafcass Cymru should specify which court forms filed by the parties (Forms C100, C7 and C1A) have been considered. In terms of the notice period, paragraph 14.2 was amended in 2018, so that the respondent(s) shall have at least 14 days' notice of the hearing, as opposed to the 10 days they had previously, but the court may specify a shorter time.

13.8.7 Applications made without notice (formerly known as *ex parte* procedures)

These are applications made without requiring the other party/parties to attend on notice. Applications for orders under section 8 of the CA 1989 may be made *without notice* in any court (rule 12.16 of the FPR 2010).

Applications made without notice must be supported by the same forms (Form C100 or Form C2), which should be brought to court or, if it is a telephone application, should be filed the next business day. In any event, they should be served on the respondents within 48 hours of any order being made. The court has the power under the rules to give directions as to service.

In the context of Article 6 of the ECHR and the interests of natural justice, applications without notice are generally frowned upon by the courts. They should be reserved for situations of urgency, such as medical or other emergencies or child abduction cases (rule 12.47 of the FPR 2010).

At the time of writing, there are a number of pilot schemes and new rules relating to the online submission of applications and supporting documents in private law applications (see Part 36 of the FPR 2010). In particular, FPR 2010 PD 36ZD is updated, so that there is express provision for the court to send information relating to proceedings to Cafcass or Cafcass Cymru in cases where the court has commissioned Cafcass or Cafcass Cymru to prepare a section 7 report or where they are otherwise engaged in proceedings progressing on the digital portal. The rules should therefore be checked carefully regarding current procedures.

13.8.8 Withdrawal, variation, discharge and appeals

Leave of the court is necessary for withdrawal of applications under section 8 of the CA 1989 (rule 29.4 of the FPR 2010) on oral application where the parties are present or by written request, setting out the reasons for withdrawal, which must then be duly served. The court may permit withdrawal without a hearing if the parties and any other person such as the Cafcass or Cafcass Cymru officer have had a chance to make representations and the court considers it appropriate.

Applications to vary or discharge an order under section 8 of the CA 1989 may be made by those entitled to seek the original order (see paras 13.1–13.2, and applications at para 13.8). The procedure is the same as the original application. Under section 91(14) and 91A, the court may order that no further application be made for a specified period without leave.

Orders under section 8 of the CA 1989 are automatically discharged by the making of a care order or an adoption order (section 91(2)).

The procedure for appeals is set out in Part 30 of the FPR 2010 and PD 30A.

13.9   Family assistance order

Section 16 of the CA 1989 creates the family assistance order, requiring a probation or local authority officer to be made available to 'advise, assist and befriend' any person named in the order (section 16(1)). But note that the court can only make this order with the consent of every person named in the order, save the child (section 16(3)).

The person to be 'advised, assisted or befriended' may be the child, his or her parent or guardian, or any person with whom the child is living or who has a child arrangements order in respect of the child (section 16(2)). It originally lasted for 6 months but was extended to a possible maximum of 12 months, or a shorter specified period (section 16(5) of the CA 1989).

The family assistance order may direct the person(s) named in the order to take whatever steps are necessary to enable the officer to be kept informed of their address, and to be allowed to visit the named person (section 16(4) of the CA 1989).

Where there is in force a family assistance order and also an order under section 8 of the CA 1989, then the officer may refer to the court the possibility of variation or discharge of the section 8 order (section 16(6)). This power should obviously be of use where a family assistance order has been made at the same time as a child arrangements order which is clearly not working. Under section 16(4A), the officer concerned may specifically also assist in facilitating a contact order, if any.

13.10   Order to local authority to investigate under section 37 of the Children Act 1989

Where, in any 'family proceedings' (see section 8(3) of the CA 1989) in which a question arises with respect to the welfare of any child, it appears to the court that it may be appropriate for a care or supervision order to be made, the court may direct the appropriate authority to undertake an investigation of the child's circumstances (section 37(1)).

A section 37 order should be made only where a public law order is being considered by the court; an investigation into what is a private law dispute should be undertaken through other means (*Re L (A Minor)* [1999] 1 FLR 984).

The local authority to which the direction is given is then under a duty to consider whether it should:

• apply for a care or supervision order;

• provide services or assistance for the child and family;

• take any other action in respect of the child.

If the local authority decides not to seek a care order, it shall inform the court within 8 weeks from the direction under section 37 of the CA 1989 of its reasons, any services or assistance provided, and any other action taken. If the decision is made to seek care or supervision, the local authority shall also consider whether it would be appropriate to review the case at a later date, and the date of any such review shall be determined.

The difference between a direction under section 37 of the CA 1989 and one under section 7 is that the former is made only when care proceedings might be necessary, and the latter is made because welfare issues have arisen and the family is already known to local government officers.

13.11   Special guardianship

Note that special guardianship orders (see Chapter 3) are private law orders, coming within Part II, sections 14A–G of the CA 1989, and may be appropriately considered in some cases as an alternative to a child arrangements order regulating living with.

14 Commencement and Transfer of Proceedings

14.1 General rules

Under section 1 of the Family Law Act 1986, a child in respect of whom a private law application is made must be either ordinarily or habitually resident in England and Wales, or physically present within the jurisdiction of the court at the time of the application. A section 8 order may be made where the court has jurisdiction in connection with matrimonial proceedings or founded on habitual residence. The provision also applies across Scotland and Northern Ireland to ensure that only one court has jurisdiction.

The general rule is that private law applications under the CA 1989 must be made to the Family Court, unless brought under the inherent jurisdiction of the High Court or there is an international element or other complexity. Details are set out in para 14.2.1.

The distribution of business in the Family Court is set out in Schedule 1 to the Family Court (Composition and Distribution of Business) Rules 2014 (as amended in 2021), between lay justices, district judges, circuit judges and Judges at High Court level. This is supported by the *President's Guidance on Allocation and Gatekeeping for Proceedings under Part II of the Children Act 1989 (Private Law)* (22 April 2014) (as amended in 2020).

The allocation of public law applications to magistrates and judges is managed by the gatekeeping team in each Designated Family Justice Centre, in accordance with the *President's Guidance on Allocation and Gatekeeping for Care, Supervision and other Proceedings under Part IV of the Children Act 1989 (Public Law)* (22 April 2014) (as amended in 2020).

14.2 Applicants and allocation of family case

There are specific provisions concerning in which court certain family proceedings must be commenced. These are considered further below.

Table 14.1   Commencement of proceedings

CA 1989 (or other legislation as specified)	Type of order	Applicant
Section 4, section 4A	Parental responsibility, by parent or step-parent	Father or step-parent or 'other female parent' can apply for order (section 4(1)(c), section 4A(1)(b), section 4ZA(1)(c)); any person with parental responsibility or child (with leave) can apply to terminate (section 4(3), section 4A(3), section 4ZA(6))
Section 5	Appointment of guardian	Any person may apply (section 5(1))
Section 6	Termination of appointment of a guardian	Application can be made by any person with parental responsibility or the child (with leave) (section 6(7)(a), (b))
Section 8	Any section 8 order	Application can be made by any parent, guardian, person named in child arrangements order as person with whom child is to live (section 10(2)(b), (4)), or other person with leave
Section 8	Child arrangements order	As with section 8, and any party to marriage, or person who had care of child for 3 years, or consent of those with parental responsibility (section 10(5)), or other person with leave
Section 14A	Special guardianship order	Guardian, person named in child arrangements order as person with whom child is to live, person who had care of child for 3 years, or consent of those with parental responsibility, or LA foster-parent for one year or more (section 14A(5)) or anyone with court leave (section 14A(3))

CA 1989 (or other legislation as specified)	Type of order	Applicant
Section 15	Financial relief order	Parent, guardian, or person named in child arrangements order as person with whom child is to live (Schedule 1, paragraph 1)
Section 16	Family assistance	Any party
Section 25 of the CA 1989 or section 119 of the SSW(W)A 2014	Secure accommodation	LA, HA, PCT, NHS Trust, NHS Foundation Trust, LEA, person carrying on care home or independent hospital
Section 31	Care or supervision order	LA, NSPCC and other authorised persons
Section 36	Education supervision order	LA
Section 43	Child assessment	LA or authorised person
Section 44	Emergency protection order	Any person can apply
Section 50	Recovery order	Person with parental responsibility by care order or emergency protection order, or designated officer
Section 42 of the Family Law Act 1996	Non-molestation order	Application can be made by or on behalf of person who has suffered molestation, and within the definition of associated person, or a child (with leave)
Sections 33–38 of the Family Law Act 1996	Occupation order	A person seeking an occupation order, and within the definition of associated person, or a child (with leave)

Key

LA = local authority; HA = health authority; PCT = primary care trust; NHS = National Health Service; LEA = local education authority.

14.2.1   Proceedings which must be commenced in the Family Division of the High Court

In the *President's Guidance: Jurisdiction of the Family Court: Allocation of Cases within the Family Court to High Court Judge Level and Transfer of Cases from the Family Court to the High Court* (24 May 2021), the President of the Family Division, Sir Andrew McFarlane, emphasised that a transfer of a case to the High Court to be heard by a judge of that court, is not the same as the allocation of a case within the Family Court to a Judge of High Court. Paragraph 17 of this guidance sets out the limited situations where certain matters must be commenced in the Family Division of the High Court, as opposed to in the Family Court. These are, first, those matters listed in Part A of the Schedule to this guidance, which are matters in respect of which the Family Court does not have jurisdiction, and which therefore must be commenced in the Family Division. Secondly, those matters listed in Part B of the Schedule to the guidance, even though the Family Court has jurisdiction, because the High Court is entitled to transfer down to the Family Court in accordance with section 38 of the Matrimonial and Family Proceedings Act 1984. Parts A and B to the Schedule contain a detailed list including: matters of the inherent jurisdiction; cases with a foreign element; radicalisation; publicity about a child; and medical treatment. It is advisable to read the full list of matters in Parts A and B to the Schedule.

14.2.2   Proceedings which must be commenced in the Family Court

Paragraph 18 of the *President's Guidance: Jurisdiction of the Family Court: Allocation of Cases within the Family Court to High Court Judge Level and Transfer of Cases from the Family Court to the High Court* (24 May 2021) specifically provides that except as specified in the Schedule to the guidance, every family matter must be commenced in the Family Court and not in the High Court. When matters are commenced in the Family Court, the allocation of cases within the Family Court is regulated by rules and guidance set out in para 14.1.

14.3   Transfers

Under rule 29.17 of the FPR 2010, a court may transfer a matter to another court where the parties consent, or the court determines at a hearing that the matter should be transferred, or the court has notified the parties that it intends to transfer the case on 14 days' notice and has not received a request for a hearing.

The President specifically set out the position regarding transfer of cases in the *President's Guidance: Jurisdiction of the Family Court: Allocation of Cases within the Family Court to High Court Judge Level and Transfer of Cases from the Family Court to the High Court* (24 May 2021). Paragraph 26 of the guidance sets out that the powers to transfer cases from the Family Court to the Family Division which are conferred by sections 31I and 38 of the Matrimonial and Family Proceedings Act 1984 are exercisable only by the Family Division, and not by the Family Court.

Section 39 confers jurisdiction on the Family Court to transfer cases to the High Court, but the exercise of this power is subject to the limitations set out in rule 29.17(3) and (4) of the FPR 2010. These are that a case may not be transferred from the Family Court to the High Court unless: (a) the decision to transfer was made by a judge sitting in the Family Court who is a person to whom rule 29.17(4) applies; or (b) one or more of the circumstances specified in PD 29C applies. Rule 29.17(4) applies to a person who is: (a) the President of the Family Division; (b) an ordinary judge of the Court of Appeal (including the vice-president, if any, of either division of that court); (c) a puisne judge of the High Court (i.e. a judge in the High Court other than a section 9 judge).

Insofar as FPR 2010 PD 29C is concerned, this provides for the transfer from the Family Court to the High Court in those proceedings where the purpose is solely for the making of an order under the inherent jurisdiction of the High Court, to require a government department or agency to disclose an address to the court. It is emphasised in the guidance that the effect of this is that the only circumstances in which a District Judge, a Circuit Judge or a Recorder (even if sitting under section 9) can transfer a case from the Family Court to the High Court are those specified in PD 29C, paragraph 1.2 (which, in practice, applies only in cases where disclosure is required from HM Revenue & Customs). Also, a transfer in these circumstances is temporary, and only for the purpose of making the disclosure order, so that once the order has been made, the matter should be re-transferred back to the Family Court.

These provisions therefore emphasise the point, as made out in the guidance, that there is no justification for transferring a case from the Family Court to the High Court merely because it requires to be heard by a judge of the Family Division or because of perceived complexity or difficulty. In such situations, the case should be re-allocated for hearing in the Family Court by a 'judge of High Court Judge level' or, if appropriate, by a judge of the Family Division.

14.4   Urgent applications

Subject to rules, guidance and case law on jurisdiction and venue, the referral procedures for urgent applications to the High Court are set out in FPR 2010 PD 12E.

Urgent applications should whenever possible be made within court hours. The earliest possible liaison is required with the clerk, who will attempt to accommodate genuinely urgent applications (at least for initial directions) in the Family Division applications court, from which the matter may be referred to another judge. When it is not possible to apply within court hours, contact should be made with the security office at the Royal Courts of Justice (020 7947 6000 or 020 7947 6260) who will refer the matter to the urgent business officer, who can contact the duty judge. The judge may agree to hold a hearing, either convened at court or elsewhere, or by telephone (preferably by recorded conference call arranged by the applicant).

FPR 2010 PD 12E includes guidance on liaising with Cafcass or Cafcass Cymru or the Official Solicitor in urgent applications.

15 Working with Children

15.1 Appointment and role of the children's guardian

The children's guardian is a person appointed by the court to act for a child aged under 18. In cases under the CA 1989, a children's guardian should be appointed in 'specified family proceedings' (section 41(6); see para 15.1.3), unless the court is satisfied that it is not necessary to do so, and may also be appointed in certain non-specified proceedings. The provisions governing the appointment and functioning of a children's guardian are in sections 41–42 of the CA 1989, and Parts 12, 14 and 16 of the FPR 2010. In *A County Council v K & Others* [2011] EWHC 1672 (Fam), the then President of the Family Division, Sir Nicholas Wall, clearly explained that the personal appointment of the guardian makes the guardian accountable to the court for his or her professional judgment in representing the child's interests during proceedings.

The children's guardian should be independent and has a duty to investigate the circumstances of the case thoroughly, interviewing parties and witnesses and examining all available evidence. The children's guardian should interview all those who may be able to give relevant information about the child's life and circumstances and also the child and her family, and may request any necessary further information or assessments and then evaluate all the evidence. The children's guardian has a duty to advise the court of the child's wishes and feelings; to inform the court of the child's circumstances, bearing in mind the welfare checklist; to evaluate all the options open to the court; and lastly to advise the court on the best way forward in the interests of the child.

Children's guardians may be employees of Cafcass, or they may be independent social workers who may have a contractual arrangement with Cafcass for the taking of cases (but not employed by Cafcass). See Chapter 4, para 4.7 for information about Cafcass, which comprises the former Children's Guardian and Reporting Officer Service, the Family Court Welfare Service and the Children's Branch of the Official Solicitor's Department, see sections 41–42 of the CA 1989, and Parts 12, 14 and 16 of the FPR 2010. In Wales, these functions are undertaken by Cafcass Cymru, which operates under the Welsh Government.

For further information, see the Cafcass website, www.cafcass.gov.uk, the Cafcass Cymru website, www.gov.wales/cafcass-cymru, and the website of NAGALRO (Professional Association for Children's Guardians, Family Court Advisers and Independent Social Workers), www.nagalro.com.

15.1.1   Official Solicitor

The Official Solicitor is an independent statutory office holder. The office, and that of the Public Trustee, is an arm's length body of the Ministry of Justice. A key role of the Official Solicitor is to act as a last resort litigation friend, and in some cases, solicitor for children (other than those who are the subject of child welfare proceedings), and for adults who lack mental capacity in litigation. Also, the Official Solicitor acts, on behalf of the Lord Chancellor, in cases of international child abduction, through the International Child Abduction and Contact Unit. The most common examples are listed in the *Practice Note: The Official Solicitor to the Senior Courts: Appointment in Family Proceedings and Proceedings under the Inherent Jurisdiction in Relation to Adults* (January 2017) (as amended).

This Practice Note for solicitors contains specific information about: (a) the appointing of the Official Solicitor as litigation friend of a child in family proceedings or a protected party; (b) requests from the court for the Official Solicitor to conduct *Harbin v Masterman* [1896] 1 Ch 351 enquiries; and (c) requests from the court for the Official Solicitor to act as, or appoint counsel to act as, an advocate to the court. The Official Solicitor will seek to determine the child's best interests within the litigation and take all measures necessary within the proceedings for the child's benefit.

15.1.2   Public funding, access to information and disclosure

A child who is subject to 'specified proceedings' is entitled to publicly funded legal representation. A solicitor may be appointed for the child by the children's guardian or by the court.

When representing the child, the solicitor will go to see the child with the children's guardian. It would be important to explain to the child (subject to his or her age and understanding), the respective roles of the solicitor and the children's guardian, and that the two professionals work in tandem, so as to ensure that the children's welfare needs are appropriately safeguarded and put to the court.

In the event of a conflict between the child and the children's guardian, a child of sufficient understanding may wish to choose his or her own solicitor, which is acceptable, provided that the appointment complies with section 41(3) of the CA 1989 and the duties of the solicitor under rule 16.29 of the FPR 2010.

The children's guardian has access under section 42(1) of the CA 1989 to all social work files and records and, if any of these documents are copied by the children's guardian, they are admissible in evidence before the court (section 42(2)). See the case of *Re T* [1994] 1 FLR 632, in which the local authority refused to disclose records of potential adopters to the children's guardian, but the Court of Appeal ordered that the children's guardian should have access to them under the terms of section 42.

The children's guardian may ask for access to medical or psychiatric records of the child, and may wish to see the health records of others involved in the child's life. Note the case of *Oxfordshire County Council v P* [1995] 1 FLR 582 concerning the issue of how confidential information should be treated by children's guardians.

The report of the children's guardian is confidential to the court and the parties, and permission of the court is required to disclose the report to others (or for use in other cases) and also to withhold information from parties. Leave to withhold information from parties may be sufficiently serious to warrant a High Court hearing, see *Re M (Disclosure)* [1998] 2 FLR 1028. See also the later case of *Local Authority v HI & Others* [2016] EWHC 1123 (Fam). Here, it was emphasised that the court needs to strike a careful balance between allowing the child's confidentiality to be respected, versus the need to enable the local authority to share relevant information if it goes towards the care plan. The power of the court to control evidence is set out in rule 22.1 of the FPR 2010.

The children's guardian in specified proceedings may bring applications on behalf of the child, or the child's solicitor may do so, if the child is of sufficient age to instruct separately (see para 15.2).

Good Practice in Child Care Cases (The Law Society, 3rd edn, 2015) is a concise guide to best practice for solicitors acting in public law cases, whether they are acting for a local authority, a parent or a child. The Law Society Practice Note, *Acting in the absence of a children's guardian* (9 December 2019) provides guidance to solicitors appointed by the court to represent children in proceedings where there are delays between the order appointing a children's guardian in specified proceedings and the allocation of a children's guardian. Note that solicitors representing children must remain mindful of the guardian's duties under FPR 2010 PD 16A, which sets out the children's guardian's duties to the court.

15.1.3   Specified proceedings

Specified proceedings are defined in section 41(6) of the CA 1989. These include any proceedings:

    (a) on an application for a care order or supervision order;

    (b) in which the court has given a direction under section 37(1) and has made, or is considering whether to make, an interim care order;

    (c) on an application for the discharge of a care order or the variation or discharge of a supervision order;

    (d) on an application under section 39(4);

    (e) in which the court is considering whether to make a child arrangements order with respect to the living arrangements of a child who is the subject of a care order;

    (f) with respect to contact between a child who is the subject of a care order and any other person;

    (g) under Part V;

    (h) on an appeal against—

        (i) the making of, or refusal to make, a care order, supervision order or any order under section 34;

        (ii) the making of, or refusal to make, a child arrangements order with respect to the living arrangements of a child who is the subject of a care order; or

        (iii) the variation or discharge, or refusal of an application to vary or discharge, an order of a kind mentioned in sub-paragraph (i) or (ii);

        (iv) the refusal of an application under section 39(4); or

        (v) the making of, or refusal to make, an order under Part V; or

  (hh) on an application for the making or revocation of a placement order (within the meaning of section 21 of the Adoption and Children Act 2002);

    (i) which are specified for the time being, for the purposes of this section, by rules of court.

15.2   Conflict between children's guardian and child

The child, if of sufficient age and understanding, may request client confidentiality with his solicitor, and/or disagree with the recommendations of the children's guardian.

In this case, the child's solicitor must decide: (a) whether the child is of sufficient age and understanding to instruct separately; and (b) whether there is a conflict between the child and the children's guardian. If both factors are present, the solicitor should discuss the matter with the children's guardian. Under rule 16.6 of the FPR 2010, a child may conduct proceedings without a children's guardian or litigation friend in specified circumstances. If a child radically disagrees with his children's guardian and is competent to instruct his own solicitor, then the court must be informed, and the solicitor may, in many cases, continue to represent the child client. The children's guardian may then proceed unrepresented or seek another lawyer where necessary. In the case of *Re W* [2016] EWCA Civ 1051, Black LJ stated (at [23]) that there is no assistance to be found in the (court) rules as to the precise nature of the understanding that will be required of a child before he or she is considered able to give instructions. There is, however, some assistance to be found in the authorities, and, in particular, in the case of *Mabon v Mabon* [2005] EWCA Civ 634. In *Re W* (above) at [27], Her Ladyship stated that the question of whether a child is able, having regard to his or her understanding, to instruct a solicitor must be approached having in mind this acknowledgment of the autonomy of children, and of the fact that it can at times be in their interests to play some direct part in the litigation about them. What is sufficient understanding in any given case will depend upon all the facts. At [36], Her Ladyship set out that understanding can be affected by all sorts of things, including the age of the child, his or her intelligence, emotional and/or psychological and/or psychiatric and/or physical state, language ability, influence, etc. The child will obviously need to comprehend enough of what the case is about (without being expected to display too sophisticated an understanding) and must have the capacity to give his or her own coherent instructions, without being more than usually inconsistent. If the judge requires an expert report to assist in determining the question of understanding, the child should be under no illusions about the importance of keeping the appointment with the expert concerned. It is an opportunity for the child to demonstrate that he or she does have the necessary understanding and there is always a risk that a failure to attend will be taken to show a failure to understand.

Note the case of *Re Z (A Child: Care Proceedings: Separate Representation)* [2018] EWFC B57, handed down by HHJ Bellamy. This case looks at the difference between access to court papers and party status when one is considering children clients. The solicitor was not under a duty to allow the child to see documents that had been served upon him but, rather, 'if the child is of "sufficient understanding", to advise the child of the contents of any documents' received. It was for the solicitor to come to a judgment about whether the child had 'sufficient understanding'. If the solicitor was uncertain whether the child had 'sufficient understanding' and whether the child should be allowed to read a document or simply be given a summary of the contents of that document, the solicitor should seek guidance from the court.

There is also the guidance set out by the Family Justice Council, *Guidance on assessing child's competence to instruct a solicitor* (April 2022). The aim of this guidance is to provide some consistency of approach when considering issues as to competence, whilst at the same time, recognising that each child is unique. Paragraphs 4 and 5 of this guidance are particularly relevant in setting out that there is a distinction to be drawn between a capacity assessment under the Mental Capacity Act 2005, which requires a determination of whether someone over the age of 16 suffers from a mental disorder, such that the person lacks capacity to make decisions, and the assessment of whether a child, for the purpose of the family proceedings under the age of 18, is competent to directly instruct his or her solicitor without a guardian. The guidance provides that a decision under the Mental Capacity Act 2005 is entirely separate from a decision about competence in the Family Court, and care should be taken in ensuring they are not confused.

The issue of separate representation was also raised as an issue in the recent case of *Re C (Child: Ability to Instruct Solicitor)* [2023] EWCA Civ 889, whereby the Court of Appeal decided that even if it is found that an application is made for separate representation (on the basis that the child is competent to instruct the solicitor separately), the court is, nonetheless, the ultimate arbiter in deciding on the issue. On the facts, the Court of Appeal set out that the first instance judge had failed to give sufficient regard to the fact that the expert (a psychiatrist) had, on two previous occasions, been satisfied that the child was not competent to give instructions separately.

15.2.1   Confidentiality

The child of sufficient age may ask his or her solicitor to keep matters confidential, and disclosure is then an issue for the solicitor to decide. The case of *Re E (A Child)* [2016] EWCA Civ 473 emphasised the need for the child's solicitor to adhere to the duty of legal professional privilege, particularly when representing children who are also alleged to have abused. Also note the most recent version of the Solicitors Regulation Authority (SRA), *SRA Code of Conduct for Solicitors, RELs and RFLs* (at the time of writing it is dated 1 December 2023).

The *SRA Code of Conduct* sets out outcomes-focused conduct requirements, so that a solicitor can consider how best to achieve the right outcomes for his client, taking into account the way that the firm works and its client base.

In particular, Chapter 6 of the *SRA Code of Conduct* covers confidentiality and disclosure. This chapter emphasises that the protection of confidential information is a fundamental feature of the solicitor's relationship with clients. The solicitor should not continue to act for a client for whom he cannot disclose material information, except in very limited circumstances where safeguards are in place. One of the provisions under Chapter 6, paragraph 6.3 is that the solicitor must keep the affairs of clients confidential, unless disclosure is required or permitted by law or the client consents.

In the context of children proceedings, a solicitor may need to consider breaching the confidentiality of an immature child client where there is a risk of serious harm to the child or to others, but a mature ('*Gillick*-competent') child may be entitled to confidentiality unless other people are at risk, or the child is in fear for his or her life or serious injury.

A possible way to avoid ethical dilemmas for solicitors representing children (or adults in family matters) is to discuss confidentiality at the outset of taking instructions, and gain the client's agreement that, if a concern arises of a risk of serious harm to the client or to others, the solicitor has permission to disclose those concerns to the children's guardian or to an appropriate helping agency. This type of agreement is often used by other professionals, for example, in mental health and medical care. Clients are usually willing to give their consent, and this avoids any subsequent ethical difficulty. Clients, especially young people and children, usually tell their problems to people they trust because they would really like to have help. If the client wishes to keep the issues secret, his reasons for this should be discussed. Is the client afraid of reprisals or is he possibly protecting someone else? Is there anyone else the client feels he could trust with this information? Once the client's fear is known, appropriate resources can be looked for and the possibility of referrals which might be acceptable to the client can be explored. Clients often worry that the helping agencies, once told about the issues of concern, might let them down by failing to provide the help needed, leaving them or others exposed to continued risk. Something can be done about that by agreeing to remain alongside the client and ensuring that he receives effective and appropriate help, in the ways that he feels are right for him.

15.3   Should I see my child client?

This is a question which will be considered by a solicitor representing the child. In the authors' view, lawyers representing children should, as a matter of good practice, meet with their child clients, unless there is a cogent reason not to do so. However, the timing of the meeting is important and should be planned carefully, and the necessary arrangements should be made in co-operation with the children's guardian, the child's parents and carers, and the local authority, see paras 15.3.1 and 15.4.1.

In the Law Society Practice Note, *Acting in the absence of a children's guardian* (9 December 2019), there is guidance to solicitors appointed by the court to represent children in proceedings where there are delays between the order appointing a children's guardian in specified proceedings and the allocation of a children's guardian. The Practice Note states that the solicitor should attempt to see the child as soon as possible, if appropriate. You should exercise professional judgement as to whether a visit is appropriate, particularly if the child is a baby or very young. Furthermore, unless there is a good reason not to, it is generally appropriate to meet the child if he or she is competent to do so and would likely benefit from the visit, or the visit would assist the court. The authors agree with Christine Liddle, who says in *Acting for Children* (Law Society, 1992), 'Although children vary in their ability to give instructions, it is still very beneficial to the solicitor's understanding of the case for him to meet his child client, whatever the age' (pages 5–6).

If a solicitor is to represent a child properly in court, it is necessary to understand the child's personality, behaviour, background and needs. This can be done through information gained by others, such as by the parent, social worker and the foster carer, but it is best done at first hand. Even a small baby can, through her non-verbal behaviour, provide the observer with a good deal about herself. Public funding in public law proceedings is granted to the child client. Initially, the solicitor is instructed through the children's guardian and the court, but the solicitor should speak with child clients who appear to be of sufficient maturity, as a vital part of the preparation of the case, see Parts 12, 14 and 16 of the FPR 2010. The solicitor's task will require him or her, in appropriate cases, to discover whether the child is sufficiently mature to instruct a lawyer separately if necessary and to find out whether a conflict exists between the child and the children's guardian. The solicitor also needs to elicit the child's wishes and feelings in order to represent them accurately to the court.

The Law Society, with Resolution and other leading organisations, interest groups and figures in this field, produced the 4th edition of *The Family Law Protocol* (The Law Society, 2015), applicable in specified family law proceedings, including matters relating to domestic abuse, honour-based abuse, forced marriage and female genital mutilation, and alternative pathways to parenthood. For solicitors involved in public law proceedings, see *Good Practice in Child Care Cases* (The Law Society, 3rd edn, 2015).

15.3.1   Meeting a child client

When arranging to meet a child, consideration should be given to the most appropriate setting and style for such a meeting. Interviews should be short and at the child's pace.

When going to see the child, the solicitor needs to ensure that he or she has clear information as to the local authority care plan/interim care plan, so as to then be able to explain this to the child, in a manner which is conducive to the child's age and understanding. It will also be necessary to be able to answer questions that the child may have. Additionally, it would be necessary to consider the issue of competency of the child and separate representation, as discussed at para 15.2. Furthermore, subject to the child's age and understanding, it would be necessary to explain to the child the court process and to prepare the child for court proceedings, as well as to consider, in appropriate cases, whether the child may want to visit the court and/or the judge.

Pat Monro and Lis Forrester in *The Guardian ad litem (Guide & Practice)* (Family Law, 1995) assume that solicitors will meet their child clients, adding practical advice:

> Where a young child is involved, the instructions will come from the children's guardian and it will usually be appropriate for the children's guardian to meet with the child in the first instance without the solicitor, who can be introduced at a later date. A young child will probably be confused by the introduction of a number of new faces, and therefore it is important for the children's guardian to get to know the child before the solicitor becomes involved. (page 46)

Note: There are rare cases where it may be inappropriate for the solicitor to meet with his or her child client, for example where the child is severely emotionally damaged and the introduction of a new person may adversely affect the child. For further notes, see para 15.4.1.

15.3.2   Decisions concerning a child's competence

The expectation is that solicitors will discuss the issue of their child client's competence with the experts in both public law and private cases. The children's guardian in a public law case is the first person to be consulted on the issue. Child psychologists, psychiatrists, social workers, counsellors and others working with the child will also have useful views.

The rights of the child are set out in Chapter 12, including the competence of a child to instruct a solicitor or to give consent to assessments and treatments depending on the child's mental capacity, maturity and level of understanding of the situation. See Chapter 12 for further discussion of the concept of '*Gillick* competence', which evolved from the case of *Gillick v West Norfolk and Wisbech Area Health Authority* [1986] AC 112. Chapter 3 addresses parental responsibility. Please note that those who hold parental responsibility for a child will make decisions for those children who do not have competence.

15.4   Taking instructions and communicating with children

Good communication with children is essential if instructions are to be effective. A basic understanding of child development, confidence in being with children (preferably accrued through practical experience) and integrity are vital. Children tend to ask direct questions; they dislike being patronised and will quickly see through prevarication. They deserve the respect of straight answers to any questions they ask, given in age-appropriate language.

Older child clients may like to receive an age-appropriate letter to let them know that they have a solicitor and to provide a channel of communication which they can take up themselves if they are worried or curious, or simply want to communicate about anything. Solicitors may communicate by telephone, text or email with older children. A few stamped envelopes (addressed to the solicitor's office) plus a mobile telephone number and an email address sent with the introductory letter enable the child to phone, text or write back if he or she wishes. It also empowers the child. That is, the child will have the information and the means to communicate and respond, and therefore will not be reliant on others to get in touch with the solicitor, and can personally get in touch confidentially and quickly if necessary.

Younger children may like to give or send their solicitor notes or drawings, etc, and may like to receive a proper reply (cards are good for this). Getting an age-appropriate, suitable card from your own solicitor is a great boost for confidence. Space may be needed on the office walls for the many drawings that will inevitably accumulate.

Everyone has their own way of communicating with others, so there are no hard and fast rules. A few guidelines which may be of use are set out below.

15.4.1   Guidelines on effective meetings and communication with children

- Discuss the timing of the first meeting with the carers for the child, the child himself and with the children's guardian.

- Consult the children's guardian about whether to accompany the guardian on his or her first visit to the child.

- Find out what the children's guardian has already told the child about the case. Ask what has been said to the child about the role of the children's guardian and solicitor and how much of the facts it is appropriate to tell the child or to discuss with her.

- Explain clearly and honestly issues of confidentiality to the child, in age-appropriate language.

- Children do not like being patronised. Answer questions as directly and openly as is appropriate, and explain and discuss issues with children in age-appropriate language.

- Informal, but professional clothing may be appropriate in some cases, but not intimidating 'power-dressing' clothes.

- Position yourself on the same level as young clients, it is acceptable to sit on the floor to talk/play.

- Take a few props to help communication if you are comfortable with using them, such as: paper, crayons or pencils (not felt tips, sharp pens, messy biros or your best fountain pen), creative bendy sticks, glove puppets, small toys, toy transport, for example, bus/car/van/bike, toy mobile or phone, etc.

- Do not worry if you do not feel at ease playing with toys. It is also totally acceptable to just *talk* with children, and even more important to listen.

- Do not take sweets, food, messy pens, biros or felt tipped pens (these can upset carers or tummies, or ruin furniture).

- It is sometimes helpful to make use of technology when seeing children. Many lawyers will use laptops, tablets or other electronic devices to take notes and explain things when seeing clients, and the use of pictures and emojis, for example, can help to communicate and break the ice. Ask the child what he or she wishes to be called. Names are important. Does the child have preferred names for herself or others?

- Try to understand the child and the environment in which he or she has been living. Get the child to talk about favourite/least favourite television programmes, activities, pop stars, food, colours, clothes, football teams, toys, friends, music, games, people and pets.

- Usually, the guardian will have introduced the solicitor to the child, but if not, then, once the child is at ease, explain your role as his or her solicitor. Many older children have seen lawyers on television and have varying ideas about the legal system, ranging from the totally Dickensian lawyer to the American advocate, or they may have ideas based on scenes from current films and TV crime series. The explanation needs to be age-appropriate. It could be something along these lines:

I am your solicitor. Part of my job is to go along to the court and talk to the court/judge/magistrates and to tell them how you feel about what is happening now, and what you would like to happen.

I would like to talk with you and I want to understand. I promise to listen, because I want to hear what you would like to tell me.

Most children feel at some level that they are not listened to, and a promise to listen carefully and really pay attention to what they say is important. There will be much more to explain and discuss with a child client, but this is a good start.

- Explain to the child what the proceedings are about, in an age-appropriate way.

- There are books to help explain who is at court, and the court procedure.

- End the meeting when appropriate. Concentrating may be difficult for any length of time for a child, especially in a stressful situation. Do not overtire a young child or overstay: an hour or less is usually enough.

- Do not press a child for facts, especially about past traumatic events, as it may cause emotional distress, which the child's carers then have to deal with afterwards.

- Avoid questioning a child intrusively. Involve the child's carers if help is needed to engage the child, and end the visit if the child seems unwilling to continue. Ensure you are clear about your role and that of the police and other professionals surrounding the gathering of evidence. Your purpose in seeing the child is not to gather evidence or to carry out ABE (Achieving Best Evidence) interviews. You could cause serious harm to the child and the court process if you go beyond your role when seeing children clients.

- Never distress a child by being 'pushy' if he or she does not want to talk or by overstaying. The children's guardian will assist with advice or help, or if the solicitor is unsure, a joint visit to the child can be made.

- A sense of calm, goodwill and appropriate humour usually help.

15.5   Child development

There is insufficient space in this book to discuss child development in any detail. There are a number of excellent reference books on the market, some of which are listed here.

For example, the contribution by Mary Sheridan in *Assessing children in need and their families: Practice Guidance* (DoH, 2000), Appendix 1, contains concise, useful information on child development from birth to 5 years.

The book by Bernard Valman, *ABC of One to Seven* (Wiley-Blackwell, 5th edition, 2009) is useful, as is the book by Carolyn Meggitt, *Teach Yourself: Understand Child Development* (Hodder Education, 2012), which is a guide to child development from birth to 16 years. It looks at, for example, matters relating to physical, cognitive, moral and behavioural aspects of a child's development.

The book by Ajay Sharma, Helen Cockerill and Lucy Sanctuary, *Mary Sheridan's From Birth to Five Years: Children's Developmental Progress* (Routledge, 5th edn, 2021) discusses the developmental progress of pre-school children and provides the knowledge required to understand children's developmental progress with age and within each developmental domain.

Many bookshops carry a range of books on child development intended for parents, which practitioners will find readable and helpful. The following are useful publications:

- R Charlesworth, *Understanding Child Development* (Cengage Learning, 10th edn, 2016).
- J Friel, *Children with Special Needs* (Jessica Kingsley, 4th edn, 1997).
- C Hobart, J Frankel and M Walker, *Practical Guide to Child Observation and Assessment* (Oxford University Press, 4th edn, 2009).
- KS Holt, *Child Development – Diagnosis and Assessment* (Butterworths, 1994).
- J Howarth and D Platt, *The Child's World: The Essential Guide to Assessing Vulnerable Children, Young People and their Families* (Jessica Kingsley, 3rd edn, 2018).
- C Megitt, *Child Development: An Illustrated Guide, 3rd edition with DVD: Birth to 19 years* (Pearson Education, 3rd edn, 2012).

15.6 Understanding your child client – race, religion, culture and ethnicity

The welfare checklist pays attention to the child's 'physical educational and emotional needs' (section 1(3)(b) of the CA 1989), and 'age, sex, background and any characteristics of his which the court considers relevant' (section 1(3)(d)).

Although the CA 1989 does not refer specifically to race, religion and culture, they are clearly included in these categories. If the child's background and needs arising from it are not clear to the solicitor and children's guardian, then expert assistance should be sought from someone who fully understands the child's cultural, religious and social needs. The child may also have physical needs which may have to be explained to a carer from a different culture, for example, food, religious duties and customs, hair and skin care, etc. Quite often, behaviour which would not make sense within one culture in a given situation makes perfect sense when understood in the context of another. The court must take the child's needs fully into account when deciding the most appropriate way forward to promote and safeguard the child's welfare.

15.7   After the case is over

Children often develop a relationship of trust with their solicitor, and, whatever the outcome of the case, may want to keep in touch. The solicitor and children's guardian's role ceases for that child when the final order is made.

It is good to have a final visit to a child client. A few sheets of blank paper and stamped addressed envelopes can be left in case the child wants to write. The child may want to phone, text, email or call into the office. If a child makes contact, make a point of responding immediately, and in a way appropriate for the child's age and understanding.

Children who are in care need to know their rights, and these should have been explained by children's services. If a child is concerned about the standard of care he is receiving, or has a need to complain, the solicitor may be the first person the child thinks of to talk to about the problem. Older children may at some time wish to instruct a solicitor on their own behalf to apply for an order under section 8 of the CA 1989, or to apply to discharge a care order, so it is essential to keep an avenue of communication open for them.

Often, the child may be concerned about an aspect of her care, and the solicitor can perform a useful function in explaining and mediating between the child and parents or child and officers or agencies when difficulties arise.

When leaving care, older children also have the right to additional services under the leaving care provisions, and they may wish to seek advice about the ways in which their needs can be met.

Case records, statements and documents should be kept at least until the child reaches 21. In adoption cases, records will need to be kept for a longer time. Guardians working from home are required to return their case papers to Cafcass for archiving and are not permitted to retain any information at all in relation to the case, including copies of reports that they have written. Thus, if there are future applications it is crucial that the child's solicitor has retained a full set of papers, particularly if the previous guardian is not available or if the archiving system is unable to quickly locate old papers. It goes without saying that cases are confidential and case notes need to be kept securely and that those that are not retained are destroyed securely. Professional duties of confidentiality are separate from, but exist alongside, data protection regulation.

15.8 Judges seeing children in children law proceedings

Judges should be very careful about when and how they see children in the course of children law proceedings, although it is increasingly common for judges to agree to meet those children who ask to do so.

The court will need to consider the guidelines of April 2010, *Guidelines for Judges Meeting Children who are Subject to Family Proceedings* [2010] 2 FLR 1872, which were issued by the Family Justice Council, with the approval of the then President of the Family Division, Sir Nicholas Wall. In the case of *Re F (Children)* [2016] EWCA Civ 546, the then President of the Family Division, Sir James Munby, set out (at [44]) that in the previous case of *Re KP (A Child) (Abduction: Rights of Custody)* [2014] EWCA Civ 554, it was emphasised that a meeting between the child and the judge is an opportunity: (a) for the judge to hear what the child may wish to say; and (b) for the child to hear the judge explain the nature of the process. Also, the purpose of the meeting is not to obtain evidence and the judge should not, therefore, probe or seek to test whatever it is that the child wishes to say, and that if the child volunteers evidence that would or might be relevant to the outcome of the proceedings, the judge should report back to the parties and determine whether, and if so how, that evidence should be adduced. In the case of *Re N-A (Children)* [2017] EWCA Civ 230, the Court of Appeal impressed that whilst the judge does follow the 2010 guidelines when seeing children, it will not necessarily be a persuasive argument on appeal to demonstrate that the judge did not do so to the letter, particularly where the alleged error was known at the time, and not pursued earlier by the aggrieved party.

16 Assessment of Children in Need and Care Planning

16.1 Developments and materials

Throughout the years, there have been various assessment materials and tools for practitioners to use in carrying out assessments and providing support and assistance.

Two major assessment materials are the companion volumes, *Framework for the assessment of children in need and their families* (DoH, 2000) and *Assessing children in need and their families: Practice Guidance* (DoH, 2000). Both of these are essential reference material for child protection practice. They replaced the old 'Orange Book', *Protecting Children: A Guide to Social Workers Undertaking a Comprehensive Assessment* (DoH, 1988), but they still referred to Mary Sheridan's very useful basic child development charts for children from birth to 5 years.

At the time of writing, the relevant statutory guidance in England is *Working Together to Safeguard Children 2023: A guide to multi-agency working to help, protect and promote the welfare of children* (DfE, December 2023), and in Wales, *Working Together to Safeguard People. Volume 5 – Handling Individual Cases to Protect Children at Risk* (Welsh Government, 2018). The position with assessments in Wales is that since April 2016, the Framework for Assessment tools for assessing children and families are now included in the *Part 3 Code of Practice*.

16.1.2 Resources for professionals

Cafcass has introduced a plethora of 'tools' for working with both children and adults, all available from the Cafcass website, www.cafcass.gov.uk.

In particular, there are various resources for professionals, separated into two key categories, namely: 'Child Impact Assessment Framework' and 'Direct work with children resources'. The 'Child Impact Assessment Framework' sets out how children may experience parental separation. The framework brings together guidance and tools into four guides which the practitioner can use to assess different case factors. These include, in particular, domestic abuse, conflict, child refusal or resistance to spending time with, and other forms of harmful parenting due to factors such as substance misuse or parental mental health difficulties. The assessment process starts when Cafcass receives the case from the court, to appoint a Family Court adviser in private family law or children's guardian (guardian) in public law to undertake an assessment of the child's welfare and best interests and to provide a report, which includes recommendations as to the child's best interests.

In relation to the 'Direct work with children resources', this covers, amongst other resources, practice aids, a diversity wheel, a needs, wishes and feelings pack, and a child impact tool. The 'My Needs, Wishes and Feelings' pack, in particular, is one of the tools Cafcass workers use to help a young person share his or her feelings directly with the court, if the young person wishes to do so. The 'diversity wheel' is used to support children and young people to talk about their identity and what is important in their life, and it is a graphic representation of protected characteristics and diversity. A document called *Cafcass Family Forum top tips: for Children's Guardians working with parents in public law proceedings* sets out the experiences of Family Forum members, who have offered advice based on their experience of working with a children's guardian and what they would consider to be best practice. There are also 'General assessments tools and guidance', which include the 'Tool for parental concerns about their child', adapted from Jeff Fowler, *A Practitioner's Tool for Child Protection and the Assessment of Parents* (Jessica Kingsley Publishers, 2002). This is a tool which can be used with the parents at the commencement of involvement, so as to assist the guardian to assess the parents'/carers' understanding of the concerns.

'Observation of contact' guidance is a tool used to consider the quality of contact and ability of the parents/carers to meet the child's needs within this context.

16.2   Assessment framework

A child who is at risk of harm is, by definition, deemed to be 'a child in need'. All the guidance materials listed above apply to children who are subject to care proceedings, and also apply to many other children who may be assessed for the provision of resources by a local authority under section 17 of, and Schedule 2 to, the CA 1989, and the equivalent Welsh provisions set out in the SSW(W)A 2014. In *Assessing children in need and their families: Practice Guidance* (DoH, 2000), the assessment framework is depicted for clarity in the form of a triangle (see Figure 16.1). This is also set out in *Working Together* (Chapter 2, paragraph 150).

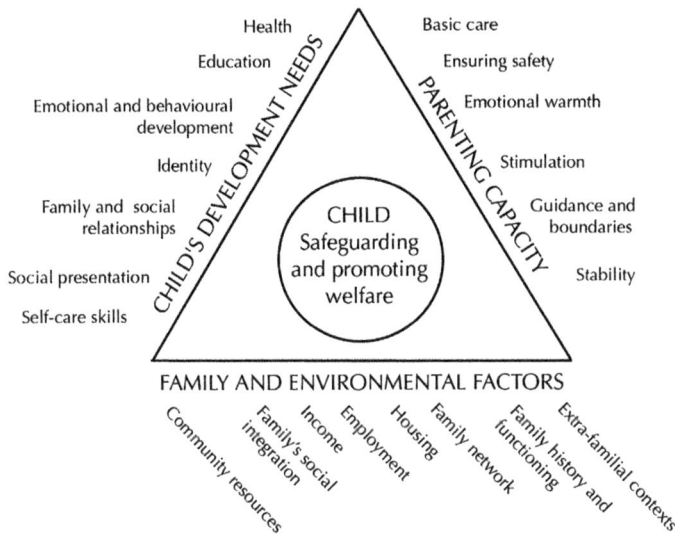

Figure 16.1   Child assessment framework

The child and the safeguarding and promoting of his welfare are central to the assessment process. Each limb of the triangle thus represents a particular area or domain of the child's world, which is further broken down into that domain's component parts, all of which inter-relate, and all of which need careful consideration both at an individual level and then as part of the whole picture.

The key areas are:

(a)   the first limb of the child's developmental needs broadly looks at the child's emotional and behavioural development and function, including a consideration of his identity; this limb also considers the child's health, social presentation, self-care skills, educational development, and family and social relationships;

(b)   the second limb considers the parenting capacity of the child's carers and, as might be expected, includes an appraisal of the provision of basic care, ensuring safety, stimulation, guidance and boundaries, stability and emotional warmth;

(c)   the third limb considers family and environmental factors, including the family history and functioning, family network, extra-familial contexts, housing, employment, income, the family's social integration and the availability of community resources.

The structure of this assessment framework has been specifically designed to provide a systematic method for the gathering and analysing of information about children, in order that different types and levels of need can be more effectively identified.

Assessing children in need and their families: Practice Guidance (DoH, 2000) looks also at the needs of children from other cultural and ethnic groups. It points out that this assessment model is equally applicable to disabled children and their families, however, the needs of the carers should be a particular factor to be taken into account. Furthermore, every assessment should reflect the unique characteristics of the child within his or her family and community context. Each child whose referral has been accepted by the local authority children's social care department should have his or her individual needs assessed, including an analysis of the parental capacity to meet those needs, whether they arise from issues within the family or the wider community. Family assessments that include all members of the family should always ensure that the needs of individual children are distinct considerations.

16.3   Care planning

Practitioners should note that case law precedent and statute has already established the requirement for a care plan in applications under section 31 of the CA 1989. The emphasis now is on the nature, format and content of the care plan. See, also, Chapter 7, para 7.8. No care order may be made unless the court has first considered a care plan submitted by the local authority (section 31(3A) of the CA 1989). The courts may require evidence in support of care plans and ask for placement details to be made available. Once the care order is made, the court loses control over implementation of the care plan. In *Re S (Minors) (Care Order: Implementation of Care Plan), Re W (Minors) (Care Order: Adequacy of Care Plan)* [2002] UKHL 10, [2002] 1 FLR 815, the House of Lords affirmed the right of local authorities to discharge their responsibility under care orders without interference from the courts. However, since this case was heard, note the changes brought about to protect the interests of children by the revised section 26 of the CA 1989, as referred to at para 7.8. Subsequently, section 26(2A) of the CA 1989 was changed as a result of the provisions of section 10 of the CYPA 2008. The functions that were to be found in section 26(2A) are now to be found in sections 25A, 25B and 25C of the CYPA 2008.

In the past, if the threshold grounds were satisfied, a lot of the court's time would have been spent on considering proportionality, and assessment and discussion of the timetable and care plan, in order to make the best decision for the child's short- and long-term future. However, the

Family Justice Review Final Report (Ministry of Justice, 2011) had identified this as a cause of unnecessary delay and recommended that courts' scrutiny of care plans be curtailed. This led to the changes brought about, set out in section 31(3A) of the CA 1989, so that when the court is deciding whether to make a care order, it is required to consider the permanence provisions of the section 31A plan for the child concerned, but is not required to consider the remainder of the section 31A plan, subject to section 34(11). Furthermore, the effect of the Children and Social Work Act 2017 is that there were further changes brought in on 31 October 2017, so that the effect of the new section 31(3B) of the CA 1989 is that the permanence provisions of a section 31A plan are: (a) such of the care plan's provisions setting out the long-term plan for the upbringing of the child concerned as provide for any of the following, (i) the child to live with any parent of the child or with any other member of, or any friend of, the child's family, (ii) adoption, (iii) long-term care not within sub-paragraph (i) or paragraph (ii); (b) such of the plan's provisions as set out in any of the following, (i) the impact on the child concerned of any harm that he or she suffered or was likely to suffer, (ii) the current and future needs of the child (including needs arising out of that impact), (iii) the way in which the long-term plan for the upbringing of the child would meet those current and future needs.

Each child must have his or her own individual care plan, and this also applies to sibling groups. The plan will often be a separate document and should not only be signed by the social worker responsible for compiling the plan, but should also be endorsed by one or more 'relevant senior officers' from within the local authority.

16.4   Adoption issues

Adoption law is governed by the Adoption and Children Act 2002. It is not within the ambit of this book to discuss adoption in detail, but adoption legislation, regulations and court rules are referred to at the Department for Education website, www.education.gov.uk.

16.4.1   Legislation and other materials

For reference, please see the following, all of which can be read in full at www.legislation.gov.uk (statutes and statutory instruments) and www.education.gov.uk (other materials):

- Adopted Children and Adoption Contact Registers Regulations 2005 (SI 2005/924).

- Adoption Agencies (Panel and Consequential Amendments) Regulations 2012 (SI 2012/1410).

- Adoption Agencies (Wales) Regulations 2005 (SI 2005/1313).

- Adoption Agencies (Wales) (Amendment) Regulations 2020 (SI 2020/163).

- Adoption Agencies and Independent Review of Determinations (Amendment) Regulations 2011 (SI 2011/589).

- Adoption Agencies Regulations 2005 (SI 2005/389).

- Adoption and Care Planning (Miscellaneous Amendments) Regulations 2018 (SI 2018/152).

- Adoption and Children Act 2002.

- Adoption and Children Act Register (Search and Inspection) (Amendment) Regulations 2018 (SI 2018/993).

- Adoption and Children (Coronavirus) (Amendment) Regulations 2021 (SI 2021/261).

- Adoption and Children (Miscellaneous Amendments) Regulations 2005 (SI 2005/3482).

- Adoption and Children (Scotland) Act 2007.

- Adoption and Children (Scotland) Act 2007 (Amendment of the Children (Scotland) Act 1995) Order 2016 (SI 2016/21).

- Adoption Information and Intermediary Services (Pre-Commencement Adoptions) Regulations 2005 (SI 2005/890).

- Adoption Information and Intermediary Services (Pre-Commencement Adoptions) (Wales) Regulations 2005 (SI 2005/2701).

- Adoption Information and Intermediary Services (Pre-Commencement Adoptions) (Wales) (Amendment) Regulations 2005 (SI 2005/ 3293).

- Adoption National Minimum Standards 2014 (DoH).

- Adoption Statutory Guidance (amended in 2013, and the draft guidance of 2014, see www.education.gov.uk).

- Adoption Support Services (Local Authorities) (Wales) Regulations 2005 (SI 2005/1512).

- Adoption Support Services Regulations 2005 (SI 2005/691).

- Adoptions with a Foreign Element Regulations 2005 (SI 2005/392) (amended in 2009).

- Adoptions with a Foreign Element (Scotland) Regulations 2009 (SI 2009/182).

- Adoptions with a Foreign Element (Special Restrictions on Adoptions from Abroad) (Scotland) Regulations 2008 (SI 2008/303) (amended in 2010–2011).

- Disclosure of Adoption Information (Post-Commencement Adoptions) Regulations 2005 (SI 2005/888).

- Family Procedure Rules 2010 (SI 2010/2955).

- Independent Review of Determinations (Adoption and Fostering) Regulations 2009 (SI 2009/395).

- Independent Review of Determinations (Adoption and Fostering) (Wales) Regulations 2010 (SI 2010/746).

- Restriction on the Preparation of Adoption Reports (Amendment) Regulations 2018 (SI 2018/674).

- Suitability of Adopters Regulations 2005 (SI 2005/1712).

16.4.2 Independent Review Mechanism

The Independent Review Mechanism helps to build public confidence in the adoption service and the adopter assessment process. For those seeking more information on the Mechanism in relation to adoptions, see www.gov.uk/government/organisations/independent-review-mechanism.

16.4.3 Publications

There are a number of excellent publications which explain the adoption law and practice. Further information about adoption law and practice issues can be obtained from the Coram British Association for Adoption and Fostering (CoramBAAF) and various adoption agencies.

In Wales, resources can be found on the National Adoption Service website, see https://adoptcymru.com/home.php?page_id=1&_act=true and the AFKA Cymru website, see https://afkacymru.org.uk/.

17 Appeals and Enforcement

17.1 Appeals and judicial review

Appeals are discussed briefly in this book under each topic, but since there is limited space, it is only possible to give further references for judicial review, complaints procedures and appeals procedures. *Hershman & McFarlane: Children Law and Practice* (Bloomsbury Professional, 2023), has an excellent section on judicial review and appeals. Another useful book is *Patterson & Karim on Judicial Review* (LexisNexis Butterworths, 3rd edn, 2019).

17.1.1 Appeal process and when permission is required

Rule 30.1 of the FPR 2010 sets out that the provisions in Part 30 apply to appeals to: (a) the High Court; and (b) the Family Court. All parties to an appeal must comply with PD 30A. Rule 30.3(1B) and (2) sets out when permission to appeal is or is not required against a decision or order of the Family Court.

However, rule 30.3(1A) of the FPR 2010 specifically provides that this rule does not apply where the route of appeal from a decision or order of the Family Court is to the Court of Appeal, namely where the appeal is against a decision or order made by a circuit judge or recorder:

   (a) in proceedings under—

      (i) Part 4 of the 1989 Act (care and supervision);

      (ii) Part 5 of the 1989 Act (protection of children);

      (iii) paragraph 19(1) of Schedule 2 to the 1989 Act (approval by the court of local authority arrangements to assist children to live abroad); or

      (iv) the 2002 Act (adoption, placement, etc.);

   (b) in exercise of the family court's jurisdiction in relation to contempt of court where that decision or order was made in, or in connection with, proceedings referred to in sub-paragraph (a); or

(c) where that decision or order was itself made on an appeal to the family court.

(Appeals in the cases referred to in this paragraph are outside the scope of these rules. The CPR make provision requiring permission to appeal in those cases.)

Rule 30.3(1B) of the FPR 2010 provides that permission to appeal *is* required: (a) unless rule 30.3(2) applies, where the appeal is against a decision made by a circuit judge, recorder, district judge or costs judge; or (b) as provided by PD 30A.

Rule 30.3(2) of the FPR 2010 provides that permission to appeal is *not* required where the appeal is against: (a) a committal order; (b) a secure accommodation order under section 25 of the CA 1989; or (c) a refusal to grant *habeas corpus* for release in relation to a minor.

In cases where permission is required, rule 30.3(3) of the FPR 2010 provides that an application for permission may be made: (a) to the lower court at the hearing at which the decision to be appealed was made; or (b) to the appeal court in an appeal notice.

17.1.2   Time limits for notice and procedure

Rule 30.4 of the FPR 2010 sets out the time limits for filing an appellant's notice at the appeal court. This specifically provides that the notice needs to be filed within such period directed by the court, or if no direction is made, within 21 days of the decision. However, where the appeal is against: (a) a case management decision; or (b) an order under section 38(1) of the CA 1989, the notice must be filed within 7 days of the decision. Rule 30.5 sets out the time limits for filing a respondent's notice at the appeal court. Any application for permission to appeal must be made in the appeal notice. Rule 30.3(4) provides that where the lower court refuses an application for permission to appeal, a further application for permission to appeal may be made to the appeal court.

The effect of rule 30.3(5) of the FPR 2010 is that subject to rule 30.3(5A), where the appeal court, without a hearing, refuses permission to appeal, the person seeking permission may request the decision to be reconsidered at a hearing.

17.1.3   If permission is refused

Rule 30.3(5A) of the FPR 2010 provides that where a judge of the High Court or in the Family Court, a judge of the High Court or a Designated Family Judge refuses permission to appeal without a hearing, and considers that the application is totally without merit, the judge may make an order that the person seeking permission may not request the decision to be reconsidered at a hearing.

Rule 30.3(5B) of the FPR 2010 goes on to provide that rule 4.3(5) will not apply to an order that the person seeking permission may not request the decision to be reconsidered at a hearing made under rule 30.3(5A).

It is expected that a request under rule 30.3(5) of the FPR 2010 must be filed within 7 days beginning with the date on which the notice that permission has been refused was served.

17.1.4   When will permission be granted?

As for the situations where permission to appeal may be given, rule 30.3(7) of the FPR 2010 sets out that it will only be where: (a) the court considers that the appeal would have a real prospect of success; or (b) there is some other compelling reason why the appeal should be heard.

The order giving permission may limit the issues to be heard, and it may be subject to conditions.

17.1.5   Judge sitting in Family Court appeals

Permission is generally required (subject to the exceptions, such as permission not being required to appeal against a committal order, as set out in para 17.1.1). The level of judge that the appeal is made to is dependent upon the level and decision of the judge sitting in the Family Court. This is set out specifically within FPR 2010 PD 30A, paragraph 2.1. Some of these situations are set out in paras 17.1.3–17.1.5.

17.1.6   Lay justices/magistrates appeals

FPR 2010 PD 30A, paragraph 2.1 provides that permission is not required to appeal against the decision of a bench of two or three lay magistrates, or a lay justice. The appeal here also lies to a judge of circuit judge level sitting in the Family Court, or a judge of High Court Judge level sitting in the Family Court where a Designated Family Judge or a judge of High Court Judge level considers that the appeal would raise an important point of principle or practice.

17.1.7   Circuit judge or recorder appeals

Permission is required and the appeal lies to the High Court Judge (sitting in the High Court), except where paragraph 5 of the table in FPR 2010 PD 30A, paragraph 2.1 applies. The appeals in paragraph 5 will require permission, and the appeal in these situations is made to the

Court of Appeal. The situations covered in paragraph 5 are where the appeal is from:

(a) a decision or order in proceedings under—

(i) Part 4 or 5 of, or paragraph 19(1) of Schedule 2 to, the Children Act 1989; or

(ii) the Adoption and Children Act 2002;

(b) a decision or order in exercise of the court's jurisdiction in relation to contempt of court, where that decision or order was made in, or in connection with, proceedings of a type referred to in sub-paragraph (a); or

(c) a decision or order made on appeal to the family court.

17.1.8 Judge of High Court Judge level appeals

Appeals lie to the Court of Appeal, and permission is required (FPR 2010 PD 30A).

17.2 Complaints procedures

If any person wishes to complain about any action by the children's services department in relation to a child, the procedure is set out in the Children Act 1989 Representations Procedure (England) Regulations 2006 (SI 2006/1738) and the Representations Procedure (Children) (Wales) Regulations 2014 (SI 2014/1795) (W 188).

If a complainant is not satisfied by the local authority's response, he or she may be able to take the matter up with the Local Government and Social Care Ombudsman (England) or the Public Services Ombudsman for Wales.

17.3 Enforcement

Enforcement of orders made under the CA 1989 is discussed briefly in this book under each topic. Further detail is available from *Hershman & McFarlane: Children Law and Practice* (Bloomsbury Professional, 2023), which has an excellent section on enforcement of orders under the CA 1989. See, also, Table 17.1.

Table 17.1   Enforcement procedures for orders under the Children
Act 1989

Breach of order	Injunction/penal notice	Surety bond	Committal or contempt	Other remedy available	Police powers and criminal proceedings
Refusal to give up a child for child arrangements order (living with)			Part 37 of the FPR 2010 Committal for breach of order or undertaking Also, see PD 37A	Search and recovery order Section 34 of the Family Law Reform Act 1986 'Seek & find' High Court inherent jurisdiction	
Threat to remove child from the United Kingdom or actual removal attempt		Can be used to ensure return of child	As above	(a) Port alert system (b) Passport restriction	(a) Police duty to assist where threat of danger or breach of the peace (b) Child Abduction and Custody Act 1985 offence
Change of name when child subject to child arrangements order (living with)	✓		✓		

Table 17.1   Enforcement procedures for orders under the Children Act 1989 *(continued)*

Breach of order	Injunction/penal notice	Surety bond	Committal or contempt	Other remedy available	Police powers and criminal proceedings
Refusal to comply with child arrangements order under section 8 of the CA 1989	To use the penal notice, the acts to be enforced must be set out clearly in the order		Committal is rare, but possible	Section 11(7) of the CA 1989 directions, including activities (sections 11A and 11B); also, section 11I warnings and enforcement orders (section 11J)	
Breach of specific issue or prohibited steps	✓		✓		Police duty to assist where threat of danger may be used in medical emergency
Removal of child from care (order under section 31 of the CA 1989)	If removal from jurisdiction is threatened, this may be necessary		✓	Port alert if threat to remove from the United Kingdom High Court Tipstaff if threat to remove from jurisdiction Recovery order (section 50 of the CA 1989)	Child Abduction and Custody Act 1985 offence Police duty to assist where threat of danger may be used in medical emergency

Change of name of child in care under section 31 of the CA 1989 without leave/consent	✓		✓	
Failure to produce records to children's guardian	Application to produce documents under section 42 of the CA 1989			Application to court to produce documents under section 42 of the CA 1989
Breach of directions of the court in CA 1989 proceedings, as to filing, service or attendance				Wasted costs order Court may impose adjournment or proceed in absence of party Evidence may be disallowed (rule 4.5 of the FPR 2010)

18 Expert Evidence

18.1 What is an expert witness?

An 'expert witness' has no specific legal definition. Many professionals style themselves as 'expert witnesses', but it is the court which makes the final decision as to who is accepted as an expert in a particular specialist field, in each individual case. This was emphasised recently in the decision of *Re C ('Parental Alienation': Instruction of Expert)* [2023] EWHC 345 (Fam), whereby the President of the Family Division stated (at [87]), that there was no definition of an 'expert' in family proceedings, save for the circular procedural definition at rule 25.2(c) of the FPR 2010: '"expert" means a person who provides expert evidence for use in proceedings'. Other than those individuals who are excluded from giving expert evidence by section 13(8) of the CFA 2014, the question of whether an expert is 'qualified to give expert evidence' (section 3 of the Civil Evidence Act 1972) is a matter for the court in each individual case.

Consequently, the authors would submit that, for example, a young, newly qualified nursery nurse may be treated by the court as an expert in the case of a particular child with whom she had worked intensively for a year. She would not have thought of claiming that status herself, but the court can regard her as an expert in that specific piece of work with that particular child. Other professionals might wish to claim expert status in their field of work, but the court may decide otherwise.

As mentioned, section 13(8) of the CFA 2014 excludes certain types of evidence from the ambit of the formalities in obtaining expert evidence, so they are not subject to the restrictions set out in the section. These include any evidence given by a person who is a member of staff of a local authority, or of an authorised applicant. The purpose is to ensure that such evidence can be adduced without the need for prior permission through the procedure under Part 25 of the FPR 2010. Similarly, evidence given by officers of Cafcass or Cafcass Cymru, and any evidence provided in connection with determining the suitability of a child for adoption, is not subject to these restrictions either.

Experts are privileged in the eyes of the law – they are not restricted to evidence of fact and can give their opinion on any relevant matter in which they are appropriately qualified. Rule 25.2(1) of the FPR 2010 defines an 'expert' as a person who provides expert evidence for use in proceedings. Acceptance of a specialist as an expert, therefore, will vary according to the issues in each case, and in order to assess expertise, the court will expect that the expert will outline his or her qualifications and experience.

18.2 Choosing and instructing expert witnesses

The choice of the appropriate expert for a case is never an easy one, and the choice may be limited by availability and time frames. See para 18.5 for ideas derived from practice.

Part 25 of the FPR 2010 relates to experts and assessors, and in children proceedings, pursuant to rule 25.4, the provision relating to control of evidence in children proceedings is contained in section 13 of the CFA 2014.

The court may refuse permission to call an expert, but be aware that it may be argued that this may prejudice the right of the party to a fair trial under Article 6 of the ECHR, see the case of *Elsholz v Germany* [2002] 34 EHRR 58, [2000] 2 FLR 486. In the course of proceedings in the High Court, the court gave helpful guidance on the use of expert witnesses, see *Re M (Minors) (Care Proceedings: Children's Wishes)* [1994] 1 FLR 749 and *Re G (Minors) (Expert Witnesses)* [1994] 2 FLR 291.

Some years later, the then President of the Family Division, Sir James Munby, set out in *Re TG (A Child)* [2013] EWCA Civ 5 (at [30]), that the revised Part 25 of the FPR 2010, as from 31 January 2013, was such that only evidence which is 'necessary to assist the court' would be sanctioned. On the facts, the expert evidence proposed fell short of what was necessary. In a later case that year, *Re H–L (A Child)* [2013] EWCA Civ 655, the Court of Appeal emphasised that one needs to ensure not to blur the lines between 'treating clinicians' and 'experts', and that this needs to be maintained. Here, the consultant geneticist's opinion was 'necessary' and the court would allow him to be formally instructed, to provide an opinion on the discrete issue in accordance with Part 25.

When deciding whether to give permission for expert evidence, the court needs to be satisfied, pursuant to section 13(6) of the CFA 2014, that it is 'necessary to assist the court to resolve the proceedings justly', by considering the criteria under section 13(7). In relation to directions that are sought as to the medical and other examination and assessment of children under section 38(6) of the CA 1989, the court needs to have regard to the factors under section 38(7B) of the CA 1989. In the case of *Re F (A Child)* [2014] EWCA Civ 789, the then President of the Family Division, Sir James Munby, stated (at [21]) that where the court does allow the instruction of an expert, there needs to be an express recital in the order to the effect that the appointment of the expert is necessary to assist the court to resolve the proceedings justly in accordance with section 13(6) of the CFA 2014. In the case *In the Matter of C (A Child) (Procedural Requirements of a Part 25 Application) and Mother and Father* [2015] EWCA Civ 539, the Court of Appeal set out that the lower court had failed to follow either Part 25 of the FPR 2010 or section 13 of the CFA 2014 in allowing the expert evidence.

In relation to capacity assessments, the case of *Re D (Children)* [2015] EWCA Civ 749 sets out that if a party takes issue with the outcome of a capacity assessment then, as with any other expert evidence, it is open to that party to make an application to the court for a second report by a different expert following the criteria under section 13 of the CFA 2014. Also, where there is a request for permission to obtain expert evidence as to substance misuse, there is a need for a letter of instruction to be provided to the drug-testing company, particularly in complex cases.

The balance between restricting the use of experts and permitting an expert has been emphasised in the 'President of the Family Division's memorandum: Experts in the Family Court', dated 11 October 2021. The President set out that there are four criteria which govern the admissibility of opinion evidence of an expert and these govern the admissibility of expert evidence of fact, where the witness draws on the knowledge and experience of others rather than, or in addition to, personal observation. The criteria, as set out in *Kennedy v Cordia (Services) LLP (Scotland)* [2016] UKSC 6 at [44], per Lord Reed PSC are:

(i) whether the proposed expert evidence will assist the court in its task;

(ii) whether the witness has the necessary knowledge and experience;

(iii) whether the witness is impartial in his or her presentation and assessment of the evidence; and

(iv) whether there is a reliable body of knowledge or experience to underpin the expert's evidence.

Furthermore, such expert evidence will only be 'necessary' where it is demanded by the contested issues rather than being merely reasonable, desirable or of assistance (*Re H-L (A Child)* [2013] EWCA Civ 655).

The Family Justice Council and the British Psychological Society have jointly produced the document, *Psychologists as Expert Witnesses in the family courts in England and Wales: Standards, competencies and expectations* (2nd edn, September 2023), available at https://explore.bps.org.uk/content/report-guideline/bpsrep.2023.inf248c. It provides a set of guidelines for how to instruct expert witnesses in family proceedings. The 2nd edition includes additional guidance in relation to the instruction of psychologist expert witnesses, specifically the scrutiny of their regulation, their qualifications and their access to psychological tests. There is reference to the case of

Re C ('Parental Alienation') [2023] EWHC 345 (Fam), regarding the use of psychologists, where the President had stated (at [98]) that, 'In every case the court should identify whether a proposed expert is HCPC registered. A sensible practice, where the expert is unregistered, is for the court to indicate in a short judgment why it is, nevertheless, appropriate to instruct them'. A CV template is given in Appendix 6 of the guidance to assist psychologist experts in meeting this requirement.

More recently, the need for expert evidence was considered by the Court of Appeal in the decision of *Re E (A Child) (Care and Placement Orders)* [2023] EWCA Civ 721. The mother had appealed against care and placement orders made in respect of her son, aged one. She had previously undergone a psychological assessment before her son was born. She had been described as having difficulties in regulating her emotions and there was the question as to whether she may be autistic. The mother applied for a further psychological assessment. This was principally on the basis that, given her background and multiple diagnoses, it was argued that a psychologist should be instructed to assess her possible complex psychological needs, any associated risks and the timescale of any treatment required to alleviate those risks. It was suggested that these issues could not properly be addressed in the social worker's or guardian's assessments and that without a psychologist's report, there would therefore be a significant gap in the evidence. Baler LJ, in handing down the leading judgment, said that the need for courts to exercise vigilance over applications for expert evidence in children's cases had been reiterated frequently, for example in the 'President of the Family Division's memorandum: Experts in the Family Court', dated 11 October 2021 and *Re H-L (A Child)* [2013] EWCA Civ 655 (above).

Therefore, sometimes parties had been too quick in applying to instruct experts. However, the Court of Appeal decided that this was not one of these cases. This was a very young mother involved in care proceedings concerning her first child. The application for a psychological assessment was based, not on speculation, nor on the hope that something would turn up but, rather, on the solid foundations of the mother's circumstances and personality – the background of serious abuse and trauma, the history of self-harm, the lengthy engagement with Child and Adolescent Mental Health Services throughout her teenage years, the diagnosis of emotionally unstable personality disorder, and the suggestion, as yet unassessed, that she may be on the autistic spectrum. The court allowed the assessment on the facts.

Having said that, it has also been recognised that cognitive and psychological assessments should be ordered only when necessary and should not be seen as routine. At para 11.2.4, the case of *West Northamptonshire Council v The Mother (Psychological Assessments)* [2024] EWHC 395 (Fam) was referred to. Lieven J stated (at [26]) that the test of necessity did not mean that a report would be 'nice to have' or might help in determining what psychological support the parent might need in the future. The assessment sought was not necessary to resolve the proceedings and, therefore, the application was refused.

18.2.1 Funding issues and prior authority from the Legal Aid Agency to instruct expert witnesses

On 3 May 2012, Sir Nicholas Wall, the then President of the Family Division, gave judgment in the case of *A Local Authority v DS, DI and DS* [2012] EWHC 1442 (Fam). In that judgment, His Lordship gave guidance on the issue of prior authority from the Legal Services Commission (LSC) (the name by which the Legal Aid Agency, was known at that time) to instruct expert witnesses in publicly funded family proceedings. The judgment is worth reading. In particular, consider [38] of the judgment:

> For present purposes, the law can be taken quite shortly. To the mind of the lawyer it remains curious that an administrative body can effectively render nugatory a judicial decision taken in what the court perceives as the best interests of a child. Where the party or parties who seek to instruct an expert are publicly funded, however, there is no doubt that the LSC has the power, given to it by Parliament, to refuse to fund the instruction or to fund the instruction in part only. Moreover, the LSC undoubtedly has the power, deriving from the same source, to cap the level of fees which may be expended by the expert at a given level. That is undoubted the law. Lawyers may complain that this is an unfair state of affairs, or that they cannot find experts who will work at the rates laid down. Their remedy, if they take the view that the decision of the LSC is *Wednesbury* unreasonable or can be struck down for any other public law reason, is to apply for judicial review.

The President gave guidance on the wording of the court order, taken from the LSC regulations, particularly if the expert is to be paid above what the funding order allowed for. The President set out that any application for prior authority needs to be made as soon as possible, and that the LSC needs to deal with applications promptly, and any urgent matter to be considered should be clearly marked.

When looking to instruct an expert, under the FPR 2010 and PDs 25A–25C, the contractual basis for the expert evidence, including funding and payment, should be set out in the letter of instruction.

Private funding is a matter of negotiation between client, solicitor and expert.

In publicly funded cases, the LAA places limitations on funding. See the LAA publication, *Guidance on Remuneration of Expert Witnesses* (September 2022, Version 7) for the rates and allowances. The most up-to-date rates and guidance issued should be followed. High-cost cases (lawyers are advised to check the current limit) are dealt with by the Special Cases Unit and the lawyer needs to present and justify an overall cost case plan. Careful negotiation of expert fees is required in advance of the case to obtain prior authority for instruction of the expert.

In the decision of *Re J (Care Proceedings: Apportionment of Expert Fees)* [2017] EWFC B49, it was emphasised that there needs to be an application made for prior authority as early as possible to cover the costs of the assessment.

Any additional unforeseen expense in respect of the expert's assessment or report preparation which arises after the initial authority must be addressed by an increase in any limitation on costs that has been imposed by the LAA.

In the case of *JG v The Lord Chancellor & Others* [2014] EWCA Civ 656, Black LJ, in handing down the leading judgment, stated (at [90]) that what could be drawn from the past legal authorities was that the court had a discretion as to what order is made as to costs of instructing experts in family proceedings, and that discretion must be exercised, bearing in mind all the circumstances of the particular case.

Experts in publicly funded cases would be wise to accept instructions and begin work only when their fee structure, an estimate of their costs, and the responsibility for who will pay, along with an agreement as to how and when payment will be made, have been clarified. This contractual arrangement should be reflected in the letter of instruction.

When the expert's evidence or other work is concluded, claims for payment on account for expert services can be submitted to the LAA, in advance of the final detailed assessment of the costs of the case (formerly called taxation).

Experts should be aware that, if the matter is publicly funded, detailed assessment may, in some circumstances, lead to a reduction in the fees allowed for the expert's work.

18.3   Expert witness evidence

Rule 25.6 of the FPR 2010 provides that unless the court directs otherwise, parties must apply for permission as mentioned in section 13(1), (3) or (5) of the CFA 2014, or rule 25.4(2) of the FPR 2010, as soon as possible, and in Part 4 proceedings, and insofar as is practicable in other public law proceedings, no later than the CMH; in private law cases, no later than first hearing dispute resolution appointment; and in adoption proceedings and placement proceedings, no later than the first directions hearing. Rule 25.7 provides that Part 18 applies to an application for court's permission as mentioned in section 13(1), (3) or (5) or rule 25.4(2).

18.3.1   Expert instruction checklist

Permission, consents and preliminary enquiries of experts

- When considering which expert to instruct, the court needs some information about the experts, so as to decide which is appropriate.

- The experts will require some information about the case to decide whether to accept instructions. The provision of such anonymised information will not require prior consent (see FPR 2010 PD 25A and, in particular, PD 25C, paragraph 3.4). However, if experts need to check on the names of the parties for conflicts of interest before accepting instructions, consent to disclose the names would be required.

- All necessary permission for the instruction of an expert (see rule 25.4(2) of the FPR 2010) and for the examination of a child should be obtained before instructing the expert (see section 13(3) of the CFA 2014, which provides that a person may not, without the permission of the court, cause a child to be medically or psychiatrically examined or otherwise assessed for the purposes of the provision of expert evidence in children proceedings).

- Once permission to instruct has been obtained, then pursuant to rule 12.73 of the FPR 2010, for the purposes of the law relating to contempt of court, information relating to the proceedings may be communicated to the expert whose instruction has been authorised by the court for the purposes of the proceedings.

- Preliminary enquiries may be necessary in order to select the right expert. An approach to an expert should comply with FPR 2010 PDs 25A and 25C. PD 25C, paragraph 3.7 provides that an application for the court's permission should be made as soon as it becomes apparent that it is necessary to make it. In addition to the matters specified in rule 25.7(2), the application for permission must state specific detail as to in particular, the discipline, qualifications and expertise of the expert, expert's availability to undertake the work, timetable for the report, responsibility for instruction, whether the expert evidence can properly be obtained by only one party, why the expert evidence proposed cannot properly be given by an officer of the service, Welsh family proceedings officer or the local authority, the likely cost of the report, and the proposed apportionment of any jointly instructed expert's fee. Under rule 25.7(2)(b), the instructing solicitor should attach a draft of the order to the application for the court's permission. Under rule 25.8, the court will give directions, approving the questions which the expert is required to answer, and, secondly, will specify the date by which the expert is to receive the letter of instruction.

- Consents should be obtained from the child and those with parental responsibility for examinations and assessments where appropriate (see Chapters 3 and 12).

- The instruction of an expert should be discussed with other parties, with the aim of agreeing joint experts wherever possible. Where two or more parties wish to put expert evidence before the court on a particular issue, the court may direct that the evidence on that issue is to be given by a single joint expert pursuant to rule 25.11 of the FPR 2010.

- The expert has an overriding duty to the court that takes precedence over the interests of any party (rule 25.3 of the FPR 2010 and PD 25B).

- Directions of the court should be obtained for:

  - the date by which the letter of instruction should be sent;
  - which documents are to be released;
  - a date for filing the report/uploading on the portal.

- The examination of a child may require directions as to venue, timing, the person(s) to accompany the child and to whom the results should be given.

Letters of instruction

These should comply with FPR 2010 PD 25C, paragraph 4.1. In brief, they should:

- set out the context in which expert opinion is sought;
- define specific questions the expert is to address;
- list the documentation provided or refer to a paginated bundle;
- identify materials that have not been produced either as original medical or other professional records or documents filed in response to an instruction from a party;
- identify all requests to third parties for information and responses;
- identify all the people concerned with the proceedings, informing the expert of his or her right to talk to them, provided an accurate record is made of discussions;
- identify any other expert instructed;
- define the contractual basis upon which the expert is instructed, including funding and payment details.

Letters of instruction should also be accompanied by a chronology with the background information, and the expert should be asked for further information or documentation if necessary.

Joint instructions are desirable, and can be directed by the court under rule 25.11 of the FPR 2010. Where joint letters of instruction are to be settled, see PD 25C, paragraph 2.1.

It is very important to remember that any delay in sending out the letter of instruction to the expert is likely to compromise the ability of the expert to file his or her report by the filing deadline. This then leads to delay to the overall court timetable, which can result in delays of many weeks.

Also see the *Templates for instructing experts in family and children court proceedings*, of April 2020, produced by the Law Society. These provide a pro forma for preliminary enquiries, a guide and sample questions for experts, a pre-proceedings letter of instruction, a letter of instruction and the standard terms and conditions to accompany a letter of instruction.

Updating, expert conferences, agreed evidence and points in issue

Experts should be kept up to date with new documents filed in the case (rule 25.18 of the FPR 2010). Therefore, unless the court directs otherwise, a copy of any order or other document affecting an expert filed with the court after the expert has been instructed, must be served on the expert within 2 days of the party receiving the order or other document. Experts may be invited to confer together, identifying areas of agreement and disputed issues. The court should regulate such meetings, and FPR 2010 PD 25E supports rule 25.16 by providing details about how and when experts discussions are to be arranged, their purpose and content.

Expert reports

- Expert reports should be objective – the expert's overriding duty is to the court.

- Parties and lawyers should not attempt to influence or 'edit' expert reports.

- Reports must be disclosed to the court and to all parties unless otherwise directed by the court.

- The requirements for the content of an expert report are set out in FPR 2010 PD 25B, paragraph 9.1.

- The expert report needs to contain statements that:

  - the expert understands his or her duty to the court and will comply with it;

  - the expert does not consider that there is any conflict of interest, nor any interest disclosed that affects his or her suitability as an expert witness. The expert will advise those instructing him or her if there is any change in circumstances affecting the expert's answers regarding interests and suitability;

- the expert is aware of the requirements of Part 25 of the FPR 2010 and PD 25B;

- in children proceedings, the expert has complied with the *Standards for Expert Witnesses in Children Proceedings in the Family Court*, which are set out in the Annex to PD 25B.

• The report shall end with a statement of truth as follows, see FPR 2010 PD 25B:

I confirm that I have made clear which facts and matters referred to in this report are within my own knowledge and which are not. Those that are within my own knowledge I confirm to be true. The opinions I have expressed represent my true and complete professional opinions on the matters to which they refer.

• Where the report relates to children proceedings, the form of statement of truth must include:

I also confirm that I have complied with the Standards for Expert Witnesses in Children Proceedings in the Family Court which are set out in the Annex to Practice Direction 25B – The Duties of an Expert, the Expert's Report and Arrangements for an Expert to Attend Court.

18.4   Expert evidence in court

With careful planning by advocates, the time and patience of expert witnesses can be saved considerably. Joint consultations and jointly compiled experts' lists of agreed and disputed issues save time, whilst arrangement of evidence in a logical sequence to fit the needs of witnesses and the run of the evidence is vital. Written evidence can be admitted by agreement, and expert witnesses' time saved by reduction of their evidence in chief and leaving more time for cross-examination. Parties should make full use of rule 25.10 of the FPR 2010, insofar as putting written questions about an expert's report to the expert, which can potentially limit the points in dispute.

In Part 35 of the Civil Procedure Rules 1998 (SI 1998/3132), the primary duty of an expert is stated to be to the court. Although it was the expectation of the courts, this duty did not specifically apply in family cases until 1 April 2008, when *Practice Direction: Experts in Family Proceedings Relating to Children* (13 February 2008), paragraph 3.1 came into effect.

Now, that overriding duty to the court is very clearly stated in the FPR 2010 and PD 25B, paragraph 3.1.

Experts should never go beyond the remit of their instructions or their expertise. There have been cases in which, regrettably, this has happened, to the detriment of a party, the child, justice, or possibly all three. The Court of Appeal gave helpful guidance for experts and lawyers in *R v Cannings* [2004] EWCA Crim 1, [2004] 1 WLR 2607.

18.5 Finding the right expert

The most effective way of finding experts is by personal recommendation by other legal practitioners in similar fields of practice. Cafcass, children's guardians, social workers, lawyers and other professionals may also provide recommendations for experts in particular specialist areas. Expert(s) should be asked to provide qualifications, current work and relevant past experience – not only for reassurance, but also because to do so is necessary for the court, pursuant to the Annex to FPR 2010 PD 25B, and, as seen, more recently emphasised in *Psychologists as Expert Witnesses in the family courts in England and Wales: Standards, competencies and expectations* (2nd edn, September 2023). It will also be necessary for other parties and the LAA to be informed. The expert should be asked how often he or she has given evidence in court before; the expert may be absolutely brilliant on paper, but may be diffident at giving oral evidence.

The sources below may be a starting point in the search for the right expert. Some organisations will send out published lists, while others provide information in response to a telephone or written enquiry and may charge an administration fee. Note with regard to psychologists, that *Psychologists as Expert Witnesses in the family courts in England and Wales: Standards, competencies and expectations* (2nd edn, September 2023) explains that only psychologists who are registered with the Health Care Professions Council (HCPC) under a protected title are regulated, and therefore their qualifications and fitness to practise can be checked by the court.

18.5.1 Registers and directories

The Academy of Experts, *Register of Experts*.

The British Psychological Society, *Directory of Chartered Psychologists*.

The Chartered Society of Forensic Sciences, internationally recognised professional body.

Forensic Science Society, *Register of Independent Consultants*.

JS Publications, *UK Register of Expert Witnesses*.

Law Society of Scotland, *Expert Witnesses Directory*.

18.5.2   Online resources

The British Psychological Society, www.bps.org.uk.

Expert Witness, www.expertwitness.co.uk.

Law Society of Scotland (Expert Witness Directory),
www.lawscot.org.uk/members/business-support/expert-witness/.

NAGALRO (Professional Association for Children's Guardians, Family
Court Advisers and Independent Social Workers),
www.nagalro.com.

UK Register of Expert Witnesses, www.jspubs.com.

19 Improving Law, Skills and Practice

It is necessary for lawyers to keep up to date with statute and case law and to constantly develop knowledge and skills, not only in law, but also, for example, in medicine, psychology and parenting.

Legal practitioners should look for training events which are run by various providers, such as The Law Society, the Solicitors Regulation Authority, the Bar Council, and those run by the associations listed in para 19.1.

It is vital to maintain a list of resources to which child clients and families may be referred and it helps to belong to organisations which can provide information and assistance. In those areas of the country where child law practitioners may find themselves isolated, discussion with a network of colleagues provides moral and practical support.

19.1 Professional and interdisciplinary associations

Legal practitioners are represented on Local Family Justice Boards, which are interdisciplinary groups attached to each care centre. The Boards were established to support the work of the Family Justice Board, by bringing together the key local agencies, including decision makers and frontline staff, so as to achieve significant improvement in the performance of the family justice system in their local areas.

A good resource for child law practice is the experience of colleagues. Listed below are some of the organisations which have been recommended to the authors as helpful in the provision of networking, training and information. By listing these, the authors are not expressing any preference, and the list is by no means exhaustive:

- Association of Child Protection Professionals (AoCPP), formerly the British Association for the Study and Prevention of Child Abuse and Neglect (BASPCAN), 17 Priory Street, York YO1 6ET, 01904 613605, www.childprotectionprofessionals.org.uk/about-us/.

- Association of Lawyers for Children (ALC), 10 Lincoln's Inn Fields, London WC2A 3PB, 07473 590332, www.alc.org.uk/.

- Children and Family Court Advisory and Support Service (Cafcass), National Office, 3rd Floor, 21 Bloomsbury Street, London WC1B 3HF, 0300 456 4000, www.cafcass.gov.uk/contact-us.

- Cafcass Cymru has various regional offices. The details of the Cardiff regional office are: Welsh Government, Cathays Park, Cardiff CF10 3NQ, 03000 628 877, cafcasscymrusouthwales@gov.wales.

- CoramBAAF Adoption & Fostering Academy, (CoramBAAF), Coram Campus, 41 Brunswick Square, London WC1N 1AZ, 020 7520 0300, https://corambaaf.org.uk/.

- Judicial College. Publications and useful information are available at www.judiciary.uk/about-the-judiciary/training-support/judicial-college/.

- Local Children's Guardian and Solicitor Groups: check with local Cafcass managers.

- NAGALRO (Professional Association for Children's Guardians, Family Court Advisers and Independent Social Workers), 01372 818504 and 0779 3949634, www.nagalro.com.

- National Youth Advisory Service (NYAS), Tower House, 1 Tower Road, Birkenhead, Wirral CH41 1FF, 0808 808 1001, www.nyas.net/get-support/support-for-young-people/advocacy/.

- Resolution, Central Office, 198 High St, Orpington BR6 6HA, 020 3841 0300, www.resolution.org.uk, info@resolution.org.uk.

- The Transparency Project runs a website that has up-to-date comment on cases and publishes guides to help make the Family Court clearer, www.transparencyproject.org.uk.

19.2 The Law Society's Children Law Accreditation

The Children Law Accreditation recognises practitioners specialising in the representation of children, families and local authorities in public and private law matters.

To achieve accreditation, applicants must be able to demonstrate awareness, knowledge and expertise in children law proceedings and the representation of children in such proceedings. The accreditation is available to solicitors and chartered legal executives who are employed by a solicitor, and who hold the Rights of Audience Matrimonial Proceedings/Family Proceedings Certificate (or other appropriate advocacy qualification) awarded by the Chartered Institute of Legal Executives. There is no minimum requirement for time spent in practice in the area of law before applying, but the applicant will need to ensure that he has sufficient experience to clearly demonstrate his abilities. It is important therefore to have sufficient experience in child and family law and a sound knowledge of child law and practice, as well as child-related issues, such as child development, as well as being able to develop skills in communicating with children.

Applicants wishing to be accepted for the accreditation must produce evidence of the appropriate qualifications and relevant experience, acquire the necessary training and pass a selection interview.

The Children Law Accreditation training courses are comprehensive, covering a wide range of topics and law relevant to the representation of children, families and local authorities and working with the children's guardian. Full information about the accreditation and application forms can be obtained from Accreditation Unit at The Law Society, 0207 320 5797, www.lawsociety.org.uk/career-advice/individual-accreditations/children-law-accreditation.

19.3 Sources of useful information and contacts for children and families, and those who work with them

- ChildLine, 0800 1111, www.childline.org.uk.

- Community Care, www.communitycare.co.uk.

- CORAM Children's Legal Centre, Wellington House, 4th Floor, 90–92 Butt Road, Colchester, Essex CO3 3DA, Coram Children's Legal Centre, Coram Campus, 41 Brunswick Square, London WC1N 1AZ, 01206 714 650, www.childrenslegalcentre.com.

- Family Law Week, www.familylawweek.co.uk (legal updates on family law).

- General Medical Council (GMC), www.gmc-uk.org.

- Government information, www.gov.uk.

- Northern Ireland Department of Health, www.dhsspsni.gov.uk.

- NSPCC, www.nspcc.org.uk.

- Scottish Government guidance, www.gov.scot.

- Thirtyone:eight (previously called Churches Child Protection Advisory Service), www.thirtyoneeight.org.

- Welsh Government guidance, www.gov.wales.

Index